The Westminster  Handbook
to Martin Luther

Other books in The Westminster Handbooks to Christian Theology series

THE WESTMINSTER HANDBOOKS
TO CHRISTIAN THEOLOGY

The Westminster Handbook to Martin Luther

Denis R. Janz

WESTMINSTER
JOHN KNOX PRESS
LOUISVILLE · KENTUCKY

First edition
Published by Westminster John Knox Press
Louisville, Kentucky

10 11 12 13 14 15 16 17 18 19—10 9 8 7 6 5 4 3 2 1

Scripture quotations from the New Revised Standard Version of the Bible are copyright © 1989 by the Division of Christian Education of the National Council of the Churches of Christ in the U.S.A. and are used by permission.

Book design by Sharon Adams
Cover design by Cynthia Dunne
Cover art: Monks copying manuscripts
(Corbis/© Archivo Iconografico)

Library of Congress Cataloging-in-Publication Data

Janz, Denis.
    The Westminster handbook to Martin Luther / Denis R. Janz. — 1st ed.
        p. cm. — (The Westminster handbooks to Christian theology)
    Includes bibliographical references (p   ).
    ISBN 978-0-664-22470-7 (alk. paper)
    1. Luther, Martin, 1483–1546.   I. Title.   II. Title: Handbook to Martin Luther.
    BR333.3.J36   2010
    284.1092—dc22

                                                            2010017891

PRINTED IN THE UNITED STATES OF AMERICA

∞ The paper used in this publication meets the minimum requirements
of the American National Standard for Information Sciences—Permanence
of Paper for Printed Library Materials, ANSI Z39.48-1992

Westminster John Knox Press advocates the responsible use of our natural resources. The text paper of this book is made from 30% post-consumer waste.

Most Westminster John Knox Press books are available at special quantity discounts when purchased in bulk by corporations, organizations, and special-interest groups. For more information, please e-mail SpecialSales@wjkbooks.com.

For
Wes Reagan
James Gaffney
and
in Memory of
Carl Ridd (1929–2003)
James Weisheipl O.P. (1923–1984)
J. Edgar Bruns (1923–1997)
Stephen Duffy (1931–2007)

Contents

Series Introduction

The Westminster Handbooks to Christian Theology series provides a set of resources for the study of historic and contemporary theological movements and Christian theologians. These books are intended to assist scholars and students in finding concise and accurate treatments of important theological terms. The entries for the handbooks are arranged in alphabetical format to provide easy access to each term. The works are written by scholars with special expertise in these fields.

We hope this series will be of great help as readers explore the riches of Christian theology as it has been expressed in the past and as it will be formulated in the future.

The Publisher

Introduction

I begin with a frank admission: few today breathlessly await a new book on the theology of Martin Luther. Yet I dare to hope that there are some groups, however limited, who might at least cautiously welcome such a volume.

First among these are the Luther experts—scholars who care about a more authentic portrait of the reformer, and who can see how new publications, if they are good, move us along in that direction. Add to these the circle of historians of early modern Europe. While skeptical perhaps of the "great men who changed the world" approach to this period, many nevertheless sense that without some grasp of Luther, the spirit of the age will elude us.

One can also hope that students—undergraduate, graduate, and seminarians—would show an interest in Luther. To become an educated person, it can easily be argued, one needs to make Luther's acquaintance. Clichés about Luther are rife in our society, most of them quite plainly wrong. Without studying Luther, we cannot help but repeat them. More generally, to understand, appropriate, or critique our cultural inheritance, we need to know something about the pillars on which it was built. And Luther was certainly one of these.

Finally, there is a group of individuals we could loosely classify as "seekers." These are not easy to pin down. Some go to church, synagogue, mosque, or temple regularly. Others never go at all. Many of them reject our current entertainment industry as mindless: they are sometimes found to be reading when more "well-adjusted" people are watching prime-time television. Some of them have switched into survival mode, determined to rescue a few last fragments of truth and goodness and beauty from the toxic slagheaps of late modern society. All of them, in one way or another, have embarked on humanity's age-old quest for self-understanding and meaning. Many of these seekers suspect, or know almost intuitively, that the great classical thinkers of our culture, despite all our disagreements with them, can help us in such matters.

These groups together are the market for this book. I wrote it for them, and if they find it helpful—cogent, lucid, thought provoking, convincing—I will count it a success.

Among all existing studies of Luther, this book is unique, obviously, in that it presents *my* interpretation of Luther's thought. What else differentiates it from the rest?

First, because of the series it appears in, the work is alphabetically arranged. Westminster John Knox's *Handbooks to Christian Theology*, a growing list of A–Z reference works, includes volumes on Thomas Aquinas, Origen, Reformed Theology, and so forth. Editor Don McKim asked me to contribute the Luther volume. I am grateful to him for this invitation, not least because it spared me a dilemma that Luther experts anguish over interminably—whether to present Luther's thought in a systematic or historical-developmental structure. Freed from this vexed question, I have happily poured my many years of Luther research into this somewhat unusual form. Thus Luther's theology is presented here in fifty-eight discrete, alphabetically arranged essays of varying lengths.

Another distinctive feature of this book, highly unusual in the field, is that it does not include a single reference to the secondary literature. This does not mean that such studies are lacking. Quite the opposite is true! Every good research library throughout the Western world devotes enormous shelf space to Luther-related publications. Several volumes appear annually listing the newest literature: the *Luther-Jahrbuch*, the *Archiv für Reformationsgeschichte: Literaturbericht*, the *Luther Digest*, and so forth. So immense is this literature that, to tell the truth, no expert I know of can keep up. We all read selectively and narrowly. I first immersed myself in this ocean thirty-six years ago, as a graduate student at the University of St. Michael's College in Toronto. With the exception of a hiatus or two, and a few scholarly detours, I persisted—until I began writing this book. It was then that I realized that by trying to do both, I would never finish: I had to stop reading other people's books to write my own! Thus I resolved to focus exclusively on Luther's writings themselves.

I certainly do not mean to imply that the secondary literature on Luther is unimportant or worthless. There is a great deal indeed to be learned from it. I studied this scholarship for many years, learned much from it, and contributed substantially to it. (For my favorites, see the "Suggestions for Further Reading" at the end of this book.) Though I do not cite it in my text, this literature has deeply shaped my general approach and orientation. Luther experts will easily be able to detect, here and there throughout this work, the influence of Ebeling, or Althaus, or Lohse, for instance. Yet only Luther himself is quoted and cited.

Readers will quickly notice too that this book is "quotation rich." Every article, sooner or later, falls back on the actual words of Luther, and sometimes very frequently. For me, this was a way of letting the color and emotional power of Luther's style creep into my text. It will, I hope, tempt readers to look into the Luther writings themselves. To put it differently, I quote Luther a great deal because he was a better writer than I am.

Needless to say, Luther's words appear here in English translation. On this, I want to add a word of explanation for newcomers to Luther scholarship. The gold standard of all collections of Luther's writings is the mighty 120-volume set known as the *Weimarer Ausgabe*. Here are the Latin and German originals, as Luther formulated them (so far as we know). About half of this material has been translated into English in the 55 volumes of the so-called American Edition. Strangely, a good number of Luther experts writing in English refuse to quote from this translation. The reasons are unclear. Perhaps they have been infected by a kind of teutonic, *wissenschaftliche* snobbery. In any case, I reject this, and happily quote from the American Edition. In my opinion, it is on the whole an excellent translation. My practice in this book, therefore, is as follows: (a) if a work of Luther is translated in the American Edition, I quote from that translation; (b) in those rare cases where I find the American Edition translation to be inaccurate or infelicitous, I give my own translation and cite the *Weimarer Ausgabe*; (c) for writings not translated in the American Edition, I provide my own translation and cite the *Weimarer Ausgabe*; (d) for the few but important writings of Luther that appear in the *Book of Concord*, I quote from the superb Kolb-Wengert translation of this work; (e) in quoting translations from the American Edition, I do not alter that source's gender-exclusive language (though this language is jarring for many of us, it serves as a stark reminder of how much Luther's world differed from ours).

In writing this book, I incurred many debts of gratitude and I am happy to acknowledge them. Friends, hosts, colleagues, archivists, and librarians facilitated my work in Chicago, Atlanta, Berkeley, Winnipeg, Cologne, Wolfenbüttel, and Toronto. Steve and Jean Godsall-Meyers of the ELCA Center welcomed me in Wittenberg. The generosity of the Rockefeller Foundation made possible a period of concentrated writing in Bellagio. My home institution, Loyola University in New Orleans, paved the way for this entire project with research fellowships, a sabbatical, and other forms of support. My wife, Jan, showed enormous patience and empathy as I expounded, perhaps far too often, on the difficulties of writing books. Without all this backing, this book would probably not have materialized.

Gratitude on a different scale is due to the persons to whom this book is dedicated. Whether they knew it or not, they functioned as mentors for me at various stages of my life. What I owe them could not be expressed in a few sentences.

On August 29, 2005, some early sections of this work, left in my home office in New Orleans, were submerged beneath the waters of Hurricane Katrina. As I returned to the empty, silent, devastated city in mid-September, I felt very keenly what Luther called "all the tragic misery and heartache, of which there is so incalculably much on earth" (BC 455). A month later citizens were returning, aid was pouring into the city, volunteers were arriving, and I was drying my flood-soaked pages on the back lawn under the kind October sun. Again, Luther's words rang true: "But now ponder in your heart the whole course of nature and of this whole life . . . and you will find more good than bad things" (LW 6, 90). For that too I am grateful.

Abbreviations

BC   *The Book of Concord: The Confessions of the Evangelical Lutheran Church.* Ed. Robert Kolb and Timothy Wengert. Minneapolis: Fortress, 2000.

LW   Luther's Works (American Edition). 55 vols. Ed. Helmut Lehmann and Jaroslav Pelikan. St. Louis: Concordia Publishing House and Philadelphia: Fortress, 1955–86.

WA   *D. Martin Luthers Werke: Kritische Gesamtausgabe, Schriften.* 84 vols. Weimar: Böhlau, 1883–.

WABr   *D. Martin Luthers Werke: Kritische Gesamtausgabe, Briefwechsel.* 18 vols. Weimar: Böhlau, 1930–85.

WADB   *D. Martin Luthers Werke: Kritische Gesamtausgabe, Deutsche Bibel.* 12 vols. Weimar: Böhlau, 1906–61.

WATR   *D. Martin Luthers Werke: Kritische Gesamtausgabe, Tischreden.* 6 vols. Weimar: Böhlau, 1912–21.

A Luther Chronology
(with important writings)

November 16: *The Freedom of a Christian*

December 10: Luther and his students burned *Exsurge Domine*

Late December: *Why the Books of the Pope and His Disciples Were Burned*

1521   January 3: excommunicated by Pope Leo X in *Decet romanum pontificem*

Defense and Explanation of All the Articles

April 17–18: appearance before the Diet of Worms

May 4 to March 1, 1522: in hiding in the Wartburg

Began German translation of New Testament

Against Latomus

November: wrote *The Judgment of Martin Luther on Monastic Vows*
    (appeared in February 1522)

1522   September: New Testament translation published

Personal Prayer Book

The Estate of Marriage

1523   *That Jesus Christ Was Born a Jew*

An Order of Mass and Communion for the Church at Wittenberg

1524   *To the Councilmen of All Cities in Germany That They Establish and Maintain*
    Christian Schools

1525   April: *An Admonition to Peace: A Reply to the Twelve Articles of the Peasants*
    in Swabia

May: *Against the Robbing and Murdering Hordes of Peasants*

June 13: marriage to Katherine von Bora

The Bondage of the Will composed in autumn, in print by late December

1526   *The German Mass and Order of Service*

Son Hans born

The Sacrament of the Body and Blood of Christ—Against the Fanatics

Whether Soldiers, Too, Can Be Saved

1527   Daughter Elisabeth born

That These Words of Christ, "This Is My Body," etc., Still Stand Firm Against
    the Fanatics

1528   Daughter Elisabeth died

Concerning Rebaptism

Confession Concerning Christ's Supper

1529   Daughter Magdalene (Lenchen) born

Marburg Colloquy with Huldrych Zwingli

March: Small Catechism

May 4: Large Catechism

On War Against the Turk

1530   May: father died

Augsburg Confession presented to Diet of Augsburg (written by Philip
    Melanchthon, approved by Luther)

The Keys

1531   Mother died

Preaching on Gospel of John (published as *Sermons on the Gospel of John*)

Began lecturing on Galatians (published as *Lectures on Galatians* in 1535)

1533   Son Paul born

1534   Daughter Margaret born

September: translation of entire Bible completed and published

1535   *Lectures on Galatians* published (begun in 1531)

Began lectures on Genesis (finished in 1545, and published as *Lectures on*
    Genesis)

1536   *Disputation Concerning Man*

List of Articles

Articles

Anfechtung   This term, which Luther used throughout his career, has no exact equivalent in English. It refers not to an idea or a belief but to an experience. Literally, it means a kind of assault or attack. The Latin term Luther most often used to refer to the same thing is *tentatio*. But to translate this simply as "temptation," as many have done, is to seriously distort what he meant. In short, the term is problematic.

At the same time it is of major importance, because Luther's theology has experience, more precisely religious experience, as its starting point. The subject matter of theology is the human person—one's guilt and redemption. Theologians try to understand this with the help of revelation. But they are driven to this task in the first place by religious experience—their own and that of others. This is what Luther meant when he said, "experience alone makes the theologian" (LW 54, nr. 46, 7). Of course, human religious experience comes in multiple, almost infinite, varieties. But Luther's analysis categorized all of it into two basic types: the negative and the positive, the experience of our sinfulness and separation from God, on the one hand, and the experience of faith, on the other. *Anfechtung* is Luther's term for the first type of experience, especially in its more intense forms. This primal religious experience *taught* Luther theology: "I didn't learn my theology all at once. I had to ponder over it ever more deeply, and my *Anfechtungen* [*tentationes*] were of help to me in this, for one does not learn anything without experience [*sine usu*]" (WATR 1, nr. 352, 146, 12–14).

(Note that in the previous paragraph, both quotations are from Luther's Table Talk. In what follows here, I quote this source repeatedly. Whenever I cite "WATR" or "LW 54" as the reference, readers should be aware that the quotation is from Luther's Table Talk. Luther experts agree that this source is of some value, but its accuracy is often suspect. As a general rule, evidence taken from the Table Talk should be regarded not as probative but as corroborative.)

This provisional definition can give us an initial orientation to the subject, but it must be tested against what Luther actually said about *Anfechtung*. He was not reluctant to speak and write about this aspect of his personal, inner life. It was a recurring experience for him: he felt it in varying degrees of intensity at every stage of his life—as a young monk, as a beginning professor at Wittenberg, at the Wartburg, in the late 1520s, and so on, into old age. Obviously this was not the kind of experience that is finally and decisively overcome in a dramatic conversion event. Moreover, his many descriptions and definitions vary widely. They leave the distinct impression that mere words are inadequate to define it. We should not be surprised: often one's most deeply felt experiences elude precise delineation in ordinary language.

Luther realized that some of his bouts of *Anfechtung* were related to physical illnesses. They can be, he says, the cause of headaches and stomach problems (LW 54, nr. 461, 74). They can also result from physical ailments that force us to face our mortality (LW 14, 141). But the "spiritual anguish exceeds bodily suffering by far" (LW 54, nr. 3799, 276). And *Anfechtung* can strike when we are in perfect health. So too Luther understood that *Anfechtung* is related to depression (LW 54, nr. 122, 17; 54, nr. 3798, 275). Severe depression can be a kind of *Anfechtung* (WABr 11, nr. 4120, 112, 7–10). But on the other hand, *Anfechtung* is by no means reducible to depression, from his point of view.

Sometimes Luther describes *Anfechtung* as an experience of God's anger—a horrifying anger because it is eternal: "in this present agony, a person sees nothing but hell, and there seems to be no way out. One feels that what is happening is endless, for it is not the wrath of a human person but of the eternal God" (WA 5, 210, 13–16). Elsewhere Luther describes this fear that God's anger is unending in other terms: "My *Anfechtung* [*tentatio*] is this, that I think I don't have a gracious God. . . . It is the greatest grief, and, as Paul says, it produces death [2 Cor. 7:10]" (WATR 1, nr. 461, 200, 6–8). Even worse, perhaps, is when one senses that one faces it alone. "When a person is tormented by *Anfechtungen*, one seems to be alone. God is irreconcilably angry only with him or her" (WA 5, 79, 14–15).

Sometimes the theme of *human* anger rises to the fore in Luther's discussion. His own early experience of *Anfechtung* in the monastery made him "angry with God" (LW 34, 337). The experience can lead to hatred of God, the "wish that there were no God at all!" (LW 22, 142),

and ultimately, blasphemously, to the desire to kill God (WA 5, 210, 1–2).

The person who experiences *Anfechtung*, Luther thought, approaches the gates of hell: "the entrance of hell . . . is near despair" (LW 31, 130). Already in his Ninety-five Theses (1517), Luther had mentioned the "horror of despair" (LW 31, 27). In the following year, in his *Explanations of the Ninety-five Theses*, he elaborated on this despair in a passage that was to become his most famous description of *Anfechtung*.

> I myself "knew a man" [Luther is referring to himself] who claimed that he had often suffered these punishments, in fact over a very brief period of time. Yet they were so great and so much like hell that no tongue could adequately express them, no pen could describe them, and one who had not himself experienced them could not believe them. And so great were they that, if they had been sustained or had lasted for half an hour, even for one tenth of an hour, he would have perished completely and all of his bones would have been reduced to ashes. At such a time God seems terribly angry, and with him the whole creation. At such a time there is no flight, no comfort, within or without, but all things accuse. At such a time, as the Psalmist mourns, 'I am cut off from thy sight' [Cf. Ps. 31:22]. . . . All that remains is the stark-naked desire for help and a terrible groaning, but it does not know where to turn for help. In this instance the person is stretched out with Christ so that all his bones may be counted, and every corner of the soul is filled with the greatest bitterness, dread, trembling, and sorrow in such a manner that all these last forever. (*LW* 31, 129)

This "abyss of despair" remained for Luther one of the standard ways of describing what he meant by *Anfechtung* (LW 33, 190; 54, 16–17).

If despair brings us near to the gates of hell, there is another form of *Anfechtung* that takes us into hell itself: the experience of the silence of God. Sometimes God "withdraws his anger" and disappears (WATR 1, nr. 1179, 585,

3–10). He abandons us: "To be abandoned by God—this is far worse than death" (WA 45, 237, 23). Here is the ultimate anguish, what Luther calls the "most perfect *Anfechtung*" (WA 5, 204, 26), the very worst human experience imaginable—hell itself.

Luther did not think that the experience of *Anfechtung* was universal. Some, such as John von Staupitz, Luther's early spiritual mentor, did not seem to understand (LW 54, nr. 1288, 133). Sebastian Münster, a Hebraist upon whom Luther relied for help in translating the Old Testament, had no such experience, in Luther's opinion (WATR 3, nr. 3505, 363, 4–6). Erasmus and Luther's "sacramentarian" opponents would change their minds if they ever experienced this (LW 49, 173). The indulgence preachers could never so crassly trivialize the gospel if they felt this (LW 31, 130). The "reprobate," Luther says, feel no such thing (LW 25, 378). Then too, "self-assured, coarse, untested, inexperienced people know and understand nothing about this" (WA 45, 237, 23–26).

At the same time Luther took comfort in the fact that he was not alone: many people do experience something similar, and some have left us with their attempts to describe it. The book of Job is one example of this (WA 5, 78, 36–37; 45, 239, 18–19). Even more poignant, from Luther's perspective, is the story of Jonah. What greater abandonment could there be than to be "cast into the deep" (Jonah 2:3; LW 19, 18–19)? What greater silence than to be in "the belly of the fish" (Jonah 2:1)? And Jonah's story was Luther's: "I sat with Jonah in the whale, where everything seemed to be despair" (WATR 3, nr. 3503, 363, 4–6). Most eloquent of all in expressing the experience of *Anfechtung*, Luther thought, were the Psalms. Indeed, this is what the whole book is about (WATR 5, nr. 6305, 592, 26–27). From the divine wrath of Psalm 6 (LW 54, nr. 3798, 275), to the "despairing spirit" of Psalm 51 (LW 25, 377), to the "faint spirit" of Psalm 142 (LW 42, 184–185), to "the

depths" of Psalm 130—"where," Luther asks, "do you find deeper, more sorrowful, more pitiful words of sadness . . . ? There again you look into the hearts of all the saints, as into death, yes, as into hell itself" (LW 35, 256). And the theme of abandonment is powerfully expressed in Psalm 22: "My God, my God, why have you forsaken me?"

With this we come to the supreme sufferer of *Anfechtung*, Jesus himself. Luther often alludes to this, but he addresses it most directly in sermons on the passion (e.g., WA 52, 734–742). Following Matthew's narrative (Matt. 26:36–46), Luther recounts how Jesus entered the Garden of Gethsemane with his disciples. There Jesus experienced an anguish (*Angst*) so great he felt he could die from it (WA 52, 734, 26–28). Faced with this *Anfechtung*, he prayed "Let this cup pass from me," three times according to Matthew. And the Father's answer? Silence! (In Luke's version, Luther notes, God sends an angel to "strengthen" Jesus [WA 52, 742, 8–9]. But still the silence is not broken [Luke 22:41–44].) No wonder, then, that shortly thereafter, from the cross, we hear his cry of dereliction, "My God, my God, why have you forsaken me?" (Matt. 27:46). Silence and abandonment—Jesus experienced "the most perfect *Anfechtung*" (WA 5, 204, 26), or what Luther elsewhere calls "the high *Anfechtung*, which is called being forsaken by God" (WA 45, 240, 26–27), a "high, spiritual suffering" that is unimaginable (WA 45, 239, 23).

Horrifying as the experience of *Anfechtung* can be, it can also be salutary. Without this, for instance, one cannot really understand the Scriptures (WATR 1, nr. 941, 472, 22–24)—not David, nor Jonah, nor Job, nor Christ. Luther wonders whether "smug people, who have never struggled with any temptation [*tentatio/Anfechtung*] or true terrors of sin and death," can really know what faith is (LW 26, 127). Moreover, Luther thought, this experience is essential for theologians. In his 1539 prescription for "a correct way of studying theology," *Anfechtung* plays a major role: It "is the touchstone which teaches you not only to know and understand, but also to experience how right, how true, how sweet, how lovely, how mighty, how comforting God's word is, wisdom beyond all wisdom" (LW 34, 286). Without experiencing the depths, in other words, the immensity of the heights can scarcely be grasped.

There is also a deeper sense in which the experience of *Anfechtung* is beneficial for us. The "broken spirit" that the psalmist calls "the sacrifice acceptable to God" (Ps. 51:17), Luther thinks, is the *Anfechtung* of despair (LW 25, 377). In fact, our despair puts us in proximity to grace (LW 33, 190). God's kindness and love lie hidden beneath his anger, as Jonah discovered (LW 19, 73; WATR 1, nr. 1179, 585, 3–10). When we experience the silence and the absence of God, Christ is "with" us: "If . . . you have been three days in hell, this is a sign that Christ is with you and you are with Christ" (LW 10, 373). Resurrection is at hand.

Is there anything that can be done to alleviate or mitigate this experience for oneself and for others? Luther offers a very substantial repertoire of advice in this regard. Some of it is found in short treatises such as his 1521 work *Comfort for a Person Facing High Anfechtung* (WA 7, 784–791; tr. in LW 42, 183–186). Even more is found in personal letters to friends and acquaintances. For instance, in 1530 Luther wrote a series of rather substantial letters to one Jerome Weller, who was going through a prolonged period of *Anfechtung* (WABr 5, nr. 1593, 373–375; nr. 1670, 518–520; nr. 1684, 546–547). Likewise in 1531 he sent a letter of advice on this theme to Barbara Lisskirchen (WABr 12, nr. 4244a, 134–136). And in 1545 he circulated a letter to pastors, detailing a kind of semiliturgical procedure for dealing with this very common problem (WABr 11, nr. 4120, 111–112). References to his own personal bouts of *Anfechtung* and how

he dealt with them are found in various writings, but above all throughout his Table Talk. What is notable in all this is the enormous variety. No single piece of advice is appropriate in every case. People differ, and *Anfechtung* manifests itself in a whole range of forms and levels of intensity.

One can easily compile a list of techniques he suggested to one or another sufferer and ones he himself used: Go to private confession (LW 51, 98). Pray, using Psalm 142 (LW 42, 184–185). Tell the devil, "Kiss my ass" (WATR 1, nr. 144, 64, 16–17). Flee solitude (LW 54, nr. 3799, 277). Drink heartily (though for some, abstinence is better) (LW 54, nr. 122, 18; WA 40:2, 115, 14–116, 2; LW 50, 48). Eat sumptuously, and think of the opposite sex (LW 54, nr. 122, 18). Tell jokes and laugh, and commit a sin to spite the devil (WABr 5, nr. 1670, 519, 42–46). Yield to God's will: focus not on "Let this cup pass from me," but rather on "Not my will, but yours" (LW 42, 183). And so on. This list could easily be extended. All of these things, Luther thought, work in certain circumstances.

Yet he also knew that in another sense none of them work. We can begin to understand this if we focus for the moment solely on the "most perfect" or "high" *Anfechtung*. Lesser *Anfechtungen* are really only weaker versions of the same thing. And this high *Anfechtung* is, as we have seen, the experience of God's silence, his abandonment of us, our God-forsakenness, hell. Luther can also speak of it as our sense that God is not really "for us" but "against us":

> My temptation [*Anfechtung, tentatio*] is this, that I think I don't have a gracious God. . . . It is the greatest grief, and, as Paul says, it produces death [II Cor. 7:10]. God hates it, and he comforts us by saying, "I am your God." I know his promise, and yet should some thought that isn't worth a fart nevertheless overwhelm me, I have the advantage . . . of taking hold of his Word once again. God be praised, I grasp the First Commandment which declares, "I am your God

[Exod. 20:2]. I'm not going to devour you. I'm not going to be poison for you." (LW 54, nr. 461, 75)

Here we see what is, to Luther's way of thinking, the only real remedy. It is the confidence that God is "for us."

This confidence or trust is what Luther called "faith." Faith alone, he believed, could alleviate the final hellishness of human experience. "[T]he afflicted conscience has no remedy against despair and eternal death except to take hold of the promise of grace offered in Christ, that is, this righteousness of faith" (LW 26, 5–6). To translate: the "grace offered in Christ" is the gospel, the good news that God is "for us." Christ is, in Luther's formula, "a mirror of the Father's heart" (BC 440). Faith, according to him, "apprehends Christ" (LW 34, 153), or accepts the good news that God is "for us." Faith is thus Anfechtung's opposite, its counterweight in human religious experience, its sole conqueror.

In 1530, in a conversation with friends at table, Luther is reported to have said: "If I would live long enough, I would like to write a book on Anfechtung, for without this nobody can understand the holy Scriptures, nor faith, or know the fear and love of God, indeed he or she cannot know what hope is" (WATR 4, nr. 4777, 490, 24–491, 1). He never wrote such a work, though he lived another sixteen years. Perhaps this has something to do with the fact that he personally was besieged by Anfechtung to the end of his life: it was no abstract, theoretical concept for him. Nor was its counterpart, faith. As he understood it, it was this that over and over again dragged him back from the abyss.

See also **Faith**; **Sin**

Angels   In early Christianity, the relatively few and scattered biblical references to angels provoked a modicum of interest and speculation. This was gathered up and massively elaborated by Pseudo-Dionysius the Areopagite

in *The Celestial Hierarchy*, around 500. Largely on this foundation, an angelology grew to full flower in the scholastic theology of the thirteenth century, developed above all by Thomas Aquinas, the "Angelic Doctor."

Luther's response three centuries later was to severely prune this luxuriant growth, retaining only a few elements that he thought were biblical. His critique began in 1520, with an attack on Dionysius's "hodge-podge about the angels in his *Celestial Hierarchy*— a book over which many curious and superstitious spirits have cudgeled their brains. . . . [I]s not everything in it his own fancy and very much like a dream?" (LW 36, 109). Luther's criticism reached its fullest development in his *Lectures on Genesis* (1535–45), where Luther again excoriated Dionysius as a fraud and his *Celestial Hierarchy* as "the silliest prattle" (LW 1, 235). Dionysius had taken names like "cherubim," "seraphim," and "archangel" literally, when in reality these are images (LW 1, 235–236). Building on this error, theologians like Thomas Aquinas had constructed a purely speculative angelology that left Scripture far behind (WA 29, 673, 17–20; 34:2, 257, 4–5; 34:2, 279, 6–7; 40:3, 50, 19–20; 45, 351, 20–22). Angels, Luther argued, should not be worshiped or venerated. They should not be prayed to, nor should we attribute all sorts of assistance to them (BC 305). Above all, Luther held, since we have God's Word, we need no further revelation from them (LW 7, 119–120).

What then did Luther have to say on the positive side? For one thing, he offered a definition, in his Table Talk: "An angel is a spiritual creature, a personal being without a body, appointed for the service of the heavenly church" (WATR 5, nr. 6229, 552, 1–2).

We also find in Luther a discussion of etymology: "angel" comes from the Greek term for "messenger" (WA 10:1:2, 166, 10–13). Yet there is ambiguity in the term's meaning. In Genesis 48, for instance, Christ is referred to as an "angel" (LW 8, 162–164). On the issue of the fall of the angels, Luther seems unsure why Moses left this out in the primeval history in Genesis. At one point Luther says that Moses purposely left it out so as to discourage speculative flights of fancy (WATR 1, nr. 319, 130, 22–24). Elsewhere Luther says that Moses "forgot" to include the story (LW 1, 22). In any case, Luther was well aware of the thin biblical basis for "fallen angels." Even so, he insisted, "this much is certain: the angels fell and the devil was transformed from an angel of light into an angel of darkness" (LW 1, 23; cf. 1, 111–113).

The role or "office" of the angels, Luther suggests, is twofold. The first takes place in heaven. It would be wrong, however, to think that they are Christ's playmates: "Christ is not someone who lolls in heaven and has fun with the angels" (LW 13, 241). Rather the angels' function there is to worship him (LW 13, 34), to "sing: 'Glory to God in the highest'" (LW 6, 88; cf. 6, 92). And this is their "higher office."

Their second duty is here on earth, and this is their "lower office." It is "to watch and govern us and the creatures, and to fight not only on behalf of the godly but also on behalf of the ungodly" (LW 6, 88). In other words, angels serve as instruments of God's providence. On occasion Luther can speak of good angels and evil angels (or devils) locked in struggle, in a way that sounds almost Manichean (e.g., WA 52, 719, 13–24). But more often he insists that these angels are not acting on their own: "God rules the world by means of the angels, though of course, he does everything by himself" (LW 20, 169; cf. 20, 170). Angels are merely instrumental in carrying out God's will.

Interestingly, Luther holds that angels act on the macrolevel as international peacemakers. They are "present at the courts of the emperor, the kings, and the princes," where they mitigate conflict and "make peace" (WA 52, 719, 32–38). Thus God, "through the angels . . . controls the empires even of the ungodly" (LW 1, 88).

More commonly, Luther speaks of the angels' function as that of personal guardians. All humans have one assigned to guard and protect them (LW 1, 171; elsewhere Luther says we all have more than one: WA 52, 720, 28–29). They come in various forms: great rulers and princes have great angels, while lowly people and children have lesser ones (WA 52, 721, 1–14). The lowest angels, in fact, do the same menial work as parents—taking care of children. Their humility is exemplary, and in reality their seemingly menial work is the noblest work (WA 34:2, 249, 14–250, 25). The belief that angels protect children from all harm—"It is good to impress this truth on children. On the other hand, children should also be told about the devil and the evil spirits. My dear child, one should say, if you will not be good, your angel will run away from you, and the evil spirit, the black monster [*der schwarze Popelmann*] will come" (WA 34:2, 251, 19–25). Childhood fear, Luther thought, was not necessarily a bad thing.

In summary, Luther was sharply critical of scholastic angelology. Yet, because of the angels' place in Scripture, Luther could not entirely abandon this belief. Thus angels remained part of his worldview, but they are decisively sidelined, relegated to the periphery. Yes, Luther says, God works through angels, but in truth "he does everything by himself" (LW 20, 169). Elsewhere Luther argues that since God's revelation in Jesus Christ is final, full, and definitive, angels (understood as "ministers," "messengers," and "forerunners") are no longer needed (LW 4, 124–125). Thus angels play no essential role in Luther's worldview.

Apocrypha   The apocryphal (or deuterocanonical) books were included in Luther's first complete German translation of the Bible, which was first printed in 1534. They appeared together under the heading "Apocrypha: These Books Are Not Held Equal to the Scriptures, but Are Useful and Good to Read" (WADB 2, 547). This summarizes precisely Luther's view of them.

In 1529 Luther had translated Wisdom of Solomon, and in 1532 he labored with great difficulty over Ecclesiasticus (or Jesus Sirach). Apparently tiring of the project, he turned the rest over to Philip Melanchthon and Justus Jonas. The books of 1 and 2 Esdras were simply left out: they "contain nothing," Luther said, "that one could not find better in Aesop" (LW 25, 350). The rest appeared in the 1534 Bible, each with a preface written by Luther in which he did not withhold his personal opinions.

Judith, he said, was of dubious historical accuracy, but nevertheless "a good, serious, heroic tragedy" (LW 35, 345). Wisdom of Solomon was surely not written by Solomon but probably by Philo (LW 35, 341). Tobit may well be fictional, "a fine, delightful, devout comedy" (LW 35, 345). Ecclesiasticus, a work of multiple authors, gives useful direction "on the virtues of a pious householder" (LW 35, 348). Baruch is "very skimpy"; Luther "nearly let it go," but then decided to "let [it] run with the pack" (LW 35, 349–350). Luther thought that 1 Maccabees had contemporary political relevance (LW 35, 350–352) and 2 Maccabees was a "good story" despite its mixed-up chronology and its apparent endorsement of a suicide in 14:41–46 (LW 35, 352–353). The Prayer of Azariah, the Song of the Three Young Men, Susanna, and Bel and the Dragon, though they are not in the Hebrew text, can be included as "beautiful religious fictions" (LW 35, 353–354).

These apocryphal texts were of virtually no theological or doctrinal importance for Luther. He included them in his Bible translation because of their edifying value. As his Bible became a bestseller, they were widely disseminated (and read?) in German Protestant parts of Europe.

Ascension   Though the ascension of Christ plays a marginal role in the New Testament (see Mark 16:19; Luke 24:51; Acts 1:2, 9), it quickly grew in importance, finding its way into all three of the classical creeds. Luther inherited it unquestioningly, as an age-old article of faith. Only in the mid–1520s did it become controversial, in the context of the dispute over the real presence of Christ in the Lord's Supper. His opponents argued that since Christ had ascended into heaven, he could not really be present in the sacrament. (*See also Lord's Supper.*)

Luther had relatively little to say about this doctrine, treating it mainly in a few sermons for Ascension Day. His understanding of it can be summarized briefly. This is an article of faith, he said, and consequently it can only be grasped by faith (WA 12, 562, 28–29). All Christians accept this, but the real question is what it means. His opponents, Luther said, take it literally (LW 37, 46). He, on the other hand, did not: Christ did not ascend "in the way that you climb the stairs into your house; rather it means that he became over, in, and outside of all creation" (WA 19, 491, 26–29). In other words, the ascension is not about a physical rising up into the clouds, but about how Christ at the end of his life on earth became ubiquitous (omnipresent) (LW 37, 214).

On the surface it might seem that the ascension represents Christ's departure from the world, and from us: "But beware that you do not think this way, that he became more remote from us. Rather, just the opposite: when he was on earth, he was too remote from us; now [after the ascension] he is near" (WA 12, 562, 24–26). Christ's presence to us depends on faith: "Those who believe it have it, and those who do not believe it do not have it" (WA 12, 565, 26–29). Ascension does not mean departure but a new kind of presence.

Luther is even more succinct when it comes to the closely related "sitting at the right hand of the Father" (the *sessio ad dexteram*). This is attested to in only one of the Gospels (Mark 16:19), but it is included in all three creeds, and thus accepted by Luther as an article of faith. Again, Luther held, it is not to be taken literally: "Scripture . . . teaches us that God's right hand is not a particular place where a body should or could be, as on a golden chair. Rather it is the almighty power of God, which can simultaneously be nowhere and everywhere" (WA 23, 133, 19–22). When Christians say that Christ sat down at the Father's right hand, they mean that he "assumed dominion" (BC 435) and "rules eternally" (BC 355).

Atonement   In their attempts to describe the work of Christ, Christians from the outset used titles like Redeemer, Savior, Mediator, Reconciler, and so forth. Throughout the history of Christianity, theologians have developed a variety of theories to explain precisely how the work of Christ is salvific, and each of these explanations has some warrant in the New Testament sources. A long debate among Luther scholars over which of these theories he sided with has proved inconclusive. In fact, Luther used them all—some more, some less—as he struggled to comprehend this central mystery of the faith, to which no single theory can do justice. Thus, rather than a single, comprehensive, and consistent theory, we find in Luther's theology a whole series of motifs, images, and theories, all of which in some way shed light on Christ's saving work. They can be summarized briefly.

The ransom image, common in the early church, is occasionally employed by Luther. "See what great price God paid for you and how great the ransom is through which you have been bought and made God's children. . . . The Father . . . let his Son Jesus Christ pour out all his blood" (WA 12, 291, 6–16). Christ is the ransom paid by God to free us, that is, to "save" us.

We also find in Luther the language of sacrifice. Christ "offers himself in order to reconcile God" (WA 10:1:1, 718, 1–2). As the sacrificial lamb in ancient Judaism, he "has taken my sins on himself and has died because of them and has allowed himself to be slain because of these sins" (WA 10:1:2, 221, 24–25). This sacrifice "takes away" our sin.

Luther endorses as well the view that part of Christ's work was to provide a model for human action (LW 22, 265). Following him as our example, however, is, strictly speaking, not salvific, and here Luther carefully avoids any kind of "Imitation of Christ" soteriology (LW 30, 117). True discipleship (following of Christ) takes place through faith, which must precede the following of Christ through works: "But you are truly following Christ if you follow him in faith and rely on him. Then another kind of following takes place, namely, following his example, doing his works, and suffering as he suffered" (LW 23, 326). Only in this attenuated sense is Christ our savior by being our example.

Luther can occasionally use the "fish hook theory," a highly mythological patristic construct, to explain Christ's work. "Here you can say that the devil attacked Christ, as the fish attacks the bait and is thus caught on the hook. . . . The worm on the hook was Christ as the world despised him; when Satan tried to swallow this worm, he was caught on the hook of the divinity and pulled out" (WA 10:3, 100, 24–30; cf. LW 22, 24). Thus the devil's power over humanity was broken by Christ.

Much more common in Luther is the motif of the "joyous exchange," which takes marriage as its central metaphor. This is prominent in his 1520 treatise *Freedom of a Christian*: "for if Christ is a bridegroom, he must take upon himself the things which are his bride's and bestow on her the things which are his." Thus "sin, death, and damnation will be Christ's, while grace, life and salvation will be the soul's" (LW 31, 351). So too in his 1535 *Lectures on Galatians* Luther explains Christ's work in these same terms: "By this fortunate exchange with us he took upon himself our sinful person and granted us his innocent and victorious person" (LW 26, 284).

More prominent still in Luther's thought on the atonement is the patristic *Christus Victor* theme. Christ saves us by fighting against what Luther calls the "tyrants" or the "powers" (sin, death, the devil, the law, etc.), and emerging victorious. "Christ's true and proper function [is] to struggle with the law, sin, and death of the entire world" (LW 26, 373). Christ's triumph "over the law, sin, and our flesh, the world, the devil, death, hell, and all evils" (LW 26, 22) means quite simply that he broke the power of evil enslaving us. When Luther approaches Christ's work from this angle, the resurrection assumes a special importance, as does Christ's divine nature.

Probably the majority of Luther's references to the atonement echo one or another version of Anselm's "satisfaction" theory. In brief, Anselm taught that humans had committed an infinite violation of God's honor; that God could have punished us but in his mercy he allowed "satisfaction" to be made; that only a "God-man" could make such a satisfaction, who as God *could* do it and who as human *should* do it; and that precisely the suffering of this "God-man" compensates God for the injury humans have done to his honor. Wherever the terms *satisfactio* or *Genugtuung* come up in Luther—and they come up frequently—we can be sure he has Anselm's theory in mind. "God has given us in the first place a man who satisfied in all things the divine righteousness for us all" (WA 10:1:1, 123, 15–16). Christ "is the eternal satisfaction for our sin" (LW 51, 92). Yet, as often as Luther used this explanation, he still recognized its inadequacy. Satisfaction, he said in a 1531 sermon, "is still too weak to fully express the grace of Christ and does not adequately honor Christ's suffering" (WA 21, 264, 28–30).

A final way in which Luther explains how Christ "saves" us falls along the lines of Abelard's so-called subjective theory of the atonement. Christ, Abelard argued, came to reveal God's love for us; in fully fathoming this we are transformed, that is, we begin to love him in return. Though Luther in his writings never mentioned Abelard, he warmly embraced the idea, especially in his sermons. In Christ, Luther held, we can learn the most essential thing there is to know about God, namely, how he is disposed toward us. Christ is "a mirror of the Father's heart," he said (*BC* 440). "What a profound and rich idea God had, to so pour out his mercy that we may know what he thinks and what he intends and through his revelation, see his heart" (WA 45, 93, 11–13). Christ's work, in other words, is to reveal to humans that they are the objects of an infinite and unconditional love.

Grasping this, or "grasping Christ"— this is what Luther means by faith, and this alone "justifies": "But Christ is grasped, not by the law or by works but by a reason or an intellect that has been illumined by faith. . . . The speculation by which Christ is grasped is not the foolish imagination of the sophists [scholastic theologians]. . . . [I]t is a theological, faithful, and divine consideration . . . of Christ hanging on the cross for my sins. . . . Hence it is evident that faith alone justifies" (LW 26, 287). And this faith, understood as the subjective appropriation of Christ, as our acceptance of God's love, is salvific. This means that it transforms us. In an Epiphany sermon from 1526, Luther asks: When we realize that God's self-revelation in Christ is for us, must not a human heart "shatter into a hundred thousand pieces because its joy is so great? For then it would peer into the depths of the fatherly heart, yes, into the inexhaustible goodness and eternal goodness and love of God that he feels and has felt toward us from eternity" (WA 20, 228, 12–15). Moreover, when Christ "saves" us in this way, there are ethical consequences for our lives. In a 1525 Palm Sunday sermon, Luther expressed this as follows: "Whose heart does not simply melt for joy at hearing this [that God's love is expressed in Christ for us]? Who can fail to love, praise, and give thanks, and not only become a servant of the whole world but gladly become even less—less important than nothing—when he sees that God himself values him so highly and so richly pours out and proves his fatherly will in the obedience of his Son?" (WA 17:2, 244, 32–37). Here then is another way of explaining how Christ "saves" us. Its importance for Luther should not be underestimated.

All of the above-mentioned motifs, images, and theories are part of Luther's effort to penetrate the central mystery of Christ's work. As indicated, Luther favors some above others, but he abandons none of them, certainly because he realizes that each has some foundation in the biblical text. Opting for one and dismissing the rest would doubtless have yielded greater systematic coherence. Luther was unwilling to do this, one suspects, because it would be a betrayal of the biblical witness and a dissolving of what is ultimately a mystery of faith.

Baptism   Luther's   understanding of baptism appears to have remained entirely conventional up until 1519. Earlier, in 1517, he had begun wrestling with the sacrament of penance, and then with the more general issue of what exactly a sacrament is. Now, in late 1519, he turned his attention to composing a sermon entitled *The Holy and Blessed Sacrament of Baptism* (LW 35, 29–43).

When we read this sermon against the background of late medieval baptismal theology, two features stand out. First, Luther insists that a true sacrament is composed of three requisite elements: a sign, a divine promise to which the sign points, and the faith by which the promise is received. This last element—

faith—"is of all things the most necessary, for it is the ground of all comfort" (LW 35, 36). "[O]nly by lack of faith in its operation is baptism cancelled out. . . . Thus everything depends on faith" (LW 35, 38). To thus locate faith at the very center of one's understanding of the sacrament was something of an innovation, and it was to raise new difficulties for Luther at a later stage.

Another feature that differentiates Luther in this early period from his medieval inheritance is his novel introduction of the language of "imputation" and "simultaneity." In baptism, he argues, "a person becomes guiltless, pure, and sinless, while at the same time continuing full of evil inclinations" (LW 35, 35). A baptized person is thus pure by the gracious imputation of God rather than by virtue of his or her own nature (LW 35, 36). In baptism, God "pledges . . . not to impute to you the sins which remain" (LW 35, 34). This language clearly foreshadows later developments in Luther's understanding of "imputed righteousness" and of the simultaneity of righteousness and sinfulness in the lives of Christians.

In his great manifesto of the following year, *The Babylonian Captivity of the Church* (1520), Luther affirms the sacramental nature of baptism and the Lord's Supper, and restricts the term "sacrament" to these two rites. As for baptism, he begins by praising God, who "has preserved in his church this sacrament at least, untouched and untainted by the ordinances of men . . . and has not permitted it to be oppressed by the filthy and godless monsters of greed and superstition" (LW 36, 57). This ringing affirmation stands in stark contrast to the denunciations that follow only a few pages later (e.g., LW 36, 67 and 70)! Several aspects of the traditional baptismal theology come under attack.

First, Luther takes issue with Jerome's statement, repeated by virtually all the scholastics, that penance is a "second plank after shipwreck." This implies, Luther argues, a mistaken view of baptism, namely, that its effect is destroyed by sin (LW 36, 58). The grace received in baptism is permanent: it is not to be understood as a kind of substance poured into us at baptism, and poured out again by sin (LW 36, 69).

Second, Luther disputes the scholastic commonplace that the sacraments are efficacious so long as the recipient places no obstacle in the way. For Luther, no "work" whatsoever is required—only faith (LW 36, 65), and this faith is indispensable: "Thus it is not baptism that justifies or benefits anyone, but it is faith in that word of promise to which baptism is added. This faith justifies, and fulfills that which baptism signifies" (LW 36, 66). Only in this sense is the other scholastic axiom—that a sacrament is an "effective sign"—true. In fact, faith can justify without it (LW 36, 66–67).

Already foreshadowed in his *Babylonian Captivity* was an issue that was shortly to become increasingly problematic for Luther and one that he never really managed to fully resolve. Luther's insistence on the necessity of faith in the recipient raised an obvious question: Are infants receiving baptism required to have faith? At first glance, Luther's answer in this work appears to be entirely conventional: the faith of the parents and sponsors substitutes for the infant. "Here I say what all say: Infants are aided by the faith of others, those who bring them for baptism.... [T]hrough the prayer of the believing church which presents it ... the infant is changed, cleansed, and renewed by inpoured faith" (LW 36, 73). Yet there are already hints here that Luther is tempted to attribute faith to infants. For one thing, the "inpoured faith" (*fides infusa*; WA 6, 538, 10–11) Luther mentions here could be understood as the infant's own. Moreover, he notes that the infant is utterly free and absolutely secure in effortlessly accepting what is being done to her or him. "We should be even as little children, when they are newly baptized, who engage in no efforts or works, but are free in every way, secure and saved solely through the glory of their baptism" (LW 36, 73). Is not this instinctual confidence and unself-conscious trust of the infant not very close to what Luther meant by "faith"?

Be this as it may, this question of the faith of infants grew into a major one for Luther. Through 1521 we find ambiguity in his position. At times he still asserts the commonly held view: infants are baptized on the faith of their parents and godparents (LW 32, 14). But by 1522 a new emphasis had emerged. In a sermon of that year, Luther asserted that people are saved only on the basis of their own faith, not somebody else's. Either infants have faith before baptism, or faith is infused in baptism itself (WA 10:3, 310, 15–27). But infant faith is a reality.

In the following year, 1523, Luther's insistence on this point became more adamant. In a work on the Lord's Supper written for the Bohemian Brethren, he expressed his view forcefully: "I have said that it would be better not to baptize any children anywhere at all than to baptize them without faith, since in such procedure the sacrament and God's holy name are taken in vain.... For without faith the sacrament should not and cannot be received or if it is received, it works greater injury" (LW 36, 300). And how did Luther think infants acquired this faith? "[T]hrough the faith and prayer of the church young children ... are endowed with faith, and thus are baptized.... And if anyone is able to overthrow this judgment of mine ... I would rather teach that children should not be baptized than (as I have said) that they should be baptized without faith" (LW 36, 301). Faith is thus divinely infused into the infant at the moment of baptism. The logic of Luther's insistence on the centrality of faith for the sacrament had driven him to this position. Yet one senses that he did not relish defending it.

It was also in 1523 that Luther took action on the liturgical front. His revised order for worship of that year included a section on baptism (LW 53, 95–103). The main change was in language—German now replaced the traditional Latin. But in its heavy emphasis on freeing the infant from "the snares of the devil" (LW 53, 96), it was quite conventional. Other traditions, such as blowing under the infant's eyes, putting salt in the mouth, putting spit in the ears and nose, and so forth, were retained, though Luther labeled them "unimportant" (LW 53, 102). In 1526 he revised this order for baptism, shortening it by deleting some traditional elements, adding nothing new, and minimizing references to the devil's snares (LW 53, 106–109). This version was appended to his Small Catechism of 1529 (BC 371–75).

In a Lenten sermon from 1525, one finds Luther returning to the issue of the faith of infants. First, he rejects outright the Catholic teaching that infants are baptized on the faith of the church (WA 17:2, 78, 30–79, 3). Second, he rejects the "Waldensian" view that infants are baptized on the basis of their future faith (WA 17:2, 81, 8–18). Rather, the intercession of the sponsors brings about faith in the infant. He explains: "This is what we call the power of another person's faith. Not that anyone can become righteous through it, but that through another person's intercession and aid, he may receive faith from God himself, through which he will be saved" (WA 17:2, 82, 30–33). That infants have no reason is not an obstacle; indeed, it may be an advantage (WA 17:2, 87, 6–7).

Nevertheless, in this sermon too a note of doubt creeps in. Luther acknowledges the difficulty of demonstrating that infants have faith. In a sense, he concedes, the decisive thing is *not* the infant's faith. We do not baptize because of the infant's faith but because of the divine command and promise (WA 17:2, 85, 36–86, 4). But this minor note is overridden by Luther's confident-sounding assertion: if infants have no faith, it would be better to stop baptizing them; indeed, the sooner the better (WA 17:2, 82, 22–26).

Ever since 1522 various controversial figures—the Zwickau Prophets, Andreas Bodenstein von Karlstadt, Thomas Müntzer—had been advocating just that. After 1525 Luther was aware that an "Anabaptist" movement was coalescing, behind leaders such as Balthasar Hubmaier. Two evangelical pastors wrote to Luther asking for guidance, and the result was his book *Concerning Rebaptism*, which appeared in early 1528. Hurriedly written, repetitious, and disorganized, it is not one of Luther's finer literary efforts. But it is his only extended treatment of the subject.

In this work, Luther confesses to be less than fully informed on the exact teaching of the Anabaptists (LW 40, 261). And he finds the vicious persecution of these people lamentable (LW 40, 230). (By 1531 he had changed his mind about this; see WABr 6, nr. 1882, 222–223.) The heart of the treatise is an enumeration of reasons why the baptism of infants is correct and should be continued:

1. It has been practiced in the church "since the days of the apostles" (LW 40, 254).
2. If infant baptism were wrong, God would not have permitted it to continue for so long (LW 40, 255).
3. Many baptized infants grow up to be true Christians. If infant baptism was invalid, this would not happen.
4. If infant baptism was invalid, there would have been no Christendom for a thousand years (LW 40, 256).
5. Saint Paul calls the church the "temple of God." If infant baptism was invalid, the church would not be this.
6. The old covenant did not exclude children; neither can the new covenant (LW 40, 257).

Absent from this list, but nevertheless relevant in Luther's view, is the witness of Scripture. Thus the instruction to baptize "all" in Matthew 28:19,

Luther argues, must include infants (LW 40, 245). He knows, of course, that Scripture gives us nothing explicit. This silence of Scripture on the issue gives rise to two lines of argument. First, he suggests, "What [God] does not will, he clearly witnesses to in Scripture. What is not so witnessed to there, we can accept as his work" (LW 40, 255). Second, the silence of Scripture means that it is incumbent on the Anabaptists to prove that infant baptism is contrary to Scripture (LW 40, 241).

In the Anabaptist view, this last point (that infant baptism is contrary to Scripture) was self-evident from passages such as Mark 16:16 ("The one who believes and is baptized will be saved"). Infants cannot "believe"; hence infant baptism is contrary to Scripture. Luther understood this and therefore felt compelled once again to make the argument that infants have faith. For "no man should be baptized before he believes" (LW 40, 239).

Luther begins with the assertion that it can never be proven that infants can *not* have faith (LW 40, 241). He then adduces various examples from Scripture that purportedly show that infants *can* have faith (LW 40, 242–243). To say that these are far-fetched is to put it kindly. When he later accuses the Anabaptists of attempting "to make the Scriptures agree with them by dragging passages in by the hair" (LW 40, 262), the reader cannot help but remember this piece of exegesis. Luther himself was not persuaded: a few pages further he acknowledges that "we cannot prove that children do believe with any Scripture verse" (LW 40, 254).

Indeed, Luther seems ready in this treatise to consider the possibility that infants do *not* have faith: "even if they [the Anabaptists] could establish that children are without faith when they are baptized, it would make no difference to me" (LW 40, 246). He is still opposed to rebaptism, because if this is the case (that infants do not have faith), faith comes later. And "when faith comes, baptism is complete" (LW 40, 246). Baptism is a real and authentic sacrament even if faith is absent: "Granted, it is not of benefit to the baptized one who is without faith, because of his lack of faith, but the baptism is not thereby incorrect, uncertain, or of no meaning" (LW 40, 252). It becomes effective for the recipient later, perhaps in adulthood, when faith is present. Here he seems close to endorsing the very position he had rejected in 1525 as "Waldensian."

In the decade following *Concerning Rebaptism*, Luther preached at least twenty-three times on the subject. And he addressed himself to the topic, briefly at least, in various other writings. His most carefully considered statements, however, are to be found in his Large Catechism and Small Catechism of 1529. Here is where his mature teaching and final position on baptism breaks through. What we find is a new clarity on what he believed about baptism and on what was to be left as an open question. It can be summarized as follows.

Baptism, Luther emphasizes, was instituted by Christ. Since it is of divine origin, it is of the highest importance (*BC* 456–59). It is not magical water (cf. *BC* 320) but plain water—"the same water with which the maid waters the cow," as he had said a year earlier (LW 51, 184). But when it is connected with God's word of promise, it becomes "God's water" (*BC* 458). In this symbolized promise, what is offered and given is baptismal grace. This is not one of several graces God offers, nor is it a special type of grace, but rather grace itself, the whole of grace. It encompasses "victory over death and the devil, forgiveness of sin, God's grace, the entire Christ, and the Holy Spirit with his gifts" (*BC* 461). We will never need a new or different grace. The whole life of the Christian is only the completion or fulfillment of baptism. In Luther's words, "a Christian life is nothing else than a daily baptism, begun once and continuing ever after" (*BC* 465).

This offered gift is valid, real and authentic in and of itself and for all time. The sheer performance of the act ensures its validity, even though faith is absent. "[W]hen the Word accompanies the water, baptism is valid, even though faith is lacking. For my faith does not make baptism; rather, it receives baptism. Baptism does not become invalid if it is not properly received or used" (*BC* 463). Faith is not needed to make God's offer of grace real. But it *is* needed to make this offer effective for the individual. In other words, the gift must be received for it to do us any good (*BC* 465). In taking this position, Luther returned to the technical terminology he had learned from the scholastics, and which they had inherited from Augustine: the sacrament is "valid" *ex opere operato* (by the sheer performance of the act); faith is not necessary for the sacrament to be "valid," but it is necessary for the sacrament to be "efficacious."

So faith is necessary to make baptism meaningful: until it is present, baptism is actually an "empty symbol": "Where faith is present with its fruits, there baptism is no empty symbol, but the effect accompanies it; but where faith is lacking, it remains a mere unfruitful sign" (*BC* 465). But when precisely does faith become present? This question, which had vexed Luther for so long, is in the final analysis left open. Infants might or might not have faith at the moment of baptism. In any case, Luther says, "we do not put the main emphasis on whether the person baptized believes or not" (*BC* 463). If the infant has faith, baptism immediately has its effect. And if the infant does not have faith, baptism has its effect in the future, when faith becomes present (*BC* 463–464). In either case, baptism is "valid."

Bible   There is a sense in which we could say that Luther devoted his life to understanding this book. Already as a novice friar in the Augustinian monastery in Erfurt he spent large parts of his day studying the Scriptures. His doctoral oath, sworn on the Bible on October 4, 1512, marked the beginning of his career as a professor of biblical studies at the University of Wittenberg. From that point on, he was ceaselessly occupied with the sacred text, lecturing on it, preaching from it, writing commentaries on it, and translating it. By the early 1530s he could claim, "The Scriptures are a vast forest, but there's no tree in it that I haven't shaken with my hand" (LW 54, nr. 674, 121). Yet he maintained to the end that the Scriptures are inexhaustible: in his last recorded words, from February 16, 1546, he said that in the presence of this book, "We are beggars. That is true" (LW 54, nr. 5677, 476). Why this extraordinary lifelong devotion to a book? Because, Luther thought, it is the only bridge we have that gives us access to the ultimate.

We may begin our summary of his engagement with this book by considering his German translations. They were by no means the first, but earlier ones were stilted and wooden renderings, quite unappealing to ordinary people. The ideal Bible translation, he said in 1520, "pierces and rings through the heart, through all the senses" (LW 35, 192). And so, late in the following year, while he was incarcerated for his own safety in the Wartburg castle, he took up the task. Using Erasmus's newly edited version of the Greek text, he finished the entire New Testament in an astonishing eleven weeks. This was published in September of 1522 and is thus known as Luther's "September Testament."

The Old Testament proved far more difficult. For one thing, Luther's competence in Hebrew, though praised by colleagues (WADB 9:1, x), was decidedly inferior to his knowledge of Greek, as he admitted (LW 40, 120). He assembled a linguistic team (Philip Melanchthon, Matthew Aurogallus, Caspar Cruciger, George Rörer, Justus Jonas, Veit Dietrich, and Bernhard Ziegler), and together they struggled mightily to complete the task. A letter of 1528 describes the arduous labor: "We are sweating over the work of putting the Prophets into German. God, how much of it there is, and how hard it is to make these Hebrew writers talk German! They resist us, and do not want to leave their Hebrew and imitate our German barbarisms. It is like making a nightingale leave her own sweet song and imitate the monotonous voice of a cuckoo, which she detests" (LW 35, 229). Finally, in 1534, it was done, and the entire Bible was published in German, together with 117 woodcuts by Lucas Cranach. Never satisfied, Luther and the team continued to revise the translation, write prefaces to the various books, and so forth. What was decisive, however, was that this German Bible became a bestseller: it impacted the development of written German; it influenced all succeeding translations; and most importantly the content of this book now began to shape the religious consciousness of an entire culture in ways it had not before.

Luther's translation improved the possibilities of widespread public access to the Scriptures. This was desirable, he thought, because the Bible's authority for believers is unique, final, and definitive. From at least some of the scholastics he had learned that the assent of faith is due only to what is in Scripture (WABr 1, nr. 74, 171, 70–74). Already in 1518 he argued that no one can require Christians to believe what is not in Scripture: "No Christian believer can be forced [to believe an article] beyond Scripture—which in the true sense is of divine right—apart from a new and confirmed revelation" (WA 59, 466, 1061–1062). All teachings must be tested against it, he said in 1521: "necessity forces us to run to the Bible with the writings of all teachers, and to obtain there a verdict and judgment upon them. Scripture alone [*sola scriptura*] is the true lord and master of all writings and doctrine on earth" (LW 32, 11–12). All must acquiesce in the presence of this authority, he reiterated in the early 1530s: "This queen [Scripture] must rule, and everyone must obey, and be subject to her. The Pope, Luther, Augustine, Paul, or even an angel from heaven—these should not be masters, judges, or arbiters, but only witnesses, disciples, and confessors of Scripture" (LW 26, 57–58; cf. LW 34, 284). Luther thus raised the Bible's authority to the level of a church-critical principle. But, his opponents asked, was not the Bible itself the product of the church, historically speaking? And if so, how could it then be elevated over the church? In response, Luther conceded that the book itself was indeed the product of the church. But the "Word of God," which one finds in the Bible, is not; rather the church is a product of *it*: "it is the promises of God that make the church, and not the church that makes the promise of God. For the Word of God is incomparably superior to the church, and in this Word the church, being a creature, has nothing to decree, ordain, or make, but only to be decreed, ordained, and made. For who begets his own parent? Who first brings forth his own maker?" (LW 36, 107). Thus the church must be subservient to the Word of God as this is found in Scripture, and subject to its critique and correction.

Just how consistent Luther was in applying his *sola scriptura* principle is open to question. He used it against the Roman Catholic Church, but selectively. For instance, he apparently accepted the doctrine of the immaculate conception with no warrant from Scripture whatsoever (WA 17:2, 288, 5–16; *see* **Mary**). So too, in his struggle with the Anabaptists, he fell back on an argument from tradition: "If the first, or child, baptism were not right, it would follow that for more than a thousand years there was no baptism or any Christendom, which is impossible. . . . But the fact that child baptism has spread throughout all the Christian world to this day gives rise to no probability that it is wrong, but rather to a strong indication that it is right" (LW 40, 256–257; *see* **Baptism**). Finally, Luther quickly realized that when untutored novices approach the sacred text, they come away with wildly divergent understandings. So he, like predecessors from Jerome to Erasmus, wrote prefaces to all the biblical books to explain "what [the reader] is to look for" in each (LW 35, 357). Here already was a serious qualification of the *sola* in *sola scriptura*.

This issue is complicated by Luther's understanding of precisely what Scripture is, and what it is not. Strictly speaking, it is not "God's Word." "God's Word," or "the gospel" as Luther sometimes calls it, exists first and foremost in oral, proclaimed form (LW 35, 123; WA 12, 259, 8–13). From this, its most authentic form, it was reduced to its less satisfactory literary form, Luther says, "to ensure that the sheep could feed themselves and hence protect themselves against the wolves, if their shepherds failed to feed them or were in danger of becoming wolves too" (LW 52, 206). The book helps to transmit the Word of God or the gospel, but the two should not be simply equated. Properly speaking, the Bible "contains" (*fasset*) God's Word (WA 10:1:2, 75, 6–7), and preachers "extract the living word" from it (LW 52, 206). While God's Word is divine, the book is not. As Luther explained in 1525, "God and the Scripture of God are two things, no less than the Creator and the creature are two things" (LW 33, 25). In no way did Luther succumb to an idolatry of the book.

Luther was tireless in emphasizing and explaining the criterion by which to judge what is authentic Scripture and what is not, or to put it another way, what should be in the canon and what should not be: "All the genuine sacred books agree in this, that all of them preach and inculcate [*treiben*] Christ. And that is the true test by which to judge all books, when we see whether or not they inculcate Christ.... Whatever does not teach Christ is not yet apostolic, even though St. Peter or St. Paul does the teaching. Again, whatever preaches Christ would be apostolic, even if Judas,

Annas, Pilate, and Herod were doing it" (LW 35, 396; cf. 22, 339; 34, 112; 25, 405; 33, 26). Here was Luther's canonical principle: "whatever teaches Christ." And if we wonder what precisely this means, Luther is elsewhere explicit: "proclaiming Christ" means depicting "in masterly fashion, how faith in Christ overcomes sin, death, and hell, and gives life, righteousness, and salvation" (LW 35, 362). Here a distinctively Pauline understanding of Christ becomes the standard against which all else is measured. For Luther this means there is a sense in which the biblical canon is really not closed. The church leaders involved in the process of forming the canon made mistakes. And we, many centuries later, can revisit the process. When we do, Luther believed, sometimes we will have to "base ourselves on Christ, *against* the Scriptures" (WA 39:1, 47, 19; emphasis mine).

This also means that Luther, in applying his canonical principle, ends up with a "canon within the canon," or what might be called a "canonical hierarchy." For not all biblical books "proclaim Christ" with equal clarity. What does Luther's version of this ranking look like? Relying on scattered references, and acknowledging some inconsistencies, we can reconstruct the New Testament portion approximately as follows: John's Gospel is at the top (LW 35, 362), followed by 1 John and then Paul's letters to the Romans, Galatians, and Ephesians (LW 35, 365). Then comes 1 Peter and the other three Gospels (LW 35, 362). Toward the bottom of the list comes the Letter to the Hebrews, which has "some wood, straw, or hay mixed in" with the gold and silver (LW 35, 395). Even worse is the book of Revelation: in 1522 Luther claimed he could find no trace of the Holy Spirit in it (LW 35, 398; but cf. his milder 1530 statement in LW 35, 399–409). Last of all, it seems, was the Letter of James, for "it is flatly against Paul and all the rest of Scripture in ascribing justification to works" (LW 35, 396; cf. 35, 362 and 34, 317). Here we have an example of Luther rejecting "Scripture" in the name of Christ. "Scripture" is "Scripture" only when it is God's Word, that is, when it proclaims Christ.

But does Luther not believe that the Holy Spirit inspired the authors of this book? At times it certainly sounds that way. He can speak unguardedly of the Holy Spirit himself as the author of Scripture (WA 40: 3, 16, 24–26; WATR 2, nr. 1610, 151, 11–14). Thus in response to those who quibble about the six days of creation (a story that sixteenth-century theologians took literally), he said: "do the Holy Spirit the honor of acknowledging that he is more learned than you are" (WA 12, 440, 16). Despite such statements, Luther certainly did not believe that all biblical books were "inspired" by the Holy Spirit. Besides, "inspiration" did not mean for him a kind of mechanical dictation, the Holy Spirit whispering into the ear of the author.

Consequently, even in the "inspired" books, inerrancy was out of the question (despite the fact that he quotes Augustine's regularly cited and contrary-sounding statement on the issue; LW 23, 11). Thus many of the predictions of the Hebrew prophets were simply wrong (WA 17:2, 39, 33). And Moses "forgot" to include an account of the "fallen angel" in his primeval history in Genesis 1–3 (LW 1, 22). As for the Gospels, Luther was fully aware of their discrepancies, but he treated these as unimportant (LW 22, 218–219). On historical/factual matters, that is, on the level of the literal, the Bible is often self-contradictory: "There are many passages in Holy Scripture that are contradictory according to the letters; but when that which motivates them is pointed out, everything is all right" (LW 41, 54). In other words, for Luther, factual errors in the text do not compromise the religious meaning, or God's Word, which the text conveys.

Finding God's Word in the book is the task of exegesis. Luther inherited the medieval exegetical tradition, which centered on various "senses" of Scripture. The literal sense, it was agreed, was primary. But beyond this one could also find a "spiritual sense," whether it was allegorical, tropological (moral), or anagogical (eschatological). Some of the scholastics focused almost exclusively on the literal sense (e.g., Thomas Aquinas and Nicholas of Lyra), while others were extravagantly inventive in their determination to find all four senses of a text. In Luther's first course of lectures on the Psalms (1513–16), one can see him wrestling with this method. By his second Psalms lectures (1519–21), he had collapsed the entire edifice.

Almost from the outset, it was allegorical interpretation above all that made Luther uneasy. "Beware of allegories," he wrote in the late 1520s (WA 31:2, 243, 20), and that could well have been his watchword. The problem with allegory is that it is too uncertain, unreliable, and arbitrary a foundation to support matters of faith (LW 9, 24–25; WA 31:2, 97, 15–21). In the final analysis, it dehistoricizes and trivializes the Old Testament narrative (LW 35, 235–236). At times, when the meaning of a passage escapes Luther, he simply confesses his ignorance rather than resorting to allegorizing (e.g., WA 5, 98, 12). Indeed, Luther ridiculed the method when he suggested in 1546 that the three frogs referred to in Revelation 16:13 refer to John Faber, John Eck, and Jerome Emser, his contemptible Roman Catholic opponents (LW 35, 408). Yet, though he came to use this method very cautiously and increasingly rarely, he did not abandon it entirely. In part it was Paul's use of allegory that prevented this (e.g., Gal. 4:22–31; 2 Cor. 3:13). For example, in his 1525 lectures on Deuteronomy, the "split hoof" mentioned in Deuteronomy 14:6 refers to the distinction between law and gospel (LW 9, 136). Gradually Luther developed two rules of thumb for when allegorizing is permissible. The first is the absurdity rule: if the meaning of a text apart from allegory is absurd, the allegorical method can be used (WA 44, 766, 6–9; LW 32, 168). The second is the uselessness rule: if a text has no other useful meaning, one can resort to allegory (WA 5, 541, 12–15). But none of this is decisive: "faith is not grounded in allegories" (WA 31:2, 97, 23–24).

The literal sense "alone holds its ground in trouble and trial" (LW 9, 24). But what precisely this *sensus literalis* means for Luther is highly problematic. His terminology, though fluid and changing, allows us a glimpse inside a complex hermeneutic. "Literal" can sometimes mean what he calls the "grammatical" sense: "Become a text critic and learn about the grammatical sense, whatever grammar intends" (WA 31:2, 592, 17–19). Sometimes by "literal" he means what we might understand as the concrete/factual sense. But inevitably Luther also means more. For instance, he understands Cain and Abel as real persons and their story as factually accurate. But for Luther the event points to a larger truth: that "Cain goes on killing Abel without interruption" in human history (LW 27, 147). This is included in the "literal sense." Or, to cite another example, Luther sometimes understands Satan in a concrete/factual sense: he is a real person. Yet "Satan" also refers to "the insane idea of self-righteousness" (LW 27, 146). So too the "literal" can encompass poetic, figurative expression and imagery, as in the case of the Song of Songs (WA 31:2, 594, 19–21). Finally, "literal" can also mean the "historical sense." The history of Israel itself is the meaning of the Old Testament in the sense that it inspires hope and consolation: just as God liberated and preserved the children of Israel, "God will also liberate you and will not abandon you" (WA 31:2, 97, 28–29). All this and more Luther subsumes under the "literal sense."

Very often, particularly with regard to the Old Testament, Luther speaks not of the "literal sense" but of what he calls the "literal prophetic sense." Of course, what he means is that the whole of the Old Testament points forward to Christ. "Here [in the Old Testament] you will find the swaddling cloths and the manger in which Christ lies. . . . Simple and lowly are these swaddling cloths, but dear is the treasure, Christ, who lies in them" (LW 35, 236). Here again Luther's canonical principle surfaces. The New Testament is "nothing but a revelation of the Old" (LW 52, 41), and "the entire Scripture deals only with Christ everywhere" (LW 25, 405). The literal prophetic sense *is* the christological sense.

Thus when the ancient Israelites longed to be liberated from their oppression, they were yearning for the coming of Christ. When they called out for God's help in time of crisis, when the psalmist appealed for God's mercy, when in times of apparent abandonment the Israelites prayed for God's presence, they were longing for Christ's advent, whether they would have expressed it this way or not (e.g., WA 38, 49, 5–17). For what does "Christ" mean other than God with us, God for us, God saving us through his mercy alone? Whenever the ancient Israelites experienced God as merciful and saving, they were encountering Christ, however veiled. And since the entire Old Testament tells the story of the encounter between a people and their loving, infinitely merciful, saving God, it points toward Christ, who, in Luther's view, "is" this God. Christ is thus the hermeneutical key to the entire Bible.

Is the Bible then to be understood as "revelation"? For Luther, the fundamental Christian position is that God has revealed himself in Jesus Christ. The Bible gives us access to this revelation. But it does not merely convey objective information. Or, to put it another way, what we find in the Bible is not revelatory for us until it has an effect on us. For instance, a person can memorize the whole Bible, Luther said, without ever apprehending and truly grasping what it means for himself or herself (LW 33, 28). Those who come to this book in need, that is, "those who are troubled, afflicted, vexed, and tempted," have a better chance of finding Christ in it

(LW 27, 148). They come, Luther said, "not only to know and understand, but also to experience how right, how true, how sweet, how lovely, how mighty, how comforting God's word is, wisdom beyond all wisdom" (LW 34, 287). This is what some interpreters have called Luther's "existential" understanding of revelation: it only becomes revelation when it has an impact on us. The Bible is important, in other words, because the "Word of God" can be heard in it. And what we hear in this book is the real "Word of God" only if it transforms us.

Christology   Who is Jesus Christ? It is hard to imagine a more decisive question for Christian theology, and indeed, every theologian from the New Testament writers until today has wrestled with it in one way or another. Luther entered this discussion, already fifteen centuries old, with a full awareness of its centrality, and with humility in the face of profound mystery. Both of these notes are sounded in his preface to the 1535 *Lectures on Galatians*: "For in my heart there rules this one doctrine, namely, faith in Christ. From it, through it, and to it all my theological thought flows and returns day and night, and yet I am aware that all I have grasped of this wisdom in its height, width, and depth are a few poor and insignificant first fruits and fragments" (LW 27, 145).

So crucial is this doctrine that among the articles of the Nicene Creed Luther could in 1538 call this the "chief article." Those who have grasped this, "[a]lthough they may have sinned and erred in other matters, they have nevertheless been preserved at the last. For whoever stands correctly and firmly in the belief that Jesus Christ is true God and man, that he died and has risen for us, such a person has all other articles added to him and they firmly stand by him" (LW 34, 207). In other words, a correct understanding of this doctrine leads to a correct understanding of all other doctrines. And all heresies, ancient or contemporary, stem ultimately from a misunderstanding of this doctrine (LW 34, 207, 210).

Luther's clear-sighted awareness of the importance of Christology and of its systematic implications was the product of a long and gradual development. To be sure the Christology of the early Luther was entirely orthodox and traditional, but it did not become for him a subject of extended reflection until the 1520s in the controversy with Huldrych Zwingli over the Lord's Supper (see his 1528 treatise *Confession Concerning Christ's Supper*, LW 37, 153–372). Later works, such as *Three Symbols or Creeds of the Christian Faith* of 1538 (LW 34, 201–229), or *On the Councils and the Church* of 1539 (LW 41, 9–178), evidence a highly developed Christology. And his promotion disputations for doctoral candidates at Wittenberg from 1534 to 1544 (WA 39:1 and WA 39:2) indicate a serious engagement with the most technical aspects of the christological tradition. As Luther faced new circumstances and as he engaged new opponents, his christological reflection deepened until it reached full maturity in these later works.

I must emphasize that from beginning to end, Luther's Christology fell well within the bounds of orthodoxy as the Catholic tradition had defined it. He was entirely convinced that the church's early theologians—Augustine, Athanasius, Chrysostom, Irenaeus, Gregory of Nazianzus, and so on—had correctly understood the biblical witness, and that their opponents (Arius, Nestorius, Eutyches, etc.) had not. The views of these leaders had been refined and summed up at the first four ecumenical councils (Nicaea, 325; Constantinople, 381; Ephesus, 431; and Chalcedon, 451). Though these councils were in principle fallible, and though they had expressed views on all manner of trivia that we may safely ignore, their pronouncements on Christology (and the Trinity) may not be ignored, for they are the most adequate summary of who Jesus Christ was. In 1528 Luther had been beset by opponents on all sides in addition to suffering a serious illness. In this context he wrote a "final confession," so that no one would be in doubt about his views after he was gone. In it one finds a ringing endorsement of traditional christological teaching, prefaced by the phrases "I know what I am saying," "I am indeed earnest," "I believe with my whole heart" (LW 37, 361). Christ was God and human, two natures in one person.

Within this framework of orthodoxy, however, one finds distinctive accents and emphases in Luther. One of these, perhaps the most important, is his constant and insistent linkage between Christology (who Christ is) and soteriology (what he does). Unlike some of the great *Summa*s of high scholasticism, Luther does not first elaborate a Christology and then follow this with a treatise on soteriology. The two are inseparable for him; indeed, soteriology is in a sense logically prior to Christology. For the whole point of Christology is soteriology: "Through the Gospels we are told who Christ is, in order that we may learn to know that he is our Savior. . . . For even though you know that he is God's Son, that he died and rose again, and that he sits at the right hand of the Father, you have not yet learned to know Christ aright, and this knowledge still does not help you. You must know and believe that he did all this for your sake, in order to help you" (LW 30, 29–30). Even a perfectly orthodox Christology, apart from soteriology, is meaningless: "We find many people who say, 'Christ is man, Son of God, born of a pure virgin . . .'—that is all nothing" (LW 34, 110–111). Acceptance of official dogmas about Christ remains empty until such knowledge is transformed by faith into a true "knowing of Christ." "You do not yet have Christ, even though you know that he is God and man. You truly have him only when you believe that this altogether pure and innocent person has been granted to you by the Father as your high priest

and redeemer, yes, as your slave" (LW 26, 288). Here one can glimpse the existential character of Luther's theology. In this case, knowledge of Christ is not true knowledge apart from its impact on us. This (and not a sheer subjectivism) is what Luther means when he says, "if you believe, then you have; if you do not believe, then you do not have" (WA 10:3, 92, 13–14).

Affirming the divinity of Christ posed no problem for Luther, steeped as he was in the tradition. From the beginning theologians had grounded this belief in the witness of Scripture, Jesus' miracles, and his statements about himself, and Luther found this more than sufficient. Why is it important? Without this, the work of redemption is unthinkable: "if Christ is divested of His divinity, there remains no help against God's wrath and no rescue from His judgment" (LW 22, 22). A purely human Christ would not be a "savior"; his death would have no significance for us. "[I]f it cannot be said that God died for us, but only a man, we are lost; but if God's death and a dead God lie in the balance, his side goes down and ours goes up like a light and empty scale" (LW 41, 103–104). Everything depends on Christ's being "true God from true God."

What then does this really mean for Luther? It means, to begin with, that humans have access to God, that they can know something about him. If Christ was not God, he would not be God's self-revelation, and human knowledge of God would be pathetically fragmentary and essentially useless. But God has revealed something about himself in Christ. Here the Johannine character of Luther's Christology becomes apparent: "He who has seen me has seen the Father" (John 14:9). The Fourth Gospel teaches us, Luther says, to "find Christ and the Father so firmly together that we learn to think of God only in Christ" (LW 24, 61). The word "only" here is important. All our confused notions of God must be set aside in favor of what God has told us about himself in this person. "There is no other God except the one called Jesus Christ. . . . He and no one else is the true God" (WA 31:1, 63, 21–28). To say that Christ is "true God from true God" means that if we want to know something about God we must look to Christ.

What precisely can humans discover about God when they do this? Many things, Luther thinks, but most decisively, how he is disposed toward us. In a justifiably famous passage in the Large Catechism, Luther describes Christ as "a mirror of the Father's heart" (*BC* 440). Luther does not mean that Christ is a mirror in which we see our own reflection, but rather a mirror that we look into at an angle, as it were, and when we do we see God's fatherly love for us. In Christ, God himself has opened his heart to us. Here we are at the core of Luther's Christology. To say that Christ is "true God from true God" ultimately means to say that we are embraced by an infinite, eternal, and unconditional love. For humans to grasp this is transformative.

At the same time, Luther, along with the tradition, insisted on the full humanity of Christ. For the person of the Son, he believed, had assumed human nature (not a human person as he pointed out in a 1540 disputation, WA 39:2, 93–96). More than half of his extant sermons are on Synoptic texts dealing with Jesus' life and teaching. Yet he was not interested in the "historical Jesus" as modern exegetes understand this. Jesus' humanity is important only because it leads us to God: "Whoever wants to reflect or speculate in a salutary way about God, let him set everything aside except the humanity of Christ" (WABr 1, nr. 329, 50–52). This requires a certain intellectual humility. "If you can humble yourself, hold to the word and hold to Christ's humanity—then the divinity will indeed become manifest" (LW 23, 102). Precisely in the humanity is where the divinity is to be found.

One of the major themes in Luther's reflection on the humanity of Christ revolves around the concept of *kenosis* (self-emptying) taken from Philippians 2:5–8. Christ renounced the "form of God" not once but continuously, an ongoing act of divine self-giving, finalized in the cross. "The 'form of God' is wisdom, power, righteousness, goodness and freedom too. . . . He relinquished that form to God the Father and emptied himself, unwilling to use his rank against us, unwilling to be different from us. Moreover, for our sakes he became as one of us and took the form of a servant, that is, he subjected himself to all evils" (LW 31, 301). His life, suffering, and death were therefore a real human life, suffering, and death.

There is also a strong "ascent motif" in Luther's statements on Christ's humanity. By this he does not mean what theologians call an "ascending Christology" or a "Christology from below," for as we shall see, Luther insists on the union of the two natures. What Luther means is that our starting point must be Christ's humanity: "Scripture begins very gently by leading us first to Christ as to a man and afterward to the Lord of all creation and finally to a God. Thus I begin easily and learn to know God. But philosophy and the wise people of this world want to begin at the top and have become fools in the process. One must begin at the bottom and afterward rise up" (WA 10:1:2, 297, 5–10). More specifically, through Christ's human love we come to know the divine love. In a 1519 sermon on the passion, Luther exhorts his listeners to "see his friendly heart, so full of love for you, which compels him to bear the heavy burden of your conscience and your sin. . . . After that ascend through Christ's heart to God's heart" (WA 2, 140, 32–36).

These two motifs, ascent and *kenosis*, Luther combines in a third motif—that of the ladder. We can "ascend" to God only because he has "descended" to us by his self-emptying. Commenting on Isaiah in 1543/44, Luther put it this way: "This order must be carefully preserved. We are not to ascend to the study of the divine majesty before we have adequately comprehended this little infant. We are to ascend into heaven by that ladder which is placed before us. . . . The Son of God does not want to be seen and found in heaven. Therefore he descended from heaven to this earth and came to us in our flesh. He placed himself in the womb of his mother, in her lap, and on the cross. And this is the ladder that he has placed on the earth and by which we are to ascend to God" (WA 40:3, 656, 21–28). Here then is Luther's version of the patristic axiom, "God became human, that humans might become God." Christ's humanity is the way for us "to look into the depths of the divine majesty and see the gracious will and love of his fatherly heart for us" (WA 17:2, 244, 28–30).

More than the humanity or divinity of Christ considered in themselves, Luther stressed the union of the two natures, especially after the Lord's Supper controversy of the 1520s. The "divinity and humanity are one person in Christ" (LW 27, 210). This union, or the oneness of the person, is crucial since neither the divinity alone nor the humanity alone do us any good. Luther explained in a late sermon:

> The devil can still stand in when a man grasps only the man Jesus and does not go beyond this. Yes, he even permits the statement that Christ is truly God to be spoken and heard. He struggles, however, to prevent the heart from joining Christ and the Father so closely and solidly together that it certainly concludes that Christ's word and the Father's word are one and the same word, heart, and will. . . . [A] heart [that] does not unite God and Christ . . . fabricates one kind of Christ and another kind of God for itself and thus misses the true God, who does not will to be found and grasped any place else than in this Christ. (WA 21, 467, 10–21)

In other words (and this is Luther's basic principle), the divinity can be salvific for us only when joined to the humanity of Christ.

It is sometimes said that one finds in medieval scholastic Christology a certain Nestorian tendency, that is, a tendency to separate the two natures. If this is so, then we can say that Luther exhibits the opposite, Monophysite tendency, namely an emphasis on the union of the two natures. Zwingli, Luther thought, shared the medieval tendency and carried it even further, finally denying the real presence of the body of Christ in the Lord's Supper. For Luther, the doctrine of Christ as "one person" means that divinity and humanity can never be separated. God participates fully in the human condition. Accordingly, Luther stresses in a special way the traditional doctrine of the *communicatio idiomata*, the communication or sharing of attributes between the two natures.

> Christ is God and man in one person because whatever is said of him as man must also be said of him as God, namely, Christ had died, and Christ is God; therefore God died—not the separated God, but God united with humanity. For about the separated God both statements, namely, that Christ is God and that God died, are false; both are false, for then God is not man. . . . On the other hand, whatever is said of God must also be ascribed to the man, namely, God created the world and is almighty; the man Christ is God, therefore the man Christ created the world and is almighty. The reason for this is that since God and man have become one person, it follows that this person bears the *idiomata* of both natures. (LW 41, 103)

Here and elsewhere, Luther does not shy away from saying that God has suffered and God has died (cf. WA 39:2, 280, 18–20). He does not mean of course what Nietzsche or the twentieth-century "death of God" theologians meant; such statements are true only when we are speaking of God as he has come to us in Jesus Christ. Nevertheless it is legitimate to speak of Luther's "deipassionism" (not patripassionism).

A further consequence of this line of thought is Luther's doctrine of the ubiquity (omnipresence) of Christ's exalted human nature. Because the divine and human are eternally united in one person, and because the characteristics are shared, we can say that the humanity of Christ is everywhere: "we believe that Christ, according to his human nature, is put over all creatures [Eph. 1:22] and fills all things.... Not only according to his divine nature, but also according to his human nature, he is a lord of all things, has all things in his hand, and is present everywhere" (LW 36, 342). Christ indeed now "sits at the right hand of the Father," Luther says, but this means everywhere: "Christ's body is everywhere because it is at the right hand of God which is everywhere, although we do not know how that occurs" (LW 37, 214). To say that Christ is alive and present in the world, the church, and the Lord's Supper is to say that he is also mysteriously present in human nature, in his body.

These then are the major contours of Luther's Christology. His answer to the question "Who is Jesus Christ?" was expressed in two very different languages. On the one hand he used the classical terminology of the tradition: one person, two natures, truly God, truly human, and so on. On the other hand he also used the quite untraditional language of concrete image and existential immediacy: Christ is the mirror of God's fatherly heart. In his mind, both ultimately meant the same thing. Translating this into a third, more modern idiom, we could put it this way: Luther held that the most profound yearning of every human being is for a love that is truly unconditional, one that humans can never deserve. Jesus Christ, he thought, is the answer to that longing.

Church   Luther did not carefully think through a doctrine of the church in abstraction from the events of his time. He was convinced that God was bringing about a "reformation" of the existing church, and most of what he wrote was self-consciously in the service of this "reform." Accordingly his ecclesiology must be pieced together from a multitude of writings that either diagnose the ills of the church, or prescribe remedies, or react to events, or counterattack opponents on all sides. It is not surprising then that we find oscillating emphases, tensions, even outright contradictions in his views on the nature of the church. His ecclesiological statements resist an easy integration into a perfectly coherent and logically consistent system.

The most fundamental tension is between what we might call an "institutional positivism" on the one hand and a "spiritualism" on the other. The Roman Catholics, in Luther's view, identified the church with a hierarchical corporation that mediates salvation. Against them, he emphasized the spiritual nature of the church. On the other hand, beginning in the 1520s Thomas Müntzer, the Anabaptists, and others seemed to Luther to reject all institutional structure. In opposition to them, he stressed the importance of the church's concrete, material, historical nature. The distinction between spiritual and material aspects of the church was made explicit by Luther already in 1520: "Therefore... we shall call the two churches by two distinct names. The first, which is natural, basic, essential and true, we shall call 'spiritual, internal Christendom.' The second, which is man-made and external, we shall call 'physical, external Christendom.' Not that we want to separate them from each other; rather it is just as if I were talking about a man and called him 'spiritual' according to his soul, and 'physical' according to his body" (LW 39, 70). Luther himself failed to consistently apply this distinction in his ecclesiological writings. But we do well to bear it in mind in evaluating his statements, along with the context, that is, the intended target of those statements. Though Luther disliked the word "church" (*ecclesia*) because it has no precise German equivalent, he resigned himself to using it and said that a seven-year-old child knows what it means, namely "holy believers" (*BC* 324). The more proper theological definition Luther gives it is taken from the Apostles' Creed, *communio sanctorum*, which should be translated as "community of saints." This term in the creed stands in opposition to "church"; it is the creed's definition of "church" (*BC* 437). "Saints" for Luther, simply refers to all those who have been made holy by the forgiveness of sins. These form a community.

While this community does not, strictly speaking, mediate salvation, it nevertheless has certain special features that are of great importance to Luther. For one thing, there is in principle absolute equality in this community: "It is enough for me that I am a member of this body and have as many rights in it and as much honor as all others" (WA 17:2, 37, 7–9). All share a common priesthood. Another feature, one of immense comfort to Luther personally, is that "in this community of Christendom all things are common, that the goods of each one belong to the other" (WA 7, 219, 11–13). What Luther means here is the mutual bearing of burdens and sharing of benefits:

> Therefore, when I suffer, I suffer not alone but Christ and all Christians suffer with me. . . . Thus others bear my burden, and their strength becomes my own. The church's faith supports my fearfulness, the chastity of others bears the temptations of my flesh, the fastings of others are my gain, the prayers of another plead for me. . . . Who, therefore, could despair in his sins? Who would not rejoice in his pains? For it is not he that bears his sins and pain; or if he does bear them, he does not bear them alone, but is assisted by so many holy sons of God, even by Christ himself. So great a thing is the community of saints, and the church of Christ. (WA 6, 131, 14–29)

The *communio sanctorum* is a "community" in the fullest sense of the word.

At the same time, this community is for Luther the body of Christ. There was no doubt in Luther's mind that Christ had established the church, and therefore God's Word, or the gospel, is inseparably bound to it: "God's word cannot be without God's people, and conversely, God's people cannot be without God's word" (LW 41, 150). But the church did not give rise to the gospel of Christ. Rather the reverse is true. "The church . . . is a creature of the gospel, incomparably less than it" (WA 2, 430, 6–7). Thus the gospel can function in Luther as an ecclesio-critical principle.

To say that the church is Christ's body means that Christ is the head of the church (in distinction to Lord of the world): "Christ certainly is a lord of all things, of those who are godly and those who are evil, of angels and devils, of virgins and whores. But he is head only of the godly, faithful Christians assembled in the Spirit. For a head must be joined to the body" (LW 39, 76). This conventional image of Christ as head of the church had taken on strong antipapal implications in John Wyclif and Jan Hus in the fifteenth century, and Luther's use of it continued this trend. If Christ is the head of the church, then the pope cannot be, at least if he ascribes to himself the plenitude of power, even over souls in purgatory, and thus usurps the place of Christ.

Because the church is Christ's body, it comes as close as anything in this world to being eternal. "The church has always existed; there has always been a people of God" (LW 13, 88). And it will endure till the end: church "should mean the holy Christian people, not only of the days of the apostles who are long since dead, but to the end of the world" (LW 41, 144). Christians are not responsible for its continuation. "For after all, we are not the ones who can preserve the church, nor were our forefathers able to do so. Nor will our successors have this power. No, it was, is and will be he who says, 'I am with you always'" (LW 47, 118). The head guarantees the continued existence of the body.

Besides being the body of Christ, the church is also the community of the Holy Spirit. His role is "to create, call, and gather the Christian church" (*BC* 436). He "has appointed a community on earth through which he speaks and does all his work" (*BC* 439). The Holy Spirit's proper task is to sanctify, to make us holy. When Christ (or the Word, or the gospel) is proclaimed, it sometimes happens that hearts unfold to receive it, forgiveness is received, life is transformed, and people become "holy." That opening, receiving, and accepting is the work of the Holy Spirit. And in this sense he creates the community of holy people called the church.

Is this visible to the world? On this question, Luther's thought points in two directions, and it is crucial to note the context in which he speaks. On the one hand, he can hold that the church is visible because of its confession of faith (WA 39:2, 161, 6–20). This aspect dominates when he engages those who seemed to him to devalue all institutional structures. More frequently, however, he emphasizes the church's invisibility, and when he does, one can be sure that his polemical target is the Roman church. "Where the word is preached and believed," he says, "there is true faith; and where faith is, there is the church" (WA 2, 208, 25–26). But faith is something hidden, as in the work of the Holy Spirit, and consequently the church is invisible. Natural reason cannot recognize it: "This article, 'I believe in the holy Christian Church,' is as much an article of faith as the rest. This is why natural reason cannot recognize it, even if it puts on all its glasses" (LW 34, 410). Ecclesiastical organizations do not dispense grace or control faith, nor can they excommunicate: "No person is able to give or take away this community—whether he is a bishop, a pope, an angel or all creation. God alone gives it through his Holy Spirit by pouring it into the heart of the believer.... [H]ere no excommunication is of any effect" (WA 6, 64, 6–11). One cannot tell who

is part of the church by the organization he or she belongs to. Christ "rejects and condemns all such judgments which attempt to establish who are Christians and the people of God and who are not" (WA 21, 333, 9–11). Whether this invisibility of the church is a constitutive element of his doctrine or a temporary polemical "spiritualism" remains a matter of debate among scholars.

Be this as it may, on another point Luther is perfectly clear: he cannot conceive of the possibility of salvation outside the church. "Whoever seeks Christ must first find the church.... For outside the Christian church there is no truth, no Christ, and no salvation" (WA 10:1:1, 140, 8–17). That was Luther's view as he expressed it in a 1522 sermon, and six years later he had not changed his mind: "Outside this Christian church there is no salvation or forgiveness of sins, but everlasting death and damnation" (LW 37, 368). This is an important qualification of Luther's much-emphasized individualism. Justification occurs to individuals, yes, but always within this community.

How then can one find the true church, from Luther's perspective? We might begin to answer this question by looking at Luther's view of the Roman Catholic Church. Was it a true church? Here we find Luther facing in two directions that cannot easily be reconciled. The first is illustrated by his 1528 treatise *Concerning Rebaptism*. In rejecting infant baptism, Luther argues, the Anabaptists have far too radically negated the Roman church. "We on our part confess that there is much that is Christian and good under the papacy; indeed everything that is Christian and good is to be found there and has come to us from this source. For instance we confess that in the papal church there are the true holy Scriptures, true baptism, the true sacrament of the altar, the true keys to the forgiveness of sins, the true office of the ministry, the true catechism" (LW 40, 231–232). It is in fact, Luther argues, the true church: "The Christendom that is now under the papacy is truly the body of Christ and a member of it. If it is his body, then it has the true spirit, gospel, faith" (LW 40, 232). Luther had already long been convinced that the pope was the antichrist, but even this does not invalidate the Roman church as church: "the Antichrist sits in the temple of God through the action of the devil, while the temple still is and remains the temple of God through the power of Christ" (LW 40, 233). Against the Anabaptists' total negation, Luther (uncharacteristically) calls for nuance: "One needs a more cautious, discreet spirit, which attacks the accretion which threatens the temple without destroying the temple of God itself" (LW 40, 233–234).

A year later, in his Large Catechism, Luther could say unambiguously that "under the papacy . . . there was no Christian church." And he explains why: "What was lacking there [in the Roman church]? There was no Holy Spirit present to reveal this truth and have it preached. Rather, it was human beings and evil spirits who were there, who taught us to obtain grace and be saved by our works" (BC 436). Likewise in the Smalcald Articles of 1537 Luther is perfectly clear: "We do not concede to them [the papists] that they are the church, and frankly they are not the church" (BC 324). And in 1541, in the incendiary rhetoric typical of the mature Luther, he denounces the Roman church as the opposite of the true church. "Thus we have proved that we are the true, ancient church. . . . [Y]ou [papists] are the new false church, which is in everything apostate, separated from the true, ancient church, thus becoming Satan's whore and synagogue" (LW 41, 199). There is no nuance here, and all attempts to reconcile this with his earlier anti-Anabaptist position are highly dubious. Even when we take into account the polemical context, Luther's distinction between the physical and spiritual church, and so forth, we must conclude that the two are a flat contradiction, explicable only

as a rather dramatic development in his thinking.

Still, the larger question of how the true church is to be recognized absorbed a great deal of Luther's attention. His answer fell along traditional lines insofar as he singled out certain "marks" or characteristics of the church. Augustine, a thousand years earlier, had identified these, in conformity with the Nicene Creed, as "one, holy, catholic, and apostolic." Luther concurred. The "oneness" and "catholicity" of the church ultimately mean the same thing, universality. (Throughout his life Luther insisted that he was a member of the "catholic" church.) "I believe," he said, "that there is no more than one holy catholic Christian church upon earth anywhere in the world, and this is nothing else than the community or gathering of the saints" (WA 7, 219, 1–3). This oneness, Luther thought, implies a strict duty to preserve the church's unity. In his 1535 Lectures on Galatians he was highly critical of the Hussites for leaving the church: "For if the bishops or priests or any persons at all are wicked, and if you were aglow with real love, you would not flee. No, even if you were at the ends of the ocean, you would come running back to them and weep, warn, and reprove, and do absolutely everything. And if you followed this teaching of the apostle [Gal. 6:2] you would know that it is not benefits but burdens that you have to bear" (LW 27, 392–393). But what about the breach of unity in which Luther himself was involved? Here Luther is emphatic: "are we, too, fleeing and seceding on this account? Perish the thought! Perish the thought! To be sure, we censure . . . but we do not on this account disrupt the unity of the spirit . . . since we know that love rises high above all things" (ibid.). Thus the question of whether Luther would have left the Roman church had he not been excommunicated is a serious one.

The church is also "holy." Here we do well to consider precisely what Luther means and does not mean by this. The church's institutional structure and functioning are often decidedly unholy, according to Luther. Indeed, seen from this aspect, the church is sometimes so sordid as to be downright offensive: "The devil can cover it [the church] over with offenses and divisions, so that you have to take offense at it. God too can conceal it behind faults and shortcomings of all kinds, so that you necessarily become a fool and pass false judgment on it" (LW 35, 410). What makes the church "holy," and indeed the only thing holy about it, is its possession and proclamation of the word, the gospel of Jesus Christ. It is "the principal item, and the holiest of holy possessions, by reason of which the Christian people are called holy" (LW 41, 149). While "[t]he appearance of the church is the appearance of a sinner" (LW 12, 263), "[i]ts holiness exists in the Word of God and true faith" (BC 325). And because this is invisible, its holiness is an article of faith (LW 35, 410). Moreover, though the church is called a community of "saints," it is not holy because its members are holy. Faith, not progress on the road to moral perfection, is what makes people holy. For faith is the acceptance of the gospel, which at its core proclaims forgiveness and absolution. Thus the church is holy because it is a community of forgiveness (BC 438), and members are holy because they have received this forgiveness. Turning away from the gospel to look at themselves, they see only sin and unworthiness. Seen from different vantage points they are "at the same time righteous and sinful" (simul iustus et peccator). And seen from different vantage points, the church is at the same time a community of saints and a community of sinners.

Finally, with Augustine and the tradition, Luther affirms that the church is "apostolic," that is, in continuity with the teaching of the apostles. Unlike the tradition, however, Luther does not think that this continuity is grounded in, and guaranteed by, an orderly and unbroken succession of bishops who understand themselves as successors to the apostles. Apostolic succession does not mean episcopal succession. Rather it means the faithful proclamation of the gospel as the apostles proclaimed it (WA 39:1, 191, 25–192, 4). A church that does not do this is not "apostolic," no matter how many bishops it has or who appointed them.

There are other "marks," or ways of recognizing, the true church. In his early years as a reformer, Luther generally listed three: "Not Rome or this or that place, but baptism, the sacrament [Lord's Supper], and the gospel are the signs by which the existence of the church in the world can be noticed externally" (LW 39, 75; cf. WA 7, 720, 32–38). Later, in 1539, he lists as many as seven: the Word of God, baptism, the Lord's Supper, the keys, the calling of ministers, worship, and bearing the cross (LW 41, 148–165). Two years later he listed ten or eleven, including baptism, the Lord's Supper, the keys, the Word of God, the creed, the Lord's Prayer, the honoring of temporal authority, the praise of marriage, the bearing of suffering, the renunciation of revenge, and maybe also fasting (LW 41, 194–198). Yet, however many he lists, one is clearly more fundamental than the rest. This point is made, for instance, in his 1521 response to Ambrosius Catharinus: "For the gospel is the unique, the most certain, and the most noble sign of the church—more so even than the bread and baptism; for it is through the gospel alone that the church is conceived, formed, nourished, born, educated, fed, clothed, cared for, strengthened, armed, and preserved—in short, the entire life and substance of the church is the Word of God" (WA 7, 721, 9–13). Luther made the point again in his 1532–34 lectures on Isaiah: "The only perpetual and infallible mark of the church was always the Word" (WA 25, 97, 32–33). Thus beneath the surface complexity of identifying the true church there lies a final, ultimate simplicity.

This centrality of the gospel (or Word of God) in Luther's thought has consequences for the problems of authority in the church. Luther's views on this issue (aspects of which are taken up elsewhere in this book) are already summarized in the title of his 1523 pamphlet, *That a Christian Assembly or Congregation Has the Right and Power to Judge All Teaching and to Call, Appoint, and Dismiss Teachers, Established and Proven by Scripture* (LW 39, 305–314). Popes, councils, and bishops, he says, have usurped this right (LW 39, 307). Canon law can safely be ignored: "need breaks all laws and has none" when it comes to appointing pastors (LW 39, 310). Nor does tradition have an authoritative status: "one should not care at all about human statutes, law, old precedent, usage, custom, etc., even if they were instituted by pope or emperor, prince or bishop, if one half or the whole world accepted them, or if they lasted one year or a thousand years" (LW 39, 306). As the Reformation progressed Luther altered and softened his views on some of these things. His confrontation with more radical reformers, for instance, and his facing up to questions of authority in his own church, seemed to demand such changes. What did not change, however, was his conviction that the gospel is the sole criterion for all that happens in the church. And for this reason, the "highest official" in the church is the preacher of the gospel. Even the sacraments, important as they are, are secondary to the proclamation of the Word (LW 39, 314).

This in outline is the shape of Luther's ecclesiology. That one finds tensions, developments, even contradictions in it should not surprise us when we consider the length and the depth of his involvement in the struggle for the church's "reformation." This reformation of the church, he insisted, was not his doing but God's. And the church that resulted was in no way "his." When associates began to call themselves "Lutherans" in the early 1520s, he wrote, "let them call themselves Christians, not Lutherans. What is Luther? After all, the teaching is not mine. Neither was I crucified for

anyone" (LW 45, 70). The community of saints belongs only to Christ.

Confirmation   The Acts of the Apostles records new believers receiving the imposition of hands by the apostles, and thereby the Holy Spirit (8:17; 9:16). Based on this, a rite of confirmation had very gradually evolved. This was finally given official status as one of the seven sacraments by the Council of Florence in 1439. Its material was holy oil or "chrism"; its minister was the bishop; the formula to be used was, "I sign you with the sign of the cross and confirm you with the chrism of salvation, in the name of the Father, and the Son, and the Holy Spirit"; and it was understood to confer the Holy Spirit on the recipient.

Though Luther never mentions it, he most probably received this sacrament while a schoolboy in Mansfeld, between 1491 and 1497. At least until 1517 he assumed that it was a sacrament (e.g., LW 29, 180). Only in 1519, in a December letter to his friend George Spalatin, do we find him expressing doubts about it (WABr 1, nr. 231, 594–595, 19–24). In the following year his mind was made up. The apostles, Luther acknowledges, laid hands on various people for various reasons. But not everything they did was a sacrament. This sign, he argues, lacks divine institution and it has no promise attached to it. It is "a certain churchly rite or sacramental ceremony . . . such as the blessing of water and the like" (LW 36, 91–92).

In the years following, Luther came to acknowledge that this rite has a certain value when used to celebrate the final examination after a course of catechetical instruction (WA 11, 66, 29–32), as long as nobody regards it as a sacrament. That "fanciful deception" should be repudiated entirely (LW 45, 24–25).

Councils   As a person with formal training in the scholastic theology of the late Middle Ages, Luther was well aware of the history of church councils, their major decisions, and their importance. They first claimed his focused attention in 1518, after the issue of teaching authority in the church was pressed on him by various opponents. In response to Silvester Prierias, he asserted that councils of the church can err (WA 1, 656, 30–33). And after his meeting with Cardinal Cajetan at Augsburg, he called for a future council to take up the disputed issues (WA 2, 34–40). In the course of this appeal, Luther referred favorably to the Council of Constance and its "conciliarism" (the view that councils have a higher authority than popes) (WA 2, 36, 23–32).

In 1519 the issue came up again at the Leipzig Disputation with John Eck. Luther quoted the respected canon lawyer Nicholas of Tudeschi (Panormitanus) (1386–1445) to the effect that councils can err (WA 59, 480, 1–3). Yet, when it comes to the essential articles of faith, they do not: "If I may speak my mind, I believe that a council and the church never err in those things that pertain to faith; in other things it is not necessary to be free of error" (WA 59, 547, 3577–3579). What Luther enunciates here is not a doctrine of "inerrancy" or "infallibility," but rather "indefectibility": the church as such will never entirely abandon the fundamental truths of the faith. And insofar as a council represents the church, the same can be said for it. In taking this position, Luther remained in the mainstream of Catholic thought. Only in his conciliarist views was he beginning to step out of that mainstream.

In the following years and throughout the 1520s, Luther had little to say on the topic, but there is no evidence that he abandoned his basic position. What was clarified, however, was his view of the foundation of conciliar teaching authority. In 1521 he could say emphatically that conciliar teaching on the articles of faith is authoritative because, and insofar as, it is based on Scripture. "In

some councils there are articles whose belief is explained by Scripture, such as Nicaea; and some things are decreed that are drawn from and based on Scripture, and these are to be held to just as much as God's Word" (WA 8, 149, 34–150, 4). Aside from this new clarification, Luther largely ignored the issue for the next decade.

Luther's interest in councils was renewed in the early 1530s, first by talk emanating from Rome about a possible future council. Sometime in those years, certainly before 1535, Luther embarked on a major scholarly research project on the history of the councils. By 1539 he seems to have read everything on the topic that was then available. It is not too much to say that in these years Luther showed a remarkable interest in this facet of church history and even that he developed a level of expertise in it.

One can see the first fruit of this research in some of his publications from 1535. First, he issued a series of disputation theses *Against the Council of Constance* (WA 39:1, 13–38). Conciliarism was not his interest here, but rather the council's condemnation of communion "in both kinds," and its treatment of Jan Hus. He also published some of Hus's letters to raise awareness of what the council had done to him (WA 50, 23–24). Then, on November 7, he met in Wittenberg with Pope Paul III's nuncio, Paul Vergerio. He had been sent to secure Luther's participation in a forthcoming council, and Luther apparently agreed (WATR 5, nr. 6388, 637, 40–41). It was probably this visit that inspired Luther to prepare a *Disputation on the Power of Councils* (WA 39:1, 184–197). Here Luther asserted that councils have no intrinsic authority. They *can* represent the universal church, but only when they follow the norm of Scripture (WA 39:1, 186, 24–32).

Pope Paul III issued the formal call for a council on June 2, 1536. This council was, for various reasons, delayed and postponed time and again until 1545 when it opened in the city of Trent.

But Luther began his preparation by composing the Smalcald Articles (published in 1537; *BC* 297–328). Here Luther listed his basic teachings, differentiating between those that were not negotiable and those that could be discussed. By 1538 Luther was doubtful that "a truly free council" would ever meet (*BC* 297). And if a council ever did meet, he thought, it would in all likelihood spend its time "clowning around" with vestments, hats, and the like (*BC* 299).

All of Luther's interest and research on the topic culminated in his 1539 work, *On the Councils and the Church* (LW 41, 9–178). The larger part of this book is a detailed account of the first five church councils: Jerusalem (Acts 15–16), Nicaea (325), Constantinople (381), Ephesus (431), and Chalcedon (451). When all is said and done, what impresses Luther about this history is: (a) how these councils in every case understood Scripture correctly when it came to the main articles of faith; (b) how again and again these councils eventually degenerated into "sheer clerical squabbling" (LW 41, 59); (c) how remarkably limited the bishop of Rome's influence was in any of this; and (d) how amazingly contradictory the councils and "church fathers" were, at least on nonessentials.

From this history there emerge, according to Luther, concrete conclusions for his own time. Councils may play a role in the life of the church, but it is a very limited one. They must not establish new articles of faith, but rather suppress these. They must not mandate new "good works," but rather condemn the old evil works. They may not impose new ceremonies, but rather must denounce these. They may not interfere in secular government. They may not make decrees that increase the hierarchy's power. And so forth (LW 41, 123–131). They should only deal with major issues of great urgency (LW 41, 136). The day-to-day governing of the church should be left to pastors and schoolteachers (LW 41, 134 and 142). In

fact, Luther concludes, now is the time for a council: correcting the pope is a matter weighty enough (LW 41, 140). Assemble about three hundred leaders, he suggests, and invite some of the laity. But, to be realistic, for the time being this is a futile dream (LW 41, 140–142).

On the Councils and the Church is in several respects a remarkable piece of work. For one thing, it is erudite by sixteenth-century standards. Here we see Luther the scholar, intensely interested in a topic, reading everything on it he can find. He clearly takes pride in his extensive grasp of the subject. His account is a detailed and relatively nuanced one. Then too, in comparison with other writings from the older Luther, this one shows an amazing level of tolerance. Sometimes when people are wrong, he says, "gentle instruction" is better than "arrogant condemnation" (LW 41, 116). Moreover, in this very lengthy work we find only one outburst of obscenity (LW 41, 138)! Readers of Luther's later works will understand how unusual this is. And Luther throws in jokes: for example, if Christians seriously adhered to the decisions of the Council of Jerusalem, the Germans would have to give up blood sausage (LW 41, 28). Lastly, we find in this work a somewhat uncharacteristic humility. Thus, with regard to the Council of Chalcedon (451), Luther candidly admits that he does not really understand what the main issue was. He tries to explain it, but then concedes that he may be wrong (LW 41, 106–117). All of this to some extent belies the stereotype of the old Luther as disgruntled, intolerant, embittered, and angry.

As events played out, the Council of Trent finally opened in December of 1545. By then Luther was utterly disillusioned: he expected nothing from this council (LW 50, 263), and he would not even consider the question of Lutheran participation unless the pope submitted to the council's authority in advance (LW 50, 266–267).

See also **Church**; **Papacy**

Creation The Christian doctrine of creation was not in dispute at the time of the Reformation (cf. *BC* 300). All agreed on the creedal affirmation of God as "creator of heaven and earth." Theologians, however, explained what this meant in varying ways. Luther's explanation was distinctive, and an integral part of his theological project as a whole.

If we attempt to organize Luther's disparate and scattered thoughts on this topic, we can see that the doctrine for him is basically about three realities. First, the doctrine teaches us something about the cosmos, nonhuman life forms, and so forth—"nature" as he called it, and how we are to relate to it. This is the least important aspect of the doctrine. (*See also* **Nature**.) Second, and more importantly, the belief in creation tells us something about God and orients our relationship to him. (*See also* **God**.) Third, and most importantly, this belief is about us: it is crucial to the self-understanding of the human person. What follows here is an explanation of this aspect of Luther's teaching on creation.

First, however, a cautionary word about the sources is in order. It may seem entirely logical to begin by turning to Luther's exposition of Genesis 1–2. Luther lectured extensively on this in mid–1535, and the records of these lectures present a worldview with rich cosmological, astronomical, and biological detail (LW 1, 3–140). Unfortunately the text we have is not from Luther himself; rather it was composed by some of his listeners on the basis of their own lecture notes. Luther himself, who had not intended this material for publication, expressed some doubts about the version these disciples published (WA 42, 1, 2–2, 35; cf. WABr 10, nr. 3935, 443, 3–444, 21). Thus caution is in order. If a position taken in the *Lectures on Genesis* (LW 1–8) is nowhere else to be found in Luther, it may well not be his. And if what is said in the *Lectures on Genesis* contradicts what Luther says elsewhere, it is probably not from him. Thus, for example, the *Lectures on Genesis* very frequently portray human sexuality as loathsome, disgusting, and sordid (the image of leprosy is used repeatedly). Yet elsewhere Luther often speaks of sexuality as one of God's beautiful gifts to us (*see* **Sexuality**). In this case, the *Lectures on Genesis* are highly suspect. None of that should cause us, however, to lose sight of the fact that the vast majority of material in the *Lectures on Genesis* corresponds perfectly with what we know from other sources. The point here is that it cannot be used as probative evidence but only as corroborative evidence.

As an alternative place to begin, we turn to Luther's Small Catechism of 1529. In response to the question of what it means to call God "creator of heaven and earth," we have what is historically one of the most memorized passages from all of Luther's writings:

> I believe that God has created me together with all that exists. God has given me and still preserves my body and soul. . . . God daily and abundantly provides. . . . God protects me against all danger and shields and preserves me from all evil. And all this is done out of a pure, fatherly, and divine goodness and mercy, without any merit or worthiness of mine at all! For all of this I owe it to God to thank and praise, serve and obey him. (*BC* 354–55)

This justifiably famous passage captures Luther's doctrine of creation in a nutshell.

The first thing that must be pointed out in this quotation is the primacy of the human. Already the first sentence suggests that humans take priority over all the rest that God creates. God in effect says to humans, "All that I do in heaven and on earth I direct to the end that it may serve you. You are my only concern; I can and will not forget you. I attend to you with such great care and love" (LW 8, 90). Humans are the pinnacle of creation, and everything was created to serve them (LW 34, 138).

What then is the line of demarcation between the human and the nonhuman in nature? Luther answers this differently in different contexts. He can identify it as the image of God, understood as righteousness or sinlessness (LW 34, 177; 1, 62–63; cf. 1, 65). Moreover, our destiny differentiates us from nonhuman animals: humans "were created to worship God and to live eternally with God" (LW 1, 131). Or to put it differently, we were created with a *capax immortalitatis*, a capacity for immortality (WA 42, 63, 37; LW 1, 84). Animals were not. Elsewhere Luther locates the difference quite simply in reason (LW 52, 60), or even (perhaps) in free will (LW 1, 84–85). In any case, a vast gulf separates the human from the nonhuman in creation, and the human takes absolute priority.

Even more pronounced in Luther's theology of creation is the primacy of the individual self: creation is not just about the human, but it is first and foremost about "me," the believing subject. Luther argues that since God is eternal, there is no past or future for him, but all things are in the present. Thus when he said, "Let us make man," he created me: my origin is in God, and this includes my individuality (LW 1, 76). To realize this is to internalize the doctrine of creation. Until we do, it remains abstract knowledge, with no impact on us—irrelevant. But if we do, it will change us.

Moreover, God's creating of us, Luther held, is ongoing: this is what it means to say that God "preserves" me (LW 4, 136; WA 21, 521, 21–25). Creation is not a moment of origin in the distant past as much as it is a continuing new beginning: it is not so much *initium* as it is *principium* (LW 1, 10; 22, 27). Creation means to "continually make things new" (WA 1, 563, 7–8). This creating extends to the "new creations" we are to become, a renewal of the creatureliness we, as sinners, have denied—a possibility to once again "walk in the garden," among the good things God has created (WA 38, 373, 30–32). And all this ongoing creation will have as its end—its *finis* and its *telos*—the eschatological new heaven and new earth (LW 34, 164; 12, 118–121).

A final essential point: to believe in the doctrine of creation means to understand life as a gift. "[W]e learn from this article that none of us has life—or anything else . . . —from ourselves. . . . [These things come from God's] fatherly heart and his boundless love toward us" (BC 433). Creation is *ex nihilo*, out of nothing, just as our new creation (justification) is *ex nihilo*, "without any merit or worthiness of mine at all" (354–55). To grasp this is to be overwhelmed with gratitude, a gratitude that will spontaneously erupt into a life of praise, service, and obedience (BC 355).

Creeds   Luther's acceptance of the historic creedal statements of the Christian tradition (Apostles', Nicene, and Athanasian) was wholehearted and unambiguous. All Christians, he said in his Large Catechism of 1529, must know the creed, and if we are too stubborn to learn it we should "have the dogs set upon us and also be pelted with horse manure" (BC 381). It superbly summarizes Christian belief: "Here in the [Apostles'] Creed you have the entire essence, will, and work of God exquisitely depicted in very brief but rich words" (BC 439). Knowing it is the minimal requirement for being called "Christian" and for being admitted to the Lord's Supper (BC 383).

The creeds have a certain authoritative status based on universal acceptance and long usage in the tradition. This authority is not absolute: the creeds are not in principle inerrant (cf. LW 36, 29; 32, 230; 32, 11). Their wording can be changed, for instance, if some do not understand terms like *homoousion* (LW 32, 244). Their authority, rather, is conditional and derivative: we accept them because they conform to the higher authority of Scripture (cf. LW 34, 229).

The real value of the creeds, for Luther, lies in the fact that they accurately summarize the essence of a very long and complex book, the Bible. In fact, as he explained in a sermon of 1534/35, the Apostles' Creed can serve as a little Bible for ordinary people. What had happened is that a layperson had been challenged on the veracity of the virgin birth; Luther's advice was to reply, "I have here a little booklet called the creed, and it contains this article [on the virgin birth]. This is my Bible; it has stood for a long time and still stands without being overthrown. I stand by this creed. I was baptized into this faith, and I shall live and die by it" (WA 37, 55, 12–15). As a summary of the Bible, the creed is accurate and reliable. But even it can be too complicated for some, and so Luther offers his own further condensation in his Large Catechism: "I believe in God the Father, who created me; I believe in God the Son, who has redeemed me; I believe in the Holy Spirit, who makes me holy" (BC 432). Though he is willing to distill the essence of Christianity in this way, Luther does not want to be misunderstood. In its stark simplicity, the meaning of the creed is inexhaustible. For ultimately what it tells us is "what God does for us and gives to us" (BC 440).

In 1538 Luther devoted a separate publication to the creeds, The Three Symbols or Creeds of the Christian Faith (LW 34, 201–229). Besides giving him an opportunity to publish his German translations of the creeds, by doing this he wanted to reassert his stance within the mainstream of the Christian tradition. He began with the Apostles' Creed, "the finest of all" in his opinion. This was followed by the Athanasian Creed, which elaborates and defends the second article (LW 34, 201). Then comes, somewhat anomalously, the "Te Deum Laudamus," which Luther calls a "symbol or creed," but which is more properly speaking a hymn of praise and gratitude (LW 34, 205). Finally, after a long polemic against christological and Trinitarian heresies, comes the Nicene Creed, which is "sung in the mass every Sunday" (LW 34, 228).

In 1528, as he was immersed in the heat of controversy, it suddenly occurred to Luther that after he was gone, his opponents (and followers too?) would doubtlessly distort his positions on various issues. So he paused, took a step back from the struggle with Huldrych Zwingli over the Lord's Supper, and penned a personal confession of faith. As we might expect, it was modeled on the Apostles' Creed. And while Luther could not resist amplifying its various articles, it was surely this creed first and foremost that he had in mind when he said, "I am determined to abide by it until my death and (so help me God!) in this faith to depart from this world and to appear before the judgment seat of our Lord Jesus Christ" (LW 37, 360).

Death   While it is true that humans have always been to some extent both fascinated and horrified by the subject of death, scholars have often noted that the level of this "horrified fascination" reached a new height on the eve of the Reformation. Some interpreters have suggested that Luther not only inherited this but allowed it to become a personal obsession. In my view, this is an exaggeration: we should probably rather speak of it as a preoccupation that periodically intensified and then receded. At times he was clearly almost overwhelmed with horror and dread at the thought of death. Invariably though, these periods gave way to an equanimity, peace, and even joy in the face of death. This oscillation corresponded directly to the dialectic of faith and doubt that characterized his experience.

One indicator of the morbid spirit of the times in the fifteenth century was the popularity of a new genre of pastoral literature, the so-called ars moriendi—books of instruction on how to die. Luther knew this literature well and in

1519 made his own contribution to the genre, his *Sermon on Preparing to Die* (LW 42, 99–115). Like previous books of this type, Luther's sermon gives many practical points of advice on how to face death. Yet there is a difference, and it lies in Luther's fundamental perception that the real and only "preparation" necessary on our part is faith—a purely passive receptivity to the "preparation" God has already made.

As for the nature of death itself, Luther vacillated between the dualistic understanding of death that he inherited from medieval theology and a more holistic understanding suggested by the biblical witness. The dualistic view, a product of the Hellenistic thought world, saw the human person as made up of two entities, body and soul. What occurs at death is their separation. Luther endorsed this traditional dualistic view of death when, for instance, he spoke of the soul's immortality (LW 5, 76). So too, in a 1532 funeral sermon, Luther could say that what dies is "not even the whole man, but only a part, the body" (LW 51:234). Later Lutheranism adopted this view as well: on the last day, bodies rise and are reunited with immortal souls already in God's presence. Yet Luther from time to time questioned this: why, he asked, would souls want a body if they were already in heaven? (WATR 5, nr. 5534; 219, 16–17). Elsewhere, he wondered "whether the body and soul are separate things" (WA 39:2, 354, 10–15). Such questions place Luther closer to the unified understanding of the human person and the unified understanding of the resurrection that is suggested in the New Testament.

Far from minimizing it, Luther acknowledged that death is difficult and terrifying for humans. This is because it is unnatural for us. Animals, for whom death is natural, have no sense of dread, as humans do (LW 13, 106). God created humans for life, not for death (LW 13, 76). Death is a result of human sinfulness and is inflicted by the wrath of God: "as life is the result of God's designing,

so death is the result of God's wrath. It is he who causes man to die. It is he who plunges him from life into death" (LW 13, 97). Death, in other words, is a punishment. And precisely because Christians understand it as God's "no" (LW 13, 78), the experience of death is worse for them than for nonbelievers: "Our [Christians'] death is more terrible . . . than the troubles and death of other men. . . . Christians . . . know that their death . . . is to be equated with God's wrath" (LW 13, 112; cf. 14, 90).

Yet, Luther argues, simultaneous with God's "no," and hidden under it, is his "yes." One way in which Luther explains this is with reference to baptism. We receive baptism "for the forgiveness of sin," but we remain immersed in sin in this life: the promise of baptism is fulfilled in death: "when we die, it [sin] is destroyed essentially" (LW 34, 164–165). As we move toward death we are moving toward perfect righteousness. Death is therefore not only punishment but also remedy. "Thus death, which previously was a punishment of sin, is now a remedy for sin. Thus here it is blessed" (WA 10:3, 76, 13). Our will, Luther says, should therefore accept it.

The dual character of the Christian as at the same time righteous and sinful (*simul iustus et peccator*) means that till the end of our lives we will continue to anticipate death with a mixture of dread and joyous hope. Insofar as we are sinners, death confronts us as an "abyss" into which we must leap (WA 19, 217, 20–25). But insofar as we are righteous by faith, this abyss is perceived not as one of eternal nothingness but of infinite love (LW 14, 90).

Luther also elucidated this duality in the Christian attitude toward death with his distinction between law and gospel. Since we always remain sinful, we are always under the law, and to that extent death is perceived as horrifying punishment. Faith, on the other hand, embraces the gospel, which assures us that we can never be separated from God's love. Thus the gospel takes away death's sting. As Luther put it, the law tells us, "'In the midst of earthly life, snares of death surround us,' but the voice of the gospel cheers the terrified sinner with its song: 'In the midst of certain death, life in Christ is ours' [because we have the forgiveness of sins]" (LW 13, 83; cf. WA 40:3, 496, 4–5 and 16–17). When we look from the vantage point of the law, we find death in the midst of life. But when we look from the vantage point of the gospel, we find life in the midst of death. Death, the negation of life, is clearly life's biggest problem. The gospel, from Luther's perspective, is the negation of this negation.

Just as Christians should not hide their anxiety about their own death under a false bravado, so too they should allow themselves to mourn the death of others. "For God has not created man to be a stick or a stone. He has given him five senses and a heart of flesh in order that he may love his friends, be angry with his enemies, and to lament and grieve when his dear friends suffer evil" (LW 51, 233). Remaining stoic in the face of death is a denial of our humanity. This was Luther's advice in a funeral sermon in 1532. He preached a good number of these in his career: in all of them, his central point is that what awaits us after death is not eternal nothingness but "eternal life." For what Luther meant by this, *see Eschatology.*

Decalogue   In the two centuries before Luther's time, the Ten Commandments had risen to a new prominence in the church, replacing the seven deadly sins as the primary vehicle for Christian moral instruction. Like almost all Christians at the time, Luther took for granted their importance: with perhaps a little exaggeration, in his Large Catechism Luther called them "the greatest treasure God has given us" (BC 431).

The Decalogue is important because it is a summary of the natural law, and thus an expression of God's will for humans (LW 34, 112; 43, 16; 47, 89; 35,

165). It informs us "of what we are to do to make our whole life pleasing to God" (BC 428). At the same time, in teaching humans how to live, it also teaches them to recognize their sinfulness. Both are summarized in the eleventh verse of Luther's 1524 hymn on the Ten Commandments:

To us come these commands, that so
Thou, son of man, thy sins may know,
And make thee also well perceive
How before God man should live.
                    (LW 53, 279)

To know our sinfulness means to understand that the commands "are beyond human power to fulfill" (BC 429): "no one is able to keep even one of the Ten Commandments as it ought to be kept" (BC 428). The utter impossibility of the demands placed on us implies the necessity of a savior. Faith, or trust in this savior, fulfills the first commandment to have no other gods. And in this first command all the others are comprehended. Thus faith is the fulfillment of the entire Decalogue (BC 430). Or, as Luther put it in his lectures on Deuteronomy, faith "uses law lawfully when it has no laws and has all laws—no laws, because none bind unless they serve faith and love; all, because all bind when they serve faith and love" (LW 9, 70). This typically paradoxical formulation also expresses in a nutshell how the gospel both fulfills and abrogates the law.

That this view of Luther was open to misunderstanding is confirmed by the fact that in the late 1530s some of his followers, known as "Antinomians," above all John Agricola, sought to "expel the law of God or the Ten Commandments from the church and assign them to city hall" (LW 47, 107). In other words, they held that the Decalogue is a fine guide to civic virtue but has nothing to do with Christianity. This Luther denounced as a crude misunderstanding of him and his teaching. In 1529 he had said so (BC 380) and now in 1539 he said it again: "I myself . . . recite the commandments daily word for word like a child" (LW 47, 109). From both a theological and personal-devotional point of view, the Decalogue was of high significance to him.

It was also for Luther an indispensable part of Christian pedagogy. For at least a century before him, all catechisms had included a section on the Decalogue, explaining and amplifying it for the sake of children and uneducated adults. Luther contributed mightily to this tradition of Decalogue commentary, a tradition that in his view reached back to the Old Testament itself. For what was the book of Deuteronomy but "a most ample and excellent explanation of the Decalog" (LW 9, 14)? "Moreover, what is the whole Psalter [Luther's favorite book], but meditation and exercises based on the First Commandment?" (BC 382). Jesus had summarized the Ten Commandments (LW 43, 16), and in fact Christ, Paul, and Peter had all made "new decalogues," clarifying that of Moses (LW 34, 112). So Decalogue explanations, to Luther's mind, had a worthy pedigree. And he wrote a good number of his own, the most important of which can only be listed here.

In 1520 he gave a brief explanation of the Decalogue in his *Short Form of the Ten Commandments, the Creed, and the Lord's Prayer* (WA 7, 205–214), and a much longer one in his *Treatise on Good Works* (LW 44, 15–113). In the following year, 1521, another appeared in *The Misuse of the Mass* (LW 36, 204–218). Here, in a diatribe against the papacy, Luther explains how the pope perverts all ten of the commandments into their opposite—a kind of left-handed Decalogue explanation. In 1522, for the reform of Christian devotion, Luther wrote a *Personal Prayer Book* with another commentary, this one imitating late medieval devotional literature by listing extensively the various sins against each command, and the various ways each is fulfilled (LW 43, 14–24). In 1524, with the pedagogical function of worship in mind, he penned two hymns on the Decalogue (LW 53, 278–279, 281). His

most famous Decalogue explanations appeared in 1529, one in his Large Catechism (BC 386–431) and another in his Small Catechism (BC 351–54). Finally, in 1535, at the request of his barber, Luther wrote *A Simple Way to Pray* and here he explained the Decalogue again, this time approaching each commandment separately from the fourfold viewpoint of instruction, thanksgiving, confession, and prayer (LW 43, 200–209).

Some say that Luther's focus on justification by faith alone had the effect of consigning ethical reflection to a back room in the theological household or even banishing it altogether. The foregoing indicates that such a view is a caricature, or at best a half-truth. Luther was deeply interested in ethical reflection (and Decalogue explanations were only one of the forms such reflection took in his writings). For if the commandments express God's will for humanity, it is important to understand them. They are important too, because without them (understood collectively as the "law"), the gospel makes no sense.

Descent into Hell   Christ's descent into hell was an ancient Christian teaching with vague origins in Roman mythology and in certain rather obscure New Testament passages (e.g., 1 Pet. 3:19–22; 4:6; Eph. 4:8–10). By the mid-fourth century it had found its way into early creedal formulations. In the Middle Ages it provided grist, in a minor way, for the scholastic theological mill. It also furnished a vivid theme for the creative imagination, expressing itself in graphic and dramatic art.

Luther accepted the *descensus ad inferos*, as the creeds (Apostles' and Athanasian) called it, as an article of faith. Thus the question of its truth was not at issue. What was open to discussion was its meaning. Yet even on this subject Luther had surprisingly little to say. Only in a few Easter or Ascension Day sermons, and in a handful of other sources, does Luther express his views.

Luther's understanding of this doctrine seems to have been developing throughout the 1520s. In 1523, for instance, we find him expressing considerable puzzlement over what the primary scriptural source (1 Pet. 3:19–22) could possibly mean (WA 12, 367, 31–32). He came back to this passage and Ephesians 4:8–10 in 1527, in a sermon for Ascension Day. What it means, he emphasized, is that Christ went "down" before he went "up." In fact he went as deep as it is possible to go, to "the devil, death, sin, and hell." Thus the triumphant Christ encompasses all things under his rule, from the very lowest to the highest (WA 23, 702, 12–16). By the 1530s Luther's understanding seems to have reached maturity, and he expressed it most fully in his 1532 sermon for Easter Day. The article of faith as he now enunciates it is quite simply that "he descended into hell that he might redeem us, who should have lay imprisoned there" (WA 37, 62, 31–32). But the question is: how should this be understood? Luther begins his sermon with a substantial polemic against those who take articles of faith like this literally, and thus make nonsense out of them. "[M]any have wanted to grasp these words with their reason and five senses, but without success. They have only been led further from the faith" (WA 37, 62, 37–63, 2). Obviously, Luther says, "it did not happen in a physical way, since he indeed remained three days in the grave" (WA 37, 62, 12–13). Crude literalism, Luther insists, makes nonsense of this (WA 37, 63, 36–41). Indeed, it is precisely the devil who tries to make us literalists and thus lead us away from the core truth (WA 37, 64, 16–19).

How then did it happen? Luther's answer is frankly agnostic: we really do not know. "I would simply leave this subject alone since I cannot even grasp everything that pertains to this life" (WA 37, 63, 20–21). What it points to, on the other hand, is "that Christ destroyed hell's power and took all the devil's power away from him. When I grasp

that, then I have the true core and meaning of it, and I should not ask further nor rack my brain about how it happened or how it was possible" (WA 37, 63, 31–34). We could learn much from "children and simple people" and artists, when it comes to expressing these things. They are not literalists, but they use their imaginations—create paintings, tell a story, perform in the children's Easter pageant, and so forth (WA 37, 63, 5–13; 64, 23). Luther gives an example of such imaginative "explanation": "he went to hell with his banner in hand as a victorious hero, and he tore down its gates and charged into the midst of the devils, throwing one through the window and another out the door" (WA 37, 65, 23–25). And we should not be afraid (as literalists tend to be) that such imaginative depictions will "harm or mislead us" (WA 37, 65, 38–39).

Once we have grasped Luther's rejection of the literal, we are in a position to understand his final answer to the question of why Christ descended into hell: to douse the fire! "[N]either all monastic sanctity nor all the world's power and might can extinguish one spark of the fire of hell. But it so happened that this man went down with his banner, and then all the devils had to flee as if for their lives. And he extinguished all the fires of hell, so that no Christians need to fear it" (WA 37, 66, 29–34) The threat of hell hovered ominously over the medieval and Reformation periods and it loomed large on Luther's personal horizon. It was in this context that Luther came to understand the descent into hell as a "powerful" and "useful" article of faith (WA 37, 63, 30).

Devil   From the milieu of popular piety into which he was born, Luther absorbed an unshakable belief in the devil. And from the theological tradition that he studied, he inherited the conventional late medieval way of understanding and speaking about the devil. Already at a young age, this was an integral part of his worldview; and it did not become less important for him as he developed from a pious, deferential monk into a critical, outspoken reformer. Nor did old age diminish the vivid realism of his belief in Satan. The existence and power of the devil were as self-evident to Luther as the existence and power of evil are to us.

Luther referred to the devil constantly, both in his formal writings and in his informal conversation (as recorded in the Table Talk). What may be striking to the modern reader is how literal, and indeed physical, Luther's understanding of the devil was. Take, for example, the following statement, made over dinner, probably in the 1530s: "It is not a unique, unheard-of thing for the devil to thump about and haunt houses. In our monastery in Wittenberg I heard him distinctly. For when I began to lecture on the book of Psalms, and I was sitting in the refectory after we had sung matins, studying and writing my lecture, the devil came and thudded three times in the storage chamber, as if dragging a bushel away" (WATR 6, nr. 6832, 219, 30–35). The devil here seems no less real than a mouse or a rat, scratching around in the woodpile. Additionally, like all theologians in the sixteenth century, Luther took the Genesis creation story literally, and so too the fallen angel mythology: Satan had originally been a good angel, but had disobeyed God and become God's enemy (LW 1, 22).

Alongside this literal/physical understanding of the devil, one also finds in Luther what we might call a symbolic/representational view. Thus "the devil" can very often be Luther's shorthand for "evil" (e.g., LW 34, 144). Or "Satan" can refer to an idea: "And yet Satan, that is, the insane idea of self-righteousness . . ." (LW 27, 146). Or "the devil" can represent death and all that is associated with it (e.g., WATR 1, nr. 832, 404, 28–29). Most conspicuously, in the Large Catechism of 1529, Luther used "the devil" to personify the hell-ish aspects of life that humans all too often experience. The last petition of the Lord's Prayer, "Deliver us from the Evil One [the devil]," means: protect us from "poverty, disgrace, death, and, in short, all the tragic misery and heartache, of which there is so incalculably much on earth" (BC 455). It is this entire negative side of life to which "the devil" refers. It would be a serious misunderstanding to think that this symbolic/representational devil is somehow less "real" than the literal/physical one. Luther oscillated between these two ways of speaking about the devil, and he saw no contradiction between them: they were different ways of describing what was for him an unquestionable reality. The problem with understanding Luther here is our modern tendency toward a literalism that enables us to see only one dimension. Luther could hold the two together.

In his theological reflection on this theme, Luther's language was unguarded, to say the least, and readers might be forgiven for suspecting dualistic tendencies here. "Dualism" in this context refers to a worldview that posits two ultimate realities—a good god and an evil god. Along these lines, one can find in Luther statements about "two Gods" (LW 33, 52) and two kingdoms, God's and Satan's (LW 33, 227). As "lord of this world" or "prince of this world" (LW 47, 113–114; 37, 18), the devil leads a ceaseless struggle against the good (LW 33, 287–288; cf. 27, 148). Unguarded language such as this inevitably led to accusations of dualism.

For at least a thousand years before Luther, ever since Augustine's great controversy with the Manicheans, the Christian tradition had decisively rejected such a worldview: there is only one ultimate principle in the universe, and it is good. Of course, Luther knew this and, when pressed, emphatically endorsed it. Satan is powerful and he is indeed lord of this world, but the outcome of the struggle is assured (WA 40:3, 68, 9–14). In his more apocalyptic moods, Luther could even affirm that Satan "knows his time is short" (LW 34, 338). The devil has no ultimacy and no power that God does not give him (LW 13, 97; cf. 12, 374). Satan, Luther thought, is both God's enemy and his instrument. God allows Satan to afflict humans for various reasons, but Satan remains subject to God's omnipotence (LW 33, 175–76; cf. 12, 373). Or, as Luther put it to his dinner guests in 1531, God permits the devil to harm us, and then watches as a child "looks through his fingers" (LW 54, nr. 1252, 128–129). But, as he constantly insisted, the outcome is assured: the devil cannot triumph in the end (e.g., LW 54, nr. 255, 34). For he has in principle been conquered by Christ (LW 54, nr. 252, 34; WATR 6, nr. 6830, 217, 5–8).

In the meantime, until the final eschatological victory, all manner of evils that beset humans are attributable to the devil. And here we might say parenthetically that much of Luther's talk of the devil is couched in the language of death and excrement (e.g., WA 1, 50, 24–25; WA 4, 681, 20–30). This aside, the devil harasses us with temptations (WATR 5, nr. 5284, 44, 8–9). There are actually different kinds of devils: menial ones tempt us with things like fornication and avarice; higher ones tempt us to unbelief, despair, and so forth (WA 52, 721, 610). There are even white ones who try to pass for angels (WA 40:1, 108, 6–109, 6). Satan prevents people from understanding their own sinfulness (LW 33, 130); he causes disease and pain (LW 54, nr. 3543a, 227); he hates life (LW 54, nr. 252, 34), and yet he makes death seem horrifying to us (WA 37, 3, 23–25); he causes sadness, fear, and depression (WATR 1, nr. 832, 404, 28–29; LW 54, nr. 122, 15–17); he offers convincing arguments to the effect that God does not exist (LW 54, nr. 518, 93); he causes insomnia (WATR 2, nr. 1557, 132, 4–5); he drives people to suicide (LW 54, nr. 590, 106); he plants doubts in our minds (LW 54, nr. 518, 93); he constantly perverts the gospel into the law (LW 54, nr. 590, 106); he causes illusions and appari-

tions (LW 54, nr. 3601, 241); he possesses people (LW 54, nr. 5207, 396–397); he has sex with women, thereby making them into witches (LW 54, nr. 3953, 298); he appears to people in specters and poltergeists (LW 54, nr. 3814, 279–280); and so forth.

What does Luther recommend for Christians in dealing with these onslaughts of the devil? What strategies are best? Luther's formal theological answer is entirely conventional: "The only way to drive away the devil is through faith in Christ, by saying, 'I have been baptized, I am a Christian'" (WATR 6, nr. 6830, 217, 26–27). Because Christians belong to Christ, the devil, fearsome as he is, has no ultimate power over them.

Furthermore, when people are besieged by the devil, there are practical things they can do. In these recommendations, Luther is not as conventional. Since the devil is associated with sadness, depression, and death, affirming life and its joys is one way of dealing with him (LW 54, nr. 522, 95–96). In fact, getting married, Luther said in 1525, is a good way to spite the devil (WA 18, 277, 26–36); and he took his own advice.

In the Table Talk, one finds plenty of personal stories from Luther, recounting how he dealt with the devil. Two things about these stories will catch the attention of the modern reader. The first is their vulgarity. In case after case, Luther tells of how he drove the devil away with a fart (e.g., LW 54, nr. 122, 16; 54, nr. 469, 78; 54, nr. 491, 83; and so forth). Or he tells the devil to kiss his "backside" (in the overly delicate American translation, LW 54, nr. 590, 106; cf. WATR 1, nr. 590, 276, 12–13). The second arresting feature of these personal reminiscences is their almost nonchalant character. For example, from 1532 we have this report from Luther: "If the devil comes during the night to plague me, I give him this answer: Devil, I must sleep now; for this is God's command: Work during the day, sleep at night" (WATR 2, nr. 1557, 132, 4–7). Or, take the passage quoted above about the devil thumping around in the storage chamber of the monastery. It continues as follows: "Finally, as it did not want to stop, I collected my books and went to bed. I still regret to this hour that I did not sit him out, to discover what else the devil wanted to do. I also heard him once over my chamber in the monastery. But when I realized that it was him, I paid no attention and went back to sleep again" (WATR 6, nr. 6832, 219, 35–40). How could Luther be this casual, offhanded, even unperturbed, in the face of a close encounter with the devil? The nonchalant vulgarity of Luther's response to Satan underscores his fundamental view: horrifying as he may seem to us, ultimately he is nothing to worry about. For though he currently reigns as "lord of this world" (LW 47, 113) and as the "prince of death" (LW 14, 84), his demise is assured. "[H]e should kiss my backside," Luther says, because "[God's] mercy is greater than sin, and life is stronger than death" (LW 54, nr. 590, 106).

Divorce By 1520 Luther had already broken decisively with the Roman Catholic system of marriage annulment and the vast body of canon law regulating it. This complex system specified not only multiple impediments to valid marriages but also grounds for annulment, and then granted dispensations for infractions and irregularities for a suitable fee. Thus, he said, church authorities have involved themselves in the sale of "vulvas and genitals": "O worthy trade for our pontiffs to ply, instead of the ministry of the gospel" (LW 36, 96). From this point on, Luther was convinced that the church should not make laws on such matters: Christian leaders can advise, but legalities should be left to the civil authorities. He himself gave much advice on such matters, but in the name of Christian liberty he consistently resisted turning general principles and advice into law.

From the outset then, Luther's general principle is that divorce is not a good thing: God's will is that there be no divorce (LW 45, 31). Nevertheless, human beings are sinful, and this means that many things that are not good must be allowed "lest greater evil occur" (LW 9, 210; cf. 21, 94). Divorce is one of these things. Moreover, relationships in real life are too complex to be governed strictly by law. How, for instance, can law mandate patience and forgiveness, which are in every case preferable to divorce (LW 21, 94–98)? Even the various New Testament statements on divorce (e.g., Matt. 5:32) must be understood as appeals and not as law.

In the course of his career, both as a theologian and pastoral adviser, Luther enumerated what he thought were legitimate grounds for divorce in various ways. In 1520 he listed adultery, impotence, ignorance of a previous marriage, ignorance that one's spouse has taken a vow of chastity, refusal to pay the "conjugal debt" (i.e., refusal to have sex—a traditional feature of the Catholic Church's marriage law), and drastic incompatibility (LW 36, 102–106). These grounds were reiterated in 1522 (LW 45, 30–33), though now Luther added that if a spouse becomes an invalid and cannot have sex, this is *not* grounds for divorce (LW 45, 34). This list, with minor variations, Luther reiterated quite frequently from that point on. The only significant addition came in 1532: "certain queer, stubborn, and obstinate people, who have no capacity for toleration and are not suitable for married life at all should be permitted to get a divorce" (LW 21, 94).

All of this Luther offered as opinion, not law. He advised pastors confronted with marital counseling to leave legalities to the civil authorities and focus on comforting troubled consciences. "[I]f you find a confusion of conscience is about to arise over the law, then tear through the law confidently like a millstone through a spiderweb, and act as if this law had never been born" (LW 46, 319). This is especially relevant, Luther said, when dealing with issues and occurrences from the past. Pastors should say, "See to it that it does not happen again, and forgive and forget" (ibid.).

Since marriage ought to be a matter of love in which law has no weight, and since in real life one must sometimes choose a lesser evil to avoid a greater one, it was even conceivable to Luther that in certain unfortunate circumstances, bigamy would be preferable to divorce. He envisioned this possibility first in 1520 (LW 36, 105), again in 1522 (LW 45, 19), and also in 1531 in relation to Henry VIII's divorce (LW 50, 33). Then in 1539 he came up against just such a situation in the case of Philip of Hesse. Among other reasons, Philip wanted to divorce his wife because of her unfriendliness, her bad smell, and her alcoholism. These were *not* legitimate grounds for divorce, in Luther's view. In the end, to keep a bad situation from becoming worse, he secretly consented (as did Philip's wife) to a bigamous marriage (LW 54, nr. 5038, 379; nr. 5046, 382; nr. 5096, 387–389).

Eschatology   In its broadest sense, "eschatology" is the area of Christian theology that deals with the future. It includes the subject of death, of course, but more conventionally it focuses on what comes after death. By Luther's time, Christians for almost fifteen centuries had described this by speaking of the kingdom of God, resurrection, eternal life, and so forth. This much Luther took for granted. The properly theological question is, What do these things mean? and Luther expended considerable effort trying to answer.

He based himself on the hints that are to be found in the Bible. As any history of Christian eschatological thinking makes abundantly clear, many of these scriptural statements are in tension with one another, if not downright contradic-

tory. This, more than anything else, can help us understand why Luther failed to elaborate a consistent eschatology. Fidelity to the biblical witness prevented this. And in the end it reminds us, as it did Luther, that what the biblical writers were struggling to express is ultimately a mystery. To insist on rigid dogmatic formulations is to reduce the mystery to the level of human intelligibility. Ultimately, when all is said and done, we must confess that we know virtually nothing: "As little as babies in their mother's womb know about what awaits them, so little we know about eternal life" (WATR 3, nr. 3339; 276, 26–27).

Nevertheless, Luther struggled to make sense of what he found in the Bible. It is a mistake, Luther thought, to take this material too literally. For instance, Paul's words about an archangel's call, a trumpet's sound, the dead rising, the alive taken into the clouds, "meeting the Lord in the air" (1 Thess. 4:16–18)—these words, Luther says, "are purely allegorical. He [Paul] was trying to paint a picture, as we must use pictures with children and simple people" (LW 51, 253).

Even more problematic, for Luther, was the book of Revelation. In his 1522 preface to this book, Luther opines that it is "neither apostolic nor prophetic. . . . I can in no way detect that the Holy Spirit produced it." Consequently, "about this book . . . I leave everyone free to hold his own opinions" (LW 35, 398). He wryly adds that according to 22:7, a blessing is promised to those who keep what is written here; "and yet no one knows what that is, to say nothing of keeping it" (LW 35, 398f). In a much more extensive preface from 1530, Luther takes basically the same approach: while "[s]ome have even brewed it into many stupid things out of their own heads," we really do not know what it means (LW 35, 400). Yet here Luther ventures his own tentative interpretation. But even this is not entirely serious. Thus he suggests, for example, that the three vile frogs in 16:13 are John Faber, John Eck, and Jerome Emser—his contemptible opponents (LW 35, 408). Details aside, Luther thinks, the "bottom line" of Revelation is clear: it is that despite all plagues, beasts, and demons, Christ's final victory is assured (LW 35, 411).

The biblical image that Luther uses most frequently to describe what happens to us after death is sleep (e.g., 1 Thess. 4:13–14). We will then rest, or sleep, or be at peace in the bosom, or arms, of Christ (e.g., LW 4, 313; 51, 231–243; WABr 2, nr. 449, 422, 29–31; WABr 5, nr. 1529, 240, 68–70). How can this be? Luther's answer is blunt: "We don't know" (LW 4, 313). But what the image evokes is clear: to be asleep in the arms of Jesus means to be at peace in the care of an infinite, maternally protective, love. Sleep obviously implies too the absence of consciousness. Luther explains in a 1525 sermon: "For just as one who falls asleep and sleeps soundly until morning does not know what has happened to him when he wakes up, so we shall suddenly rise on the last day; and we shall not know how we died or how we came through death" (WA 17:2, 235, 17–20). Thus Luther can speak of an immediate life with Christ after death (as 2 Cor. 5:6–10 and Phil. 1:23 seem to), *and* a resurrection on the last day (as 1 Cor. 15:51–52 and Phil. 3:20–21 seem to). Moreover, none of this causes Luther to lose sight of the more fundamental truth, that Christ meets us in death.

What comes next, according to Luther, is the resurrection of the "last day"—a return to consciousness. "[W]e will sleep until he comes and knocks on the grave and says, 'Dr. Martin, get up.' Then I will arise in a moment and be eternally happy with him" (WA 37, 151, 8–10). We should also note here that while this is Luther's usual explanation, he can at times say the opposite, that is, that we go to heaven immediately after death (e.g., WA 53, 400, 14–19; WABr 6, nr. 1930, 301, 6–8). Still elsewhere he "resolves" the difficulty by noting that in sleep we lose track of time. Time after

death is "one eternal moment," and therefore we can say that the last day comes "immediately" after death *and* "at the end of time" (WA 10:3, 194, 10–12).

Be this as it may, there will be a resurrection, which will be followed by a final judgment, as the creed specifies. Late medieval pastoral practice emphasized this judgment as a "day of wrath," and we do not go far wrong in surmising that large numbers of Christians lost sleep over the prospect. The young Luther had experienced this himself, and from one point of view his entire theological program aimed at alleviating such anxiety. We will not be judged, he insisted, on our moral or religious achievements, but rather on whether we have opened our hearts in pure receptivity to God's mercy and love. Grasping what the gospel means is grasping "that we need not fear the final judgment" (LW 22, 380; cf. 34, 328). The doctrine of justification transforms the horror of the last day into a comfort.

What follows then, in the Christian hope, is eternal life, heaven. Our present righteousness in the world is an eschatological reality: it is a hoped-for righteousness: "Our being justified perfectly still remains to be seen, and this is what we hope for. Thus our righteousness does not yet exist in fact, but it still exists in hope" (LW 27, 21). This "incipient" righteousness will reach its consummation and perfection "in heaven" (LW 27, 22). Eternal life is the state in which we will be "perfectly pure and holy people, full of integrity and righteousness, completely freed from sin, death, and all misfortune, living in new, immortal, and glorified bodies" (BC 438). From the vantage point of our lives now, in this world, we can scarcely imagine such a perfect righteousness, fulfillment, and happiness.

And what about the "damned"? Compared with some other Christian theologians, Luther has surprisingly little to say about them. Hell, understood as a place of fiery punishment, is the traditional answer, and some statements in

Luther could be read as an endorsement of this tradition. More often, however, we can observe Luther struggling to extricate himself from this conventional wisdom. (For more on this, *see* **Hell**.) The following statement from his late Genesis lectures is typical. Referring to John 5:29 he says: "I am unable to say positively in what state those are who are condemned in the New Testament. I leave this undecided" (LW 4, 316). In his view we simply do not know, and in his more circumspect moments he realized that about such matters it is wiser to say less than more.

So much for an eschatology of the individual. What then did Luther have to say about a collective eschatology, about the future of the world and humankind? Perhaps the most common Christian category, in this regard, is the "kingdom of God." Luther speaks of it in various ways: it does battle with the current "devil's kingdom" (WA 41, 317, 14); it is present now in faith and will be present in its fullness in the future (LW 12, 118); it is not a "worldly kingdom" but a "heavenly kingdom" (WA 30:2, 213, 11–14; cf. *BC* 50–51); and so forth. Very commonly, Luther "individualizes" this collective concept. Thus he says in his Small Catechism of 1529, when we pray "Your kingdom come," we are saying may it come "to us" (*BC* 356). In his Large Catechism of the same year he elaborates. In the Lord's Prayer we are asking that this kingdom "may be realized in us" (*BC* 447). When it is, then God rules us "as a king of righteousness, life, and salvation against sin, death, and an evil conscience" (*BC* 446). Beginning in our lives now through faith, it will be perfected in the future: It destroys "the devil's kingdom . . . so that he may have no right over us until finally his kingdom is utterly eradicated and sin, death, and hell wiped out, that we may live forever in perfect righteousness and blessedness" (*BC* 447). In Luther's explanation, the social implications of the collective concept of "kingdom" are not prominently featured.

What about the consummation of history, the end of the world, the return of Christ, and the "last day"? This complex of ideas about our collective future became increasingly important to Luther as he got older. At times it seemed to him that the end was imminent; and at other times this sense of an impending end receded in his consciousness. Thus it is legitimate to speak of Luther's "apocalypticism," as long as we understand that he was inconsistent in this regard.

Strictly speaking, Luther's view has nothing to do with what is sometimes called "millenarianism." The thousand-year period referred to in Revelation 20:3–7 fascinated him from time to time, and in his *Computation of the Years of the World* of 1541–45 (WA 53, 1184), it figured into his calculations (WA 53, 152–154). In the end, however, Luther thought that this "millennium" does not refer to the end of the world but rather to the time of the church, and in this he followed Augustine (LW 35, 409). Thus the "millennium" is in the past; it is not for Luther an eschatological concept.

Nevertheless, he was sure that the world would end. The only question was, when? In this regard, Luther realized, the Bible leaves us with a dilemma: on the one hand it tells us that we cannot know, and on the other hand it gives us "signs": "For these two things will and must occur together, as they are both preached together by Christ and the apostles: first there will be many and great signs. And second, the coming of the last day will be unexpected" (WA 10:1:2, 93, 24–28).

Very often, especially toward the end of his life, Luther "read" these signs to mean an almost immediate end. One of these was that the antichrist (i.e., the pope) now ruled, attacking Christendom from within (e.g., LW 41, 263–376). Another was that the devil (i.e., Islam, or "the Turk") was besieging Christendom from without (e.g., WA 30:2, 149–197). These signs, coupled with a perceived moral deterioration of the world in general, were sometimes overwhelming to Luther. Already in 1530, he spoke of these "wretched last times" (e.g., LW 35, 315). By 1541 he expressed this even more forcefully: "As for me, I content myself with the fact that the last day is at the door. For almost all the signs that Christ and the apostles Peter and Paul announced have already occurred. . . . Certainly things are coming to an end" (WADB 11:2, 124, 15–20). In noting this expectation of an imminent end, we should not discount the role of nontheological factors such as the older Luther's illness, his experience of being besieged from all sides, his periodic disillusionment, and even what we would today call depression.

Elsewhere, and especially in the earlier Luther, we find an expectation that the Parousia delay will continue for the long term. We find this alternative reading of the signs, for instance, in a letter of 1519 (WABr 1, nr. 177; 400, 20–22). So too we find it in a sermon of 1522: the signs of the last day "are yet to be fulfilled" (WA 10:1:2, 93, 21–22). Even in 1530 we can find Luther saying that his time is really "a golden age" in comparison with the past (LW 35, 410). Thus we must be cautious about attributing to Luther an unrelenting pessimism about this world and an unwavering conviction that it was very soon coming to an end.

It is easy for Christians to allow all the various issues dealt with here to obscure the fundamentals. This happened in Luther's case: from time to time he argued passionately for one position or another on various eschatological questions. But in the final analysis, he realized, all these positions must be held tentatively. What we really "know" about the future is that we do not know (WATR 3, nr. 3339; 276, 26–27). That, and one other thing: not even death "will be able to separate us from the love of God in Christ Jesus our Lord" (Rom. 8:38–39; cf. LW 25, 360).

Ethics Summarizing Luther's thought in the area of ethics (*see also* **Ethics, Social/Political**) presents us with two kinds of difficulties. The first is that he wrote so much about it. Questions of ethics come up in some form in everything he produced, whether exegetical or devotional, in lectures, in scholarly treatises, in disputations, in letters, and so forth. The second difficulty is that his ethical reflection is anything but systematic or orderly. He never laid out a coherent "ethics" in the sense of a single work that begins with basic questions, assumptions, definitions, and so forth, and then develops a structured body of thought on that foundation. One who wishes to give a brief account of Luther's ethics, therefore, must comb through his works, gather up his scattered comments, try to isolate his foundational principles, and give the whole some kind of logical order. What follows is one such attempt.

We can begin with the question of what is the good, and how humans come to know this. Standing in the Christian theological tradition, Luther answers in a largely conventional way. God is by definition the *summum bonum*, the "highest good" (LW 44, 50; 44, 52), the source of all good in the universe (*BC* 388–389). God has created human beings and has expressed his will for them, that is, he has told them what he wants them to do. This "moral instruction" he built into the human person from the moment of creation. By this "natural law" every human being knows what is morally good.

The natural law implanted in us is identical with divine law (WATR 2, nr. 2151, 338, 3–5). And it is universal (LW 46, 27). Located specifically in human reason (LW 45, 128), this set of rules would be wholly sufficient and adequate for humans, if only they would follow it (WA 17:2, 102, 10–14). Nothing more than this would be needed for the regulation of human life, the human relationship to nature, family life, government, and so forth (LW 24, 228). This is the splendid treasure we all brought with us when we came into the world (WA 39:1, 540, 24–26). "Positive laws," on the other hand, are not universal but rather written laws fashioned by human beings and specific to certain places and times (LW 54, nr. 3911. 293; cf. 40, 98). They should in every case be derived from natural law (WATR 2, nr. 2151, 338, 1–5), or, to put it differently, they ought to be derived from reason and "subject to reason" (LW 45, 129). (*See also* **Reason.**)

Noble and precious as the natural law is, it has been somewhat obscured by human sinfulness: its light does not shine as brightly in us as it should. For that reason God revealed it again to Moses—in order to reawaken our awareness of it. Of course, not the whole of the Mosaic law is natural law; much of this in fact is positive law, and therefore not applicable to us. But the Decalogue *is* natural law, indeed, an incomparable expression of the natural law. It reminds us of what we already know instinctively but perhaps vaguely (LW 40, 97–98). (*See also* **Decalogue.**)

The Mosaic law, specifically the Decalogue, is in its turn summarized, clarified, and deepened most profoundly by the "law of Christ," according to Luther. Asked to sum up the law, Jesus had answered: "You shall love the Lord your God with all your heart. . . . You shall love your neighbor as yourself" (Matt. 22:37–39). This is what Luther sometimes calls Christ's "new decalogue" (LW 34, 112–113). It interprets the Mosaic law, but it neither adds nor subtracts from it (LW 24, 228).

Furthermore, this law of Christ—love of God and love of neighbor—is finally reducible to one thing only, namely, love of neighbor. If we ask what precisely it means for humans to "love God," and how they are to do this, Luther's answer is that this love is best expressed in love of neighbor: "It is there [in the needy one] God is to be

found and loved, there he is to be served and ministered to, whoever wishes to minister to God and serve him; so that the commandment of the love of God is brought down in its entirety into the love of neighbor. . . . For this was the reason he put off the form of God and took on the form of a servant, that he might draw down our love for him and fasten it on our neighbor" (WA 17:2, 99, 18–31; cf. WA 10:1:1, 100, 13–16). Thus, in the final analysis, "The law of Christ is the law of love" (LW 27, 113).

This law of love—"love your neighbor as yourself"—is the sum and substance of the whole moral teaching of Jesus in the New Testament. Indeed, it is a summary of Jesus' Sermon on the Mount (LW 21, 235–236). An alternative way of expressing the same thing is the Golden Rule: "Do to others what you would have them do to you" (Matt. 7:12; Luke 6:31) (LW 27, 56; 40, 97; 42, 68; 45, 128; 45, 292; 46, 110–111, and 114). This then is the moral demand that God places on his creatures. It comes to us by way of the natural law, the Mosaic law, the law of Christ, and it is quite simply the law of love. That is "the good," and how we come to know it. (Occasionally Luther suggests that the law of Christ demands more than the natural law, namely, suffering [e.g., LW 46, 29]. That, however, is seldom expressed, and it stands outside the main current of Luther's ethical thought.)

With this we come to a second fundamental question: Why should we do the good? Does God attach an incentive system to his moral demand on humans? Are we even capable of doing what is demanded? Here is where Luther parted company with conventional approaches (though not entirely with the theological tradition).

First, Luther teaches, we can never act out of a pure love for God because we always act out of love for ourselves. We do things "for God," Luther says, "to earn something or escape something" (LW 44, 241). "[T]here is not one in a thousand who does not put his confidence in the works, and presume that by having done them he wins God's favor and lays claim to his grace. They turn the whole thing into a fairground" (LW 44, 32). But surely a higher motive than benefiting oneself is required. Acting out of love means "seeking no reward, fearing no punishment" (LW 44, 241). Love cancels out greed and fear.

Luther's analysis of love for our neighbor is similar. This mandate may appear simple, but from Luther's perspective, it is highly problematic. For fulfilling it would entail putting an end to our egocentrism. "'Love your neighbor as yourself,' but not in the sense that you should love yourself. . . . [Y]ou do wrong if you love yourself, an evil from which you will not be free unless you love your neighbor in the same way, that is, by ceasing to love yourself" (LW 25, 513–514). "Sin" is what blocks humans from doing the good, and the essence of human sinfulness is self-love: acting always in our own interests, however disguised, we cannot act in the best interests of our neighbor. Our love of self blocks us from doing God's will, acting out of love for the other. (*See also* **Sin**.)

Accordingly, for Luther, motive is everything. Truly good acts "have, and ought to have, a far higher and nobler incentive" than our calculated self-interest (LW 44, 44). Our actions must proceed from "a pure, free, cheerful, glad, and loving heart, a heart which is simply gratuitously righteous, seeking no reward" (LW 44, 241). Without such a motive, all our ethical striving is worthless. As Luther puts it elsewhere, "it is most important that a person have the right head. For where one's head is right, one's whole life must also be right, and vice versa" (BC 390).

What gets our "head right," what corrects all baser motivation, is faith. Faith accepts what Luther calls the "good news" of the gospel, namely that God loves us, forgives us, and gives us all good things. "If you see [this], that God is so kindly disposed to you that he even gives his own Son for you, then your heart in turn must grow sweet and disposed toward God. And in this way your confidence must grow out of pure good will and love—God's toward you and yours toward God" (LW 44, 38). To accept God's love in faith means that one does not have to earn it. One already possesses everything important. All moral striving for the sake of getting a reward or avoiding punishment becomes pointless. Greed and fear can now give way to love and gratitude. In this way faith frees us from the heavy weight of impossible moral demands. It gets our "head right" (*See also* **Faith**.)

Thus the foundation of all Christian ethical reflection, for Luther, is his understanding of justification. (*See also* **Justification**.) No ethical act, no human moral achievement of any kind, can change God's mind about us or improve our standing before God. God's self-giving love—his "grace"—is given to us despite the fact that we in no way deserve it. Opening ourselves up to this gift in faith transforms us, enabling us to begin acting out of love, for God and for our fellow human beings. As Luther put it, "We do not become righteous by doing righteous deeds but, having been made righteous, we do righteous deeds" (LW 31, 12; cf. 31, 361).

An ethics based on such a foundation dramatically undercuts the human propensity to self-righteousness. It assiduously avoids an oppressive moralism that robs Christians of their freedom and spontaneity. And it programmatically excludes an understanding of the Christian life as a course in self-improvement, as the "pursuit of holiness." In short, for Luther Christianity is not "legalistic," a religion that is about following rules. Rather it is a religion that frees us from rules in order that we can act out of love.

(For examples of how Luther applied these principles, *see* **Ethics, Social/ Political; War; Sexuality**.)

Ethics, Social/Political I must concede at the outset that Luther was not a social/political thinker of the first order: those who expect from him perfect systematic consistency on these issues face disappointment. Nevertheless, his fundamental theological project had unmistakable implications for ethics: briefly stated, Luther held that God's love for humans, when they open themselves up to it in faith, frees them, impels them, and empowers them to act out of love toward their fellow human beings (*see* **Faith; Grace; Justification**). The difficult question was what this meant concretely on the social and political level. Luther's answer was not worked out in the abstract or in hindsight, but rather in the immediacy of the tangled events that made up his own social/political context. Fairly quickly he achieved clarity in his own mind on several principles that henceforth remained foundational for him. As time went on he freely amplified them and adjusted them to fit new circumstances. Occasionally he compromised, and even betrayed them. But he never abandoned them. These basic principles are conventionally referred to as his doctrines of the "two kingdoms," "two governments," and "three estates."

Here as elsewhere Luther's thought is best understood against its medieval background. The dominant ideology, though highly idealized and often rudely belied by events, portrayed Christendom as a seamless whole, an undivided body under the ultimate authority of the pope. This theoretical construct of a *Corpus Christianum* received its classical formulation in Pope Boniface VIII's bull *Unam Sanctam* in 1302. Both the "spiritual sword" and the "temporal sword," Boniface had said, are in the church's hands. The former is to be used by the church, the latter by "kings and captains" but only "at the will and by the permission" of the church. Thus all temporal authority is subject to spiritual authority, which

in turn is from God. Final authority and power are thus localized in the person of the pope, and this is subject to no human judgment whatsoever. What followed this declaration was two centuries of confused struggle—between temporal and spiritual, state and church, emperor and pope—and this, so Luther thought, to their mutual detriment. The general aim of his thinking then, was to sort out the mess, to disentangle the chaos, to redraw the jurisdictions, and thus to achieve a new moral clarity and integrity for both.

By the early 1520s Luther was regularly speaking of "two kingdoms" (*zwei Reiche*) and "two governments" (*zwei Regimente*). (Note: These amount to different aspects of the same thing. The first refers to a "sphere of rule" and the second to a "means of rule." But Luther often conflates them or uses them interchangeably. In what follows, I treat them together.) What he meant was that reality is divided into two spheres of existence. One is called the "kingdom of Christ" or the "spiritual kingdom," and the other is the "kingdom of this world" or the "secular kingdom." There are many differences between them, but one thing they have in common is that they are both established by God. The divine origin of the spiritual kingdom needed no argument: on this all agreed. But Luther now asserted the same about the secular realm: "worldly government is a glorious ordinance and splendid gift of God, who has instituted it and established it and will have it maintained as something men cannot do without" (LW 46, 237). Its validity and legitimacy are not derived from the spiritual. Worldly government stands on its own, grounded in God's will.

While the two kingdoms have this in common, they differ, first, in their purpose. In 1523 Luther described this difference: the purpose of the spiritual is to "produce righteousness" while the purpose of the secular is "to bring about external peace" (LW 45, 91). The kingdom of Christ makes people truly righteous in the eyes of God, while the kingdom of this world enforces an external, superficial righteousness that is nevertheless necessary for human well-being. A 1530 description emphasizes this function of the secular: "If there were no worldly government, one man could not stand before another; each would necessarily devour the other, as irrational beasts devour one another. . . . [I]t is the function and honor of worldly government to make men out of wild beasts. It protects a man's body . . . a man's wife . . . a man's child . . . a man's house . . . a man's fields and cattle" (LW 46, 237). In other words, it is the purpose of the worldly kingdom to rein in and suppress the more rapacious instincts, to civilize humans, and to make their lives less "nasty, brutish, and short."

In accordance with their different purposes, the means of rule in the two kingdoms differs. The kingdom of Christ, Luther says, is ruled only by Christ, the Word of God, and the gospel (LW 45, 88–90). This kingdom has to do with "the right relation of the heart to God" (LW 21, 108), and in such matters there can be no coercion: "even if all Jews and heretics were forcibly burned no one ever has been or will be convinced or converted thereby" (LW 45, 115). (This position, taken by Luther in 1523, was later betrayed by him in his stance against the Anabaptists.) The kingdom of the world, on the other hand, should not be ruled with the gospel (LW 45, 91). Here it is not mercy and kindness but justice and force that are necessary. "[T]he kingdom of the world, which is nothing else than the servant of God's wrath upon the wicked . . . should not be merciful, but strict, severe, and wrathful in fulfilling its work and duty. Its tool is not a wreath of roses or a flower of love, but a naked sword; and a sword is a symbol of wrath, severity, and punishment" (LW 46, 70; cf. 45, 264). Tolerance, which is "the rule" in the spiritual kingdom, has no place in the secular kingdom (LW 21, 113).

Luther gave what is perhaps his clearest summary of these ideas in his 1526 work *Whether Soldiers, Too, Can Be Saved*:

God has established two kinds of government among men. The one is spiritual; it has no sword, but it has the word, by means of which men are to become good and righteous, so that with this righteousness they may attain eternal life. He administers this righteousness through the word, which he has committed to the preachers. The other kind is worldly government, which works through the sword so that those who do not want to be good and righteous to eternal life may be forced to become good and righteous in the eyes of the world. He administers this righteousness through the sword. And although God will not reward this kind of righteousness with eternal life, nonetheless, he still wishes peace to be maintained among men and rewards them with temporal blessings. . . . Thus God himself is the founder, lord, master, protector, and rewarder of both kinds of righteousness. There is no human ordinance or authority in either, but each is a divine thing entirely. (LW 46, 99–100)

In short, the two kingdoms or realms are Luther's way of speaking about human existence before God on the one hand, and before humanity on the other. The first falls under the aegis of the gospel, the second under the aegis of law (*see Gospel; Law*). The former corresponds with the first table of the Decalogue, the latter with the second table (*see Decalogue*). In the spiritual kingdom the ethic of Jesus' Sermon on the Mount (Matt. 5–7) is given pride of place; in the secular kingdom the ethic of Romans 13 and 1 Peter 2:13–17 is decisive.

Initially, and at least until 1520, the distinction between the two kingdoms was not this clear to Luther. In that year he wrote his appeal *To the Christian Nobility of the German Nation Concerning the Reform of the Christian Estate*, calling on the secular authorities to reform the Roman church (LW 44, 123–217). But that, he later insisted, had been an emergency measure, necessary only because the church refused to reform itself. Soon thereafter, by 1523, he was insisting that the secular should "not extend too far and encroach upon God's kingdom and government" (LW 45, 104). And in subsequent writings he was increasingly insistent on sharply distinguishing the two: the papacy, he said in 1530, has "so jumbled these two together and confused them with each other that neither one has kept to its power or force or rights" (LW 46, 266; cf. 21, 109). The result is that now not only the pope but certain "enthusiasts" try to apply gospel norms to secular government (LW 13, 194). And political authorities see themselves as the heads of Christendom or defenders of the faith (LW 46, 185–186; 13, 194). This kind of confusion is fatal, a recipe for disaster. "Constantly I must pound in and squeeze in and drive in and wedge in this difference between the two kingdoms. . . . The devil never stops cooking and brewing these two kingdoms into each other" (LW 13, 194). Just as the law/gospel distinction is crucial for theology, so the secular realm/spiritual realm distinction is crucial for social and political ethics.

Yet, different as they are, the two are at the same time related and they require each other (LW 45, 91). The temporal serves the spiritual by providing stability and peace—conditions conducive to the preaching of the gospel. And the spiritual, Luther points out, serves the secular. How? As he explained, for instance, in 1530, "a preacher confirms, strengthens, and helps to sustain authority of every kind, and temporal peace generally. He checks the rebellious, teaches obedience, morals, discipline, and honor; instructs fathers, mothers, children, and servants in their duties; in a word, he gives direction to all the temporal estates and offices" (LW 46, 226). In other words, the spiritual endorses, legitimizes, and stabilizes the temporal. Secular rulers need not fear that the spiritual kingdom will become critical or subversive of the existing order.

What complicates the lives of Christians is that they are members of both realms. In essence, Luther said, "two persons . . . are combined in one man. In addition to being a Christian, he would be a prince or a judge or a lord or a servant or a maid—all of which are termed 'secular' persons because they are part of the secular realm" (LW 21, 109). As members of both kingdoms they owe allegiance, subjection, and obedience to both: "according to the Spirit, they are subjects of no one but Christ. Nevertheless, as far as body and property are concerned, they are subject to worldly rulers, and owe them obedience" (LW 46, 99; cf. 21, 109).

In the final analysis this dual citizenship means that the Christian combines in the self a "*duplex persona*" (LW 21, 23). The tension this generates is reflected nowhere more obviously than in the Bible itself, where the demands of the Sermon on the Mount (Matt. 5–7), for instance, and those of Romans 13 and 1 Peter 2:13–17, are not easily harmonized. The former requires Christians to love their enemies, while the latter could well require Christians to kill their enemies (in war, for example). (*See also* **War**.)

Luther's solution is to say that in the Sermon on the Mount, Christ was instructing his followers on how to live as members of the spiritual kingdom. In the secular kingdom, demands such as love of enemies do not apply (LW 21, 106–107). In the kingdom of Christ, turning the other cheek is required, whereas in the kingdom of this world it would be a foolish mistake (LW 21, 109). Christians as Christians "should not make war or resist evil" (LW 46, 167). But as citizens of the earthly kingdom they may. A Christian leader may declare war—not in one's person as a Christian but in one's role as a leader of the worldly kingdom (LW 46, 122; cf. 186). Not only in war but in all other areas as well, separating the two roles is the key: "A Christian may carry on all sorts of secular business with impunity—not

as a Christian but as a secular person—
while his heart remains pure in his
Christianity as Christ demands" (LW
21, 113).

Luther's two-kingdoms doctrine
thus leads ineluctably in the direction
of an ethical dualism. The same person
may be required to do opposite things
depending on which persona one is
acting in. Christians acting as soldiers
or businesspeople or judges or heads
of families may do all kinds of things
in those roles, providing their "heart"
remains pure (LW 21, 113; cf. 108). Thus
the government official, for instance,
must wield the sword in anger, but as he
does so "he should keep his heart sweet
and friendly, free of any malice" (LW 21,
76). Christians should bring lawsuits,
but they should do this "out of a true
Christian heart" (LW 45, 104). Indeed,
this kind of ethical dualism in Luther
can become grotesque: in the Old Testament, he says, Moses and David "exe-
cuted people like chickens—but at the
same time they were no less meek, mild,
and friendly in their hearts" (WA 10:3,
253, 11–15). Christians, it would seem,
may do anything that non-Christians
can, with the only difference being the
sweetness in their hearts!

Finally, Luther's social/political
ethic is rounded out by his so-called
doctrine of the "three estates." Sometimes he speaks of these as "offices,"
"hierarchies," "orders," "institutions,"
"stations," or even "vocations." There
are in reality many of them (LW 46, 246).
But very often he names three that sub-
sume all the rest (e.g., LW 37, 364): the
ordo ecclesiasticus (church), the *ordo oeco-
nomicus* (family), and the *ordo politicus*
(government) (LW 1, 104). They have
been built into creation by God himself
to create life and preserve it (LW 46, 246–
248; 13, 370). Each has its own duties;
Luther culled these from Scripture and
placed them in his Small Catechism of
1529 (BC 365–367). Most humans belong
to several at once, and if like the pope
they belong to none, they should be
resisted (WA 39:2, 39–91). The estates

are often occupied by wicked people,
of course, but they are not thereby dis-
credited: "the estate itself is good and
remains good. . . . [T]he estates themselves are God's institution, work, and
ordinance" (LW 46, 248).

The estate of marriage/family is
in some ways fundamental to all the
rest. It is the means God has instituted
to perpetuate the human race (LW 46,
246–248). Within it, the role of children
is governed above all by the fourth commandment. Wives/mothers are to bear
and raise children. At the top of this
hierarchical structure is the husband/
father, who sees to the welfare of all and
to whose will all must submit (BC 400–
410). This patriarchal family structure is
God's will for society.

While this first estate requires no particular education, the other two do. Thus
the main point of Luther's 1530 *Sermon
on Keeping Children in School* is that the
churchly and political estates require
educated persons if they are to function
in a healthy way (LW 46, 213–258). The
spiritual estate is "the office of preaching and the service of the word and
sacraments. . . . It includes the work of
pastors, teachers, lectors, priests (whom
men call chaplains), sacristans, school-
masters, and whatever other work
belongs to these offices and persons"
(LW 46, 220). God has established this
estate, obviously, to lead us to eternal
life (LW 46, 219–220), but also to instruct
the various other estates on how to conduct themselves (LW 46, 226).

The political estate too has been
established by God, specifically to "preserve peace, justice, and life" (LW 46,
237). Luther sometimes calls these people the "jurists," meaning "chancellors,
clerks, judges, lawyers, notaries, and
all who have to do with the legal side
of government; also the counselors at
the court" (LW 46, 240). Though Luther
told some lawyer jokes late in his career
(e.g., LW 54, nr. 5663, 473–474), he also
spoke very highly of this profession. It
is "glorious and divine work," he said,
unlike merchants, who are "like hogs

wallowing forever with their noses in the dunghill" (LW 46, 241). The boys with the best minds should be trained for government and politics because in this estate one must act on the basis of reason (LW 46, 242)! All these estates together, for Luther, constitute the divinely intended structure of the social order.

This then is the foundation of Luther's social and political ethic—two kingdoms, two governments, three estates. As noted above, his aim from the outset had been to disentangle the spiritual and the temporal. This he did, to some extent, but with highly ambiguous results. He emphasized the distinction, the separate jurisdictions, the differing "means of rule" of the two kingdoms, but ended up with a kind of ethical dualism: different moral standards apply in each. And it is certainly not the business of the church to "christianize" the social order. He established the independent validity of secular authority, grounding it in the divine will. But he emphasized this so strongly that revolt was unthinkable and protest unlikely. He identified existing social institutions and structures as established by God in creation; as such they are virtually immune to critique and change. In all these ways, Luther's social/political ethic is profoundly conservative: far from issuing a challenge to the existing order, Luther's Christianity tends most often to legitimize, endorse, and stabilize that order.

Historically speaking, what followed Luther in northern European church/state relations was a system known as *landesherrliche Kirchenregiment*—secular authorities governing a basically subservient church. Some historians see this as a direct consequence of Luther's social/political ethic. Others lay this development at Philip Melanchthon's feet instead. The complexities of this debate will not be sorted out here. But a word of caution is in order. To attribute this entire development directly to Luther is to impose a simplistic clarity on something essentially ambiguous.

Insofar as Luther emphasized the divine origin of the secular, he contributed to this development. And insofar as he emphasized the distinction between the two kingdoms, he did not.

Evil, Problem of   Like all major thinkers in the Western intellectual tradition, Luther wrestled with the problem of evil, or the "theodicy" problem, as it later came to be called. For him, it assumed the form of the question "Why?" in all its variants: Why, if God is both omnipotent and good, does he allow humans to sink to appalling depths of moral evil? Why would a God like this create a world with such horrific natural evils? Why does this God stand by while patent injustices go on and on, with no end in sight? Why are the truly wretched among us viciously struck down one more time? And so on.

The issue loomed larger on Luther's horizon than is commonly recognized. From a strictly rational viewpoint, it seemed to him to compel us toward atheism, or to the conclusion that God is unjust (LW 33, 291), or to reduce all talk of God to "absurdity" (LW 33, 173). Yet it was also far from being a merely theoretical issue for Luther. Rather it was intimately related to his frequently recurring experiences of *Anfechtung*: sometimes, he tells us, it drove him to the "abyss of despair" (LW 33, 190). Other times he was tempted to conclude that this God was "worthy of hatred rather than of love" (LW 33, 63). In short, the problem of evil was no abstract puzzle for Luther. Nor did he endorse a facile solution without attempting to move beyond it.

Before going on here to outline the novel aspects of Luther's approach to the problem, we must frankly recognize that on this theme, we find stark inconsistencies in his thought. He thoroughly understood the Christian theological tradition and its conventional "solution" to the problem. He was dissatisfied with this, explicitly rejected it, and took some hesitant steps in the direction of a new approach. Yet one also finds Luther, from time to time, in various contexts, repeating the traditional answer. In other words, on this issue we find Luther setting out in a new direction and fairly frequently also regressing into the conventional.

Luther wrote about this issue at every stage of his career. Personal experience drove him to it continually. So too did his engagement with the Bible: to his mind, this book raised the "Why?" question everywhere, from the patriarchal narratives of Genesis, to Jeremiah, to Job, to the psalms of lamentation, to the very heart of the New Testament. Consequently Luther's comments on theodicy are scattered throughout his exegetical writings. His most systematic treatment, however, is to be found in his 1525 work, *On the Bondage of the Will*. In 1524 Desiderius Erasmus of Rotterdam had launched a major attack on Luther in *On the Freedom of the Will*. The primary issue in the debate was whether humans have free choice (*see* **Free Will**). As a secondary but related issue, Erasmus had raised the problem of evil.

Erasmus's approach, nuanced as it may have been, was the traditional one, current in the Latin theology of the West since the time of Augustine. In short, this solution to the problem sought in every way to avoid tracing the origin of evil back to God. God created humans with free will, and he "permits" them to choose moral evil. Natural evil can be said to be "willed" by God, as punishment or pedagogy, but ultimately for the greater good. The evil of injustice he permits for a time, but this will ultimately be rectified in the life of the world to come.

Luther rejected this sort of tidy rational solution in *On the Bondage of the Will* for two basic reasons. First, he argued that humans do not have free choice: "whatever is done by us is not done by free choice, but by sheer necessity" (LW 33, 58). Thus, obviously, the so-called free-will defense cannot be used. In

the final analysis, this kind of theodicy attempts to exonerate God by blaming humans. It seeks to distance God from evil by placing all evil on the human side of the ledger. This Luther found unconvincing. Second, Luther rejected this conventional answer because he thought that the God implicit in it is a "ridiculous God" (LW 33, 189). If God is omniscient as Christians believe, he has perfect foreknowledge. But perfect foreknowledge means that the future is in no way contingent on human choices. Otherwise we would have to conclude that God's foreknowledge is wrong in many cases. Moreover, if we say that this omnipotent God wills the good but "permits" humans to choose evil, we must conclude that he wills the good somewhat halfheartedly. Thus, following the logic of the traditional theodicy, we end up with a "ridiculous God."

What then does Luther recommend? Giving up! From a strictly logical point of view, the problem is insoluble (LW 33, 291): "there is no avoiding the absurdity" (LW 33, 173). Reason forces us to trace evil back to God himself, who, in the final analysis, "works all in all" (LW 33, 175). Here Luther introduces his distinction between the hidden God (*Deus absconditus*) and the revealed God (*Deus revelatus*). In some respects, Luther argues, "God hides himself and wills to be unknown to us. . . . [I]n this regard we have nothing to do with him. . . . It is enough to know simply that there is a certain inscrutable will in God, and as to what, why, and how far it wills, that is something we have no right whatever to inquire into, hanker after, care about, or meddle with, but only to fear and adore" (LW 33, 139–140). On the question of the origin of evil, reason points us toward the *Deus absconditus* but then stops cold: about this God we know, and can know, nothing. Such an agnosticism is of course a "nonanswer" to the problem of evil. Here rationality reaches a dead end, and humans must accept that.

At the same time, life goes on: humans (Christians in particular) have to live in the absence of a solution. What enables them to do so, from Luther's perspective, is faith. Here is where Luther's concept of the revealed God (*Deus revelatus*) comes into play (LW 33, 139–140). Christians believe that God has revealed something about himself, most obviously and directly in the person of Jesus Christ. What he has revealed is that he is infinitely good, loving, and merciful, and that despite all appearances to the contrary, some day life will triumph over death and good will triumph over evil. Faith clings to *this*; in other words, faith ignores the *Deus absconditus* and embraces the *Deus revelatus*.

Living in the absence of a solution, however, does not mean ignoring the problem. The "Why?" question continues to assert itself in all its urgency and poignancy at every stage of life. But it is met now not by speculative rationality, but rather by a struggling, lamenting, doubting, even accusing faith. No tidy solution here, and certainly no smug satisfaction—only hope, and in the meantime, anguish.

There is comfort, from Luther's perspective, in the belief that our anguish is shared. Christ took on human nature and suffered like us (WA 5, 602, 21–25; 603, 4–22). And at the moment of ultimate human extremity and despair, on the cross, he too asked "Why?": "My God, my God, why have you forsaken me?" (Matt. 27:46; Mark 15:34). Thus not only is evil traced back to the inscrutable *Deus absconditus*, but Jesus himself places the anguished and unmistakably accusatory "Why?" question before God.

That, in summary, is the new direction in Luther's thought on the theodicy problem. By no means did he pursue this line of thought to its final consequences: many loose ends remain and many questions arise. Tantalizing as all this may be, Luther went no further. In fact, he fairly frequently slipped back into one or another version of the traditional answer. For example, he could interpret episodes of the plague as God's judgment (LW 43, 113–138). So

too, the frightening new Turkish threat menacing Western Europe he explained as God's punishment on a wicked society (LW 46, 155–205). Had Luther consistently followed the logic of his new approach, he would have abandoned such timeworn answers to the "Why?" question. His answer, or rather non-answer, would have been, "We don't know." Faith alone makes it possible for us to live in this state of anguish, in the absence of an answer. "If . . . I could by any means comprehend how this God can be merciful and just who displays so much wrath and iniquity, there would be no need of faith" (LW 33, 63). Faith, in other words, stands in the place of a theodicy.

See also **Anfechtung; Faith; God**

Extreme Unction   The anointing of the sick, known as "extreme unction" in Luther's time, had been officially named as a sacrament of the Catholic Church by the Council of Florence in 1439. As late as 1519 Luther still accepted it as a sacrament (LW 42, 100, and 108), though he already had doubts about it (see his letter to George Spalatin in WABr 1, nr. 231, 594–595, 19–24).

These doubts were resolved by the time he wrote *Babylonian Captivity of the Church* in 1520. In this work Luther decisively rejected its sacramental status. One reason was the absence of any grounding in Scripture. True, Mark 6:13 reported that the twelve apostles anointed the sick with oil and healed them. Luther did not question this, but in his view, such healing "has long since ceased" (LW 36, 121). Then too James 5:14–15 instructs presbyters to anoint sick people with oil and heal them. But Luther doubted the apostolicity of this book, and besides, he argued, apostles cannot institute sacraments—only Christ can (LW 36, 118).

The other reason Luther adduced for rejecting extreme unction as a sacrament is that it does not work. Sacraments are by definition "effective signs." This one, with its promise of healing, is administered only to the dying. But it almost never heals them: "Scarcely one in a thousand is restored to health" (LW 36, 119–120). If the promise fails, it cannot be a sacrament.

Luther's rejection of extreme unction as a sacrament does not mean that for him prayer and comfort for sick and dying people were unimportant. In 1539 a new church order for Brandenburg included extreme unction, and Luther was asked to approve it. He did, with the stipulation that the gospel was to be proclaimed, no one was to call it a "sacrament," and it was to be done "without superstition" (WABr 8, nr. 3420, 623, 38–57).

Faith   Nothing is more fundamental for an understanding of Luther than his concept of faith. For him it was at the same time the profoundest and the most important mystery of human life. In a real sense his theological career was a lifelong struggle to grasp and explain it. At the midpoint of that career, in 1531, he confessed that he had barely made a start: "For in my heart there resides this one doctrine, namely, faith in Christ. From it, through it, and to it all my theological thought flows and returns day and night; yet I am aware that all I have grasped of this wisdom in its height, width, and depth are a few poor and insignificant firstfruits and fragments" (LW 27, 145). By the end of his career he had approached the subject from every conceivable angle, seeing ever new dimensions and implications, explaining it hundreds of times in scores of different ways, searching always for more adequate language, and finally acknowledging the poverty of the human intellect in the face of this, one of life's ultimate mysteries.

To begin to understand what Luther meant by faith, we must have a firm grasp of definitions he rejected. Trained in scholasticism, he had inherited the dominant medieval understanding of faith as an infused intellectual virtue or habit from which the "act of faith" proceeds. Such an act of faith, then, is essentially the assent of the intellect to propositional truths. Luther's early marginal notes (1509/10) on Augustine and Peter Lombard indicate his agreement with this traditional view (e.g., WA 9, 92, 38–93, 7). But already by 1515 he regarded this understanding of "faith as belief" as an impoverished, superficial distortion of what it really means.

Of course, he did not simply make up a new definition. Rather his new understanding emerged from a deeply personal engagement with the text of Scripture, and especially the writings of Paul. Here he found a language of faith that, in his view, overturned the traditional one. Simply acknowledging certain events to be true, for instance, falls far short of what Paul meant by "faith" in his letter to the Romans: "Faith is not the human notion and dream that some people call faith. . . . [W]hen they hear the gospel, they get busy and by their own power create an idea in their heart which says, 'I believe'; they take this then to be a true faith. But it is a human figment" (LW 35, 370).

In an academic disputation of 1535, Luther used the example of beliefs about Jesus to illustrate the point. "[T]he infused faith of the sophists [scholastics], says of Christ: 'I believe that the Son of God suffered and rose again,' and here it stops. But true faith says: 'I certainly believe that the Son of God suffered and rose, but he did this all for me, for my sins, of that I am certain'. . . . Accordingly, that 'for me' or 'for us,' if it is believed, creates that true faith and distinguishes it from all other faith which merely hears the things done. This is the faith that alone justifies us" (LW 34, 110). Or, as the Augsburg Confession had put it in 1530, faith does indeed acknowledge these events, but then so does the devil. True faith goes beyond this by believing the effect of this history (*BC* 57). Simple belief that these things happened (*fides historica*) certainly does not justify: Luther's slogan "justification by faith alone" makes no sense if this is what faith means.

Luther's understanding of faith has rightly been called "existential": knowledge of God or Christ is not real knowledge but rather it remains useless information until we see its implications for us. This is what Luther had in mind when he said in his *Lectures on Galatians*, "Faith is the creator of the Deity, not in the substance of God, but in us" (LW 26, 227). It is in faith that God becomes real for us. In those same lectures Luther explained that for Christians this happens through Christ. The "doctrine [or content] of faith," he says, "proclaims that Christ alone is the victor over sin, death, and the devil" (LW 26, 224). Faith itself then "is a sure confidence that takes hold of Christ" (LW 26, 348). In other words, faith is the confidence that "sin, death, and the devil" have been overcome for me. It is the subjective appropriation of what has objectively happened; and until there is such a subjective appropriation, what has happened objectively (Christ's victory) does me no good.

This appropriating, or apprehending, or grasping, or accepting is what Luther means by "faith." "Faith apprehends Christ," Luther says (LW 34, 153), and he means that in faith the entire being of the person recognizes, grasps, and accepts the ultimate import of Christ for him or her. And who is Christ? Most fundamentally for Luther, Christ is "a mirror of the Father's heart" (*BC* 440). To "apprehend Christ" means therefore to grasp that I am the object of the divine love. As the Augsburg Confession put it, faith is the belief that we "are received into grace [i.e., into divine favor]"; it is by faith that "forgiveness of sins and justification are taken hold of" (*BC* 41). Or as Luther says in his 1522 preface to Paul's letter to the Romans, "Faith is a living daring confidence in God's grace, so sure and certain that the believer would stake his life on it a thousand times. This knowledge of and

confidence in God's grace makes men glad and bold and happy in dealing with God and with all creatures. And this is the work which the Holy Spirit performs in faith" (LW 35, 371). In the final analysis, faith is for Luther the confidence that, because we are objects of an infinite and unconditional love, the negativities of human existence can have no finality or ultimacy for us: fear, despair, death, and all troubles have been conquered. They are stripped of their power by the conviction that the very deepest of all human longings has been fulfilled. For if we really are loved infinitely and unconditionally by an omnipotent being, nothing can hurt us.

To live one's life with such a trust, according to Luther, makes all the difference in the world. But before describing Luther's view of this "new creature," we must emphasize that for him faith exists very often in tension with experience. There are mountaintop moments in life when humans have a profound sense that all is right with the world. But there are other moments, Luther knew all too well, when bitter experience suggests that "sin, death, and the devil" (Luther's formulaic way of referring to all the evils that oppress humans) will have the last word. At such times, Luther said, "faith slinks away and hides" (WA 17:1, 72, 17). This was the experience of Christ on the cross, and so too is it our experience. Reason, at such moments, interprets experience so as to contradict faith, and only faith can overcome it: "It [reason] can be killed by nothing else but faith, which believes God. . . . It [faith] does this in spite of the fact that he speaks what seems foolish, absurd, and impossible to reason [namely that he loves us]" (LW 26, 231). The miracle is that faith, weak as it now may be, persists. Only in the life of the world to come will our experience cease to contradict faith: then what we believe now, that all evil has been overcome, will be apparent.

Faith, this trust that death and all troubles have been conquered, can sometimes seem as self-evident to us as "three plus two equals five" (WA 10:3, 260, 23–261,1). But more often in real life it coexists, in a complex relationship, with doubt. Luther even wonders at times whether people without doubt, "smug people, who have never struggled with any temptation or true terrors of sin and death," can really know what faith is (LW 26, 127). In his preface to his 1535 *Lectures on Galatians*, Luther warns that we have little hope of understanding Paul here unless we too are "miserable Galatians in faith," that is, "troubled, afflicted, vexed, and tempted" (LW 27, 148). The presence of doubt does not imply the absence of faith. Faith is a mysterious reality that hides itself beneath doubt and even beneath its absolute opposite, despair. So it is difficult to tell where faith is. "For it happens, indeed it is typical of faith, that often he who claims to believe does not believe at all; and on the other hand, he who doesn't think he believes, but is in despair, has the greatest faith" (LW 40, 241). Faith sometimes "crawls away and hides" beneath doubt and despair, and then it reemerges. Ultimately, Luther thinks, humans do not control this. If they did, faith would be nothing more than "the power of positive thinking."

It is, Luther insists, a gift. Having true faith is really a divine work (WA 12, 442, 4–9) that comes to us through the proclamation of the gospel—the good news that God loves us though we are unworthy of that love (LW 35, 368). Some—not all—who hear it accept it, and that acceptance is what Christians call the work of the Holy Spirit in us (LW 21, 299). In other words, when humans receive and accept God's grace, that itself is the result of grace. "For here we work nothing, render nothing to God; we only receive and permit someone else to work in us, namely God" (LW 26, 4–5). Faith thus comes to us, Luther says, as the dry earth receives the rain, in utter passivity (LW 26, 6). Human striving cannot induce it to fall, but when it does, new life erupts. And whenever we see signs of this new life,

we can be sure that it has fallen: "True faith is not idle. We can, therefore, ascertain and recognize those who have true faith from the effect or from what follows" (LW 34, 182). "O it is a living, busy, active, mighty thing, this faith," Luther exclaimed (LW 35, 370). And he never tired of explaining its functions and effects. On hundreds of occasions, over a period of about thirty years, Luther groped for words adequate to express the dramatic difference faith makes in people's lives. Here I can only list some of the ways he describes this.

The change that it brings about, he thought, was total: "[It] makes us altogether different men, in heart and spirit and mind and powers" (LW 35, 370). Faith is the way in which Christ becomes present to us: "It takes hold of Christ in such a way that Christ is the object of faith, or rather not the object but, so to speak, the one who is present in the faith itself. Thus faith is a sort of knowledge or darkness that nothing can see. Yet the Christ of whom this faith takes hold is sitting in this darkness" (LW 26, 129–130). In fact, it unites us with Christ: "by it [faith] you are so cemented to Christ that he and you are as one person which cannot be separated but remains attached to him forever and declares: 'I am as Christ'" (LW 26, 168). We begin to understand what Luther means by this when we recall that for him Christ is the supreme representation of God's love. Our reception of this love (what Luther calls faith) "unites" us to Christ, makes us new persons (WA 39:1, 282, 16). In accepting God's love, faith accepts his forgiveness (LW 26, 11). In other words, it "justifies" us and makes us "righteous" (LW 26, 227).

The righteousness that faith brings, Luther explains, is not an active but a passive righteousness. It is not a righteousness achieved by doing good things, but it is a "righteousness of faith," one that is "heavenly and passive. We do not have it of ourselves; we receive it from heaven. We do not perform it; we accept it by faith" (LW 26, 8).

Moral effort, Luther says, can result in "political righteousness," "ceremonial righteousness," or the "righteousness of the law," but it cannot lead to "Christian righteousness" or the "righteousness of faith" (LW 26, 45). Only God can grant this, and only faith can receive it, and it alone has value in the order of salvation. Therefore, Luther can say, "Wherever there is faith, eternal life has already begun" (LW 14, 88; cf. 26, 11).

Luther was explicit in spelling out the consequences of faith for human emotional life, and in this he very directly brought his own experience into play. As is well known, throughout his life and fairly frequently he was vigorously assaulted by what he called *Anfechtungen*. This is an untranslatable word that connoted for him a combination of doubt, fear, dread, the temptation to despair, and the suspicion that God is not good and that human destiny is death and eternal nothingness thereafter. Luther vividly described his *Anfechtungen* as the experience of hell itself. Ultimately the only answer, he thought, was faith: "the afflicted conscience has no remedy against despair and eternal death except to take hold of the promise of grace offered in Christ, that is, this righteousness of faith" (LW 26, 5–6). Losing faith means losing Christ as savior, and from this "sure despair and eternal death follow" (LW 26, 11). Losing faith, in other words, means losing confidence that the source and heart of all reality is an infinite love, and losing trust that we are unconditionally objects of that love. Hence, Luther says, when assaulted by fear and death, "we must look at no other God than this incarnate and human God. . . . When you do this, you will see the love, the goodness, and the sweetness of God" (LW 26, 29–30). Faith alone is what enables us to experience life as sweet, in the deepest sense. It brings peace and happiness—in short, salvation (LW 26, 11).

Faith not only has consequences for the inner person but also for human action. To begin to grasp this, we must first understand that for Luther there is a sense in which faith is the only thing God demands of us. In *Treatise on Good Works* he put it this way: "The first, highest, and most precious of all good works is faith in Christ. . . . For in this work all good works exist, and from faith these [other] works receive a borrowed goodness" (LW 44, 23). Or, as he put it a year earlier in his Galatians lectures of 1519, "faith is the fulfillment of all the laws for the sake of Christ, the fulfiller" (LW 27, 231). Each of the Ten Commandments, he explained, requires faith for its fulfillment (e.g., LW 44, 103–112). Moreover, all of the commandments are really contained in the first one ("You shall have no other gods"). And it is faith, Luther thinks, which is the real work of the first commandment. For faith is the acknowledgment of God as the source of all good; in faith humans "allow" God to be who he is: "When the soul firmly trusts God's promises, it regards him as truthful and righteous. Nothing more excellent than this can be ascribed to God." (LW 31, 350; cf. 26, 229). The first commandment demands trust, and faith is that trust. From such a trust, the rest follows automatically: "faith does everything through the first commandment" (LW 44, 34). Thus faith is, for Luther, the fulfillment of the law. It is literally "purity of heart" (LW 27, 257).

At the same time, and paradoxically, faith frees us from the law. Luther's most famous explanation of this is found in his 1520 *The Freedom of a Christian*, but like the rest, it became a lifelong theme. Christians are radically free from all laws because God accepts them and grants them righteousness apart from any moral effort on their part. Faith receives this gift, thus freeing us from the oppressive weight of all legal demands and moral codes. As he puts it, "A Christian is a perfectly free lord of all, subject to none" (LW 31, 343). Through faith, "the entire law has been abrogated for believers in Christ" (LW 26, 447). Throughout his career as a reformer, Luther understood himself as a defender of this "glorious freedom" against a papal tyranny that reimposed the law and indeed made new laws. His plea throughout consciously echoed the plea of Paul to the Galatians: "For freedom Christ has set us free. Stand firm, therefore, and do not submit again to a yoke of slavery" (Gal. 5:1; cf. LW 27, 3–9).

Again paradoxically, the same faith that frees us from the law inevitably results in good works. According to Luther, faith, though it alone justifies, never exists without morally good acts. If it does, he says, it is a "false faith" (LW 26, 155). He explains in his 1536 *Disputation Concerning Justification*: "It is one thing that faith justifies without works; it is another thing that faith exists without works. . . . We say that justification is effective without works, not that faith is without works" (LW 34, 175). In other words, faith alone makes us righteous, or rather it receives this righteousness (forgiveness) from God. Having then been made good, we spontaneously do good. "When I have this righteousness within me, I descend from heaven like the rain that makes the earth fertile. That is, . . . I perform good works whenever the opportunity arises" (LW 26, 11). Faith is passive receptivity, and yet it is "a busy, active, mighty thing. . . . It is impossible for it not to be doing good works incessantly" (LW 35, 370).

Another vantage point from which we can approach the paradox has to do with God's will, and our motive for fulfilling it. With Luther, we can summarize by saying that God's will is for humans to act out of love for him and out of love for our fellow human beings. We cannot do this as we should because as humans we always act to some extent out of self-love. That is, we want to do God's will because we want him to love us; this then is not love but only a higher form of selfishness. Faith is the realization that there is nothing we can or must do to earn God's love, coupled with the realization that we already have it. And if we do, we no longer have to act in our own self-interest. We can begin then to act out of a pure love for God and for our fellow human beings, moved to do so only by a spontaneous gratitude. "Thus a Christian who lives in this confidence toward God knows all things, can do all things, ventures everything gladly, and willingly, not that he may gather merits and good works, but because it is a pleasure to him to please God in doing these things" (LW 44, 26). The certain consciousness that one is loved unconditionally frees humans to love unconditionally. Faith, therefore, is what makes good works good, since it eliminates the intrusion of calculating self-interest: "Because of it [faith], without compulsion, a person is ready and glad to do good to everyone, to serve everyone, to suffer everything, out of love and praise to God who has shown him this grace" (LW 35, 370). Love, human love, needs faith to purify it. Faith in this sense frees us from ourselves to truly do God's will.

Faith helps humans to leave behind their tendency to want to calculate the relative value of various works of love. In fact from this perspective, all virtuous acts are equal in value: "where faith is present and operating, there is no distinction between works. . . . Works done in faith are not pleasing to God on their own account, but on account of faith" (WA 6, 217, 12–24). Thus, for Luther, all Christians are "saints," not only those who, as tradition had it, were persons of "heroic virtue." Faith frees Christians from conventional scales of value and moral codes to do what love demands: "Now everyone can notice and feel for himself when he does what is good and what is not good. If he finds his heart confident that it pleases God, then the work is good, even if it were so small a thing as picking up a straw" (LW 44, 24). "God smiles with all the angels and creatures," said Luther, "when diapers are washed, not because they are washed, but because it is done in faith" (WA 10:2, 296, 31–297, 1).

It should already be clear that Luther's understanding of faith had immense implications touching almost every area of Christian belief and practice. As a final example, consider the following: Luther's view that faith is the key to truly good moral action called into question the conventional Christian emphasis on moral exhortation. By Luther's time, this had become perhaps the chief element in preaching: indeed, many late medieval sermons were little more than this. Already in 1523 Luther clearly saw the implications of his understanding of faith for promoting moral goodness: "to get someone to do good works, all one needs to do is say, 'Only have faith, and you will be able to do everything yourself.' Thus you do not have to demand good works at length from someone who has faith . . . for faith is so noble that it makes everything good in a person" (WA 12, 559, 25–31). The only effective way to promote moral goodness is to promote faith.

This topic of faith has brought us to the very heart of Luther's understanding of Christianity. Its meaning, according to him, cannot be exhausted: "he who has had even a faint taste of it can never write, speak, meditate, or hear enough concerning it" (LW 31, 343). If one were forced to choose a summary statement from Luther, the following one from 1522 may well be the best. It is noteworthy that it comes not from a theological lecture or academic disputation but from a sermon.

All Christian teaching, works and life can be summed up briefly, clearly, and fully under the two categories of faith and love: humans are placed midway between God and their neighbor, receiving from above [faith] and dispensing below [love], and becoming as it were a vessel or a tube through which the stream of divine benefits flows unceasingly into other people. How clearly those are conformed to God who receive from God everything he has to give, in Christ, and in their turn, as though they were gods to others, give them benefits. . . . We are children of God through faith, which makes us heirs to all the divine goodness. But we are gods through love,

which makes us active in doing good to our neighbor; for the divine nature is nothing other than pure goodness . . . and friendliness and kindness, pouring out its good things every day in profusion upon every creature, as we can see. (WA 10:1:1, 100, 8–101, 2)

Faith, ultimately, is the ability to understand and accept ourselves as the objects of God's love. This, Luther thought, is the key to finding happiness in life. And it is inevitably transformative: it opens up the possibility of loving others, and it gives us the power to do so.

Free Will   Ever since Augustine's controversy with Pelagius in the early fifth century, the issue of human freedom had occupied a permanent place on the theological agenda of the Christian West. The perennial question was how best to acknowledge the primacy of grace in human salvation while preserving a role for the human will—how to avoid "Pelagianism" on the one hand and determinism on the other. By the time Luther entered the debate, the literature was enormous, and the various positions rivaled one another in their subtle complexity.

Luther staked out his position early in 1518, in the thirteenth theological thesis of his *Heidelberg Disputation*: "Free will, after the fall, exists in name only, and as long as it does what it is able to do, it commits a mortal sin" (LW 31, 40). This apparent denial of free choice was singled out for condemnation in Pope Leo X's bull *Exsurge Domine* in 1520, and Luther's response was quick and succinct: "So it is necessary to retract this article. For I wrongly said that free choice before grace is in reality only a name. I should have said simply: free choice is in reality a fiction, or a name without reality. For . . . everything (as Wycliffe's article condemned at Constance rightly teaches) happens by absolute necessity" (WA 7, 146, 3–8). While minor figures now entered the controversy, it was Desiderius Erasmus of

Rotterdam, by repute the most learned man of the age, who provoked a major response from Luther. Erasmus's book appeared in 1524 under the title *De libero arbitrio* (often translated as *On Free Will*, but better translated as *On Free Choice*). Luther was hard at work on his reply in the fall of 1525, and by late December it appeared in print as *De servo arbitrio* (often translated as *On the Bondage of the Will*, but better translated as *On Unfree Choice*). Thus was born what many consider to be the greatest intellectual debate of the Reformation period.

Luther had the highest regard for Erasmus's linguistic competence and for his literary eloquence. But in Luther's estimate Erasmus was no theologian, and consequently his book was "like refuse or ordure being carried in gold and silver vases" (LW 33, 16). Yet Erasmus alone among his Catholic opponents had been perceptive enough to fasten on the heart of the matter rather than on "trifles" like the papacy, purgatory, and indulgences (LW 33, 294). Erasmus deserved high credit for seeing that "this is the cardinal issue . . . what free choice can do, what it has done to it, and what is its relation to the grace of God . . . the distinction between God's power and our own" (LW 33, 35). *On Free Choice*, Luther thought, was certainly worthy of a careful, extended reply.

We can begin by outlining Erasmus's position on the issue, as Luther understood it. An overt Pelagianism that denied the necessity of grace for salvation was out of the question for Erasmus. But on the other hand both Scripture and reason attest to a role for the human will in this process. The will's power is limited: it cannot fulfill the divine law without the help of grace, it cannot love God above all things without the help of grace, and so forth. But it can at least turn the person toward God or away from God. Thus Erasmus defines free choice as "a power of the human will by which a man can apply himself to the things which lead to eternal salvation, or turn away from them"

(LW 33, 102–103). Thus there is a real, even decisive, role for free choice in human salvation.

Luther's book is lengthy, touching on a myriad of related issues. And his basic argument against Erasmus is repeated, as he admits, "with quite nauseating frequency" (LW 33, 156). It can be summarized briefly as follows: Human beings in general are under the illusion that they are "free, happy, unfettered, able, well, and alive" (LW 33, 130). This is irrational: the "omnipotence and foreknowledge of God, I say, completely abolish the dogma of free choice" (LW 33, 189). The doctrine of God's omnipotence means that he "works all in all," as Paul had said (1 Cor. 12:6; LW 33, 35). It means that God's "will can neither be resisted nor changed nor hindered" (LW 33, 43). If humans have free choice, this would imply that they could overrule God's will (LW 33, 106). And if we say that God "permits" this, the conclusion must be that what God wills he wills somewhat halfheartedly. Thus we end up, logically, with a "ridiculous God" (LW 33, 189). As for the doctrine of God's foreknowledge, it means that he foresees the future infallibly (LW 33, 37–38). If human free choice changes the future, then we have to say that God's foreknowledge is frequently mistaken. And again we end up with a "ridiculous God" (LW 33, 189). The truth is quite the opposite: "whatever is done by us is not done by free choice, but by sheer necessity" (LW 33, 58).

Luther adds two caveats that are meant to elucidate his position. First, though he uses the term "necessity," he dislikes it, "for it suggests a kind of compulsion, and the very opposite of willingness, although the subject under discussion implies no such thing" (LW 33, 39). He seems to mean that while the human will always and inevitably chooses what the divine will has decided, it does so willingly. Humans do indeed have a will, and this "would not be a will if it were compelled; for compulsion is rather (so to say) 'unwill'"

(LW 33, 65). For instance, before receiving the gift of grace, the human will inevitably and infallibly wills only evil, but it does so willingly, not compulsorily (LW 33, 67). With the gift of grace God can change our will, and then it willingly, inevitably, and infallibly wills differently (LW 33, 243).

Luther's second caveat is that by his denial of free choice, he does not mean to put humans on the same level as the animal or the vegetable. One way in which humans differ from trees and animals is that they have a certain "disposing quality or passive aptitude [*aptitudo passiva*]." This aptitude or potency for the divine, Luther defines as "that by which a man is capable of being taken hold of by the Spirit and imbued with the grace of God." And if this aptitude is what is meant by "free choice," Luther adds, then "no objection could be taken" (LW 33, 67).

Luther's final position on the issue, then, could be stated as follows: All things happen by absolute necessity. There is such a thing as the human will; and what it wills, it wills necessarily but not under compulsion (in this sense, but in this sense only, it is a "free" will). Finally, there is no such thing as human free choice; this belongs to God alone.

Luther's argument for this position, it should be noted, is based largely on reason. The divine attributes of omnipotence and omniscience (including foreknowledge) lead inexorably to the exclusion of human free choice. Interestingly, it was Erasmus who had deployed Scripture across the entire spectrum of his argumentation. And it was in response to the specifics of Erasmus's appeal to Scripture that Luther was compelled to say something about Scripture as well. Three examples will illustrate this.

First, Erasmus pointed out that everywhere in Scripture moral demands are placed on humans. Why would God do this if humans have no power to choose the good? In response, Luther argued that their purpose is to demonstrate to us our incapacity for choosing the good (LW 33, 126; cf. 33, 130).

Second, Erasmus focused on the many places where Scripture speaks of "merit." What sense would this make if humans have no free choice? Luther realized that Erasmus's position was somewhat nuanced; he was not espousing a crudely Pelagian position. Together with the mainstream of scholastic theology, Erasmus held that the human will after the fall was severely hampered in its ability to choose the good. And the concept of "merit" did not imply any kind of equivalence between the value of the human work and that of the divine reward. At best we are speaking here of a "congruence" between work and reward. (Some apply the term "semi-Pelagian" to this position.) But precisely this was the object of Luther's critique. Erasmus, he said, wants to preserve "a little particle" of free choice (LW 33, 123) so that there can still be "a little scrap of merit" (LW 33, 269). Luther, as we have seen, rejected "free choice" and therefore "merit" in its entirety. Of course, it is true that Scripture speaks everywhere of merit and reward. But this does not mean "worthiness." Paul, for example, rejects the concept of earning something from God (LW 33, 267). Rather these terms refer to "consequence." All our good and evil acts have their "reward" in this sense (LW 33, 152–153).

Third, Erasmus cited a good number of biblical examples that seemed to raise doubts about the logic of Luther's position. One example was the case of Judas: if God foresaw that he would betray Jesus, did he do so necessarily? Luther's answer: "if God foreknew that Judas would be a traitor, Judas necessarily became a traitor . . . though he did what he did willingly and not under compulsion, but that act of will was a work of God, which he set in motion by his omnipotence, like everything else" (LW 33, 185). That God "set in motion" the betrayal of his son—this was a conclusion Luther was driven to by the logic of his position, a conclusion that sounded radical to Erasmus, but one that Luther refused to draw back from.

Erasmus expressed some displeasure that Luther wanted to discuss these issues before "the common herd . . . by taking the subject out of the universities and into the taverns" (LW 33, 46). Erasmus seems to have considered it a rather arcane debate that might unsettle the laity and further disturb the peace of Christendom. Luther, for his part, had gone public precisely because he thought it was so important. Everything was at stake here: this is "the question on which everything hinges" (LW 33, 294). What did he mean?

Like Augustine one thousand years before him, his most penetrating rationale was christological, or more precisely, soteriological. Against Pelagius, Augustine had tirelessly quoted the Gospel saying of Jesus: "Those who are well have no need of a physician" (Matt. 9:12; LW 33, 282). At the heart of Christianity stands the figure of a savior, and if humans can save themselves, he becomes superfluous. Luther can only reiterate Augustine's insight: "To sum up: If we believe that Christ has redeemed men by his blood, we are bound to confess that the whole man was lost; otherwise we should make Christ either superfluous or the redeemer of only the lowest part of man, which would be blasphemy and sacrilege" (LW 33, 293). Erasmus had argued that in our highest selves, we have a spark of free choice remaining, and therefore we can produce at least some tiny fragment of merit. What this would mean, Luther saw, is that Christ "has redeemed only what is lowest in us, and that what is most excellent in man can take care of itself and has no need of Christ" (LW 33, 227). And if that is the case, this entire religion is nonsense, in Luther's view.

Did Luther in later years modify the position on free choice that he defended in 1525? It appears that he did not. Though he wrote on the subject infrequently and less forcefully, we find Luther reiterating his position, in part, in the Smalcald Articles of 1537 (BC 311), and more fully in the *Lectures on Genesis* of 1535–45 (LW 5, 42–50). And in 1537, in a letter to Wolfgang Capito, he identified *On Unfree Choice* as one of two of his works that he still held in high regard (LW 50, 172–173).

God   For most of his life, Luther was deeply immersed in an intellectual struggle with the idea of God. This was no doubt related to his personal existential struggle: while he was a lifelong believer, he was time and again plagued by profound doubt. It also certainly had to do with the ultimate nature of this unfathomable mystery. In his view, there is simply nothing more important to think about. Consequently almost everything in his massive authorship is, in one way or another, about God. Yet Luther never devoted a single work to the systematic explanation of this doctrine. Only by sifting through the whole can one begin to sketch the main contours, and this is what I attempt to do here. What emerges is a doctrine of God that stands in continuity with the medieval theological tradition in the sense that not one of its major themes is radically new. Yet Luther's emphases, his approach, his interpretation, and his way of relating these themes combine to form a doctrine of God that is, to say the least, distinctive within the tradition. This doctrine of God Luther held to with a remarkable consistency from the beginning of his career as a reformer to the end of his life. Of course there were developments in detail, emphases shifted in response to changing contexts, implications of basic insights were sharpened, and so on, but on the major themes outlined here we cannot say that Luther changed his mind in any significant way.

"What does 'to have a god' mean, or what is God?" (BC 386). Precisely what we mean when we speak of God is important for Luther. One can of course find numerous "God is" statements in his writings: "God is a glowing oven full of love" (WA 36, 425, 13); "God is an eternal fountain who overflows with pure goodness" (*BC* 389); "God is the poet, and we are the verse" (LW 7, 366); even "God is a great cook" (LW 19, 185). Luther reveled in this type of vividly descriptive metaphor when speaking of God, and in this he imitated the language of the Bible. But he clearly understood that these "God is" statements are not formal definitions of God, nor are they to be taken literally.

Luther also understood the scholastic theological tradition that had indeed given formal definitions to this term, ones that were ontological/metaphysical in character. For example, Anselm had defined God as "that being than which none greater can be thought," and Thomas Aquinas had suggested "self-subsisting being." These kinds of definitions Luther sets aside, not because he thought they are formally wrong but because they are theologically insignificant.

His answer to the question above is this: "A 'god' is the term for that to which we are to look for all good and in which we are to find refuge in all need. Therefore, to have a god is nothing else than to trust and believe in that one with your whole heart. . . . For these two belong together, faith and God. Anything on which your heart relies and depends, I say, that is really your God" (*BC* 386). Because this definition is found in Luther's Large Catechism, one might be tempted to think that it is for children, less than fully serious. This would be a fundamental mistake. Luther insists on defining God in this way, and the definition is in fact programmatic for his entire theology.

It is what we would today call an "existential" definition, in the sense that we cannot speak of something without taking into account its impact on us. This is what Luther means when he says that faith and God "belong together." By "faith" in this context, he means trust or reliance or dependence. Separated from this, the concept of God is an empty abstraction, not the real thing, an idol. No knowledge of God, considered apart from its impact on us, is "true." Faith, in this sense, "makes" God.

This existential understanding must be carefully distinguished from a sheer subjectivism. At times Luther's language can give an impression of the latter. "[I]t is the trust and faith of the heart alone that make both God and an idol. If your faith and trust are right, then your God is the true one" (*BC* 386). These kinds of statements led the great nineteenth-century philosopher Ludwig Feuerbach, in his view of God as a human projection, to regard himself as Luther's spiritual heir. This is certainly not what Luther had in mind. What he meant was that any abstract conception of God divorced from human response is not real. God is not God apart from his impact on us. God assuredly exists apart from, and antecedent to, us. But "true" knowledge of him comes only in the context of relationship.

Luther concedes that there is such a thing as natural knowledge of God. By reason alone God "could be, and can be known from the beginning of the world" (LW 25, 156). From a process of deduction along the lines of a cosmological argument we can conclude that there is a God (WA 45, 90, 2–4). Moreover, reason can teach us something of God's character: "Let us learn from nature and from reason what can be known of God. . . . Natural reason must concede that all that is good comes from God. . . . [I]t regards God as kind, gracious, merciful and benevolent. And that is indeed a bright light" (LW 19, 54). This "philosophical or metaphysical" knowledge of God sees God as "a being separate from the creatures, as Aristotle says—a being that is truthful and contemplates the creature within itself" (LW 4, 145). "But," Luther continues with the key question, "of what concern is this to us?" (ibid.).

Such natural knowledge of God, according to Luther, is weak, superficial, inadequate, and inevitably distorted. The first great defect is this: "reason does admittedly believe that God is able and competent to help and to bestow; but reason does not know whether he is willing to do this also for us" (LW 19, 54). It therefore leaves the most important question unanswered. The second great defect is: "Reason is unable to identify God properly. . . . Thus reason also plays blindman's buff with God; it consistently gropes in the dark and misses the mark. . . . [I]t rushes in clumsily and assigns the name God and ascribes divine honor to its own idea of God. Thus reason never finds the true God, but it finds the devil or its own concept of God, ruled by the devil" (LW 19, 54f). The human mind, with its capacities for distortion and self-deception, inevitably corrupts what is known by the light of reason.

Philosophical speculation tries to focus its gaze on God as he is in himself, that is, "nude" (WA 40:2, 330, 1). "Do not get mixed up with this God," Luther says. "[L]eave the majestic God alone. . . . We know no other God than the God clothed with his promises" (WA 40:2, 329, 10–330, 5). The "clothed" God is the God who has revealed himself, first and foremost in the person of Jesus Christ. Here is where "true" knowledge, that is, saving knowledge, of God is available, and nowhere else. "Thus you may find God in Christ, but you will not find God outside Christ, even in heaven" (WA 40:3, 56, 11–12). Here is where we can learn about God's intention toward us, and here is where our distortions and self-deceptions are corrected.

Apart from this, Christians have to confess that they know very little about God. Medieval scholastic doctrines of God had traditionally, at the very outset, issued what we can call the apophatic warning: there is far more that we do not know about God than that we do know. Luther inherited this insight and if anything applied it more consistently than the scholastics. For example, he showed little interest in compiling lists of the divine attributes. God is "an inexpressible being, above and beyond all that can be described or imagined" (LW 37, 228). He is "inscrutable" (LW 19, 228), a "labyrinth" (LW 2, 45). This means that the Christian response to many, if not most, human questions about God should simply be, "We do not know." Such a Christian agnosticism is the safe course to take. In the final analysis, "God in his essence is altogether unknowable, nor is it possible to define or put into words what he is, though we burst in the effort" (LW 2, 45). By mucking around in the "mazes" of the divine majesty, humans become disoriented, losing sight of what is important for us to know. About *that*, and only about that, God has spoken.

God's self-revelation, however, is not transparent. Luther could say that God not only reveals himself but he also hides himself (*Deus revelatus—Deus absconditus*). Those aspects of himself that he hides from us do not in any way concern us: "To the extent, therefore, that God hides himself and wills to be unknown to us, it is no business of ours. . . . [I]n this regard we have nothing to do with him, nor has he willed that we should have anything to do with him. But we have something to do with him insofar as he is clothed and set forth in his Word, through which he offers himself to us" (LW 33, 139). Unlike the "hidden God," the "revealed God" is of intense, indeed ultimate, human concern.

Yet even in his self-revelation there is a kind of concealment. For God accomplishes things in ways that are contrary to human logic: "he killed death by death, punishment by punishment, suffering by suffering, disgrace by disgrace, so that in Christ death . . . is eternal life, punishment is joy" (LW 11, 377–378). Not only does he act this way, but he appears to us hidden under his opposite. He is to be found in the weakness of an infant, in the humiliation of a trial, in the suffering of a cross (LW 31, 52). He appears where humans do not expect him. That is why God's self-revelation is not obvious and self-evident to all human beings. Only faith, which Luther can call "an understanding in concealment" (LW 25, 224), can discern it.

God reveals something of his innermost nature to us, Luther holds, through his acts. He does many things of course, but all that he does can be subsumed under two kinds of action: creating and loving. This is in fact all God does, and since both are ultimately acts of self-giving, even these two finally coalesce into one.

The doctrine of God as creator is of high significance for Luther. The first article of the creed "is the shortest possible way of describing and illustrating the nature, will, acts, and work of God the Father" (*BC* 432). It means, of course, that the entire universe, physically speaking, had its origin in God. But Luther insists that God's creative activity is ongoing. Scripture uses words like "mighty" or "omnipotent" to express this, "For the word 'mighty' does not denote a quiescent power. . . . But it denotes an energetic power, continuous activity, that works and operates without ceasing" (LW 21, 328). Omnipotence is not an abstract, potential capacity for action, "but the active power by which he potently works all in all" (LW 33, 189). This means that God creates us as individuals and also our personal realities, not only the original world but *our* world.

To say that God is the creator of all reality also means that he is present in all reality. He "exists at the same time in every little seed, whole and entire, and yet also in all and above all and outside all created things" (LW 19, 228). Creation implies not only transcendence but immanence. And immanence most importantly means that God is present to *our* reality, even in situations of apparent abandonment. God, Luther says, "is present everywhere, in death, in hell, in the midst of our foes, yes, also in their hearts. For he has created all things, and he also governs them, and they must all do as he wills" (LW 19, 68).

Luther also endorses the traditional Christian teaching that when God creates, he does so *ex nihilo* (from nothing). Occasionally one finds in Luther statements suggesting that human beings are in some sense cocreators with God. "All creatures are God's larvae and masks that he will allow to work with him and help in all sorts of things, but that he otherwise can and does do without their help" (WA 17:2, 192, 28–30). God may hide his creative action behind human "masks" and "mummery," but in no way do we "create" in the proper sense, that is, *ex nihilo*. Strictly speaking, only God creates, and everything that is, is created by him. Moreover, "[i]t is his nature to create all things out of nothing" (WA 40:3, 154, 11–12). That includes the world, humans, and also humans in their "new creation." The divine creative act that Luther calls "justification" is also *ex nihilo*.

Luther's doctrine of God as creator *ex nihilo*, with its corollaries of omnipotence and omnipresence, has vast implications for humans. In a 1523 sermon he said that this belief in God the creator was "without a doubt, the highest article of faith. . . . Whoever genuinely believes this has already been helped, has once again been set aright, and arrived at the place from which Adam fell. Few reach the point of believing that he is the God who creates and makes all things. For such a man must have died to all things, to good and to evil, to death and to life, to hell and to heaven, and confess from his heart that he is able to do nothing by his own power" (WA 24, 18, 26–33). Thus the doctrine of creation demands that we abandon our illusion of self-sufficiency and entrust ourselves entirely to the divine will.

This doctrine also functions in Luther as an enormous comfort against all anxiety over the uncertainties of human existence.

> Where does a man who hopes in God end up, except in his own nothingness? But when a man goes into nothingness, does he not merely return to

that from which he came? Since he comes from God and his own nonbeing, it is to God that he returns when he returns to nothingness. For even though a man falls out of himself and out of all creation, it is impossible for him to fall out of God's hand, for all creation is surrounded by God's hands. . . . So run through the world; but where are you running? Always into the hand and lap of God. (WA 5, 168, 1–7)

Luther holds that, sporadically, when our lives "come to nothing," as they sooner or later do, they come to God. In the final analysis then, nothing ultimately serious can go wrong. (*See also* **Creation**.)

In his creative activity, Luther says, God "has given to us himself" (*BC* 433). This theme of self-giving connects creation with the other category of divine activity, namely loving. This too is captured by the first article of the creed, specifically in the word "Father." In his "Fatherhood," God not only originates all creatures but he loves his creatures and gives them all good things. God's love is not merely one aspect of his character but it is his very nature: "This is what it is to be God: not to take good things but to give, that is, to return good for evil" (WA 4, 269, 25–26). Furthermore, God's love, unlike all human love, is unconditional. It is given to all, including the unworthy. "For God is he who distributes his gifts freely to all; and this is his praise of his own deity" (LW 26, 127). It flows on, even when humans try to obstruct it: "The fact that he neither becomes tired nor ceases to do good because of any evil really is, and deserves to be called, divine goodness" (LW 14, 51). This love gladly "wastes" itself even on those who ignore it: God's love "gladly loses its good deed on the unthankful" (LW 14, 106).

From Luther's point of view, the very deepest and most universal human longing is for a love that is truly unconditional. God himself, who is such a love, is the final fulfillment of this longing. And this love, when it is received,

is transformative. In Luther's language, it makes us become what God is, "righteous" (WA 56, 172, 3–10). In the final analysis, of all the things that can be said about God, this is the most important, that he is love. Precisely this is what he has revealed about himself in Jesus Christ.

Of the thousands of statements about God made by Luther, the following one from a 1532 sermon perhaps expresses his deepest and most heartfelt conviction. "If I were to paint a picture of God I would so draw him that there would be nothing else in the depth of his divine nature than that fire and passion that is called love for people. Correspondingly, love is such a thing that is neither human nor angelic but rather divine, yes, even God himself" (WA 36, 424, 2–5). To say this is to believe, despite all evidence to the contrary, that the most fundamental, powerful, all-pervasive reality in the universe is love.

Of course there is much evidence to the contrary, and Luther was acutely aware of this. The power of evil, the suffering of humanity, and our own pain are sometimes an overwhelming refutation. Luther often refers to this as the experience of God's "wrath." But real as it may be, it is not ultimate: "God hides his eternal goodness and mercy under eternal wrath, his righteousness under iniquity. This is the highest degree of faith, to believe him merciful when . . . he seems . . . to delight in the torments of the wretched or to be worthy of hatred rather than of love" (LW 33, 62–63). Faith clings to the loving God even when experience suggests that he is hateful.

This problem, the theodicy problem, is all the more acute for Luther because he insists that "nothing takes place but as [God] wills it" (LW 33, 293). (For a will that is omnipotent, "willing" and "permitting" are finally identical.) If God wills all things that happen, do we not have to conclude that God wills evil? The theological mechanism Luther frequently used to deal with this problem was his distinction between God's "alien" and "proper" work (*opus alienum, opus proprium*). Basing himself on Isaiah 28:21, he says that God's proper works are his works of grace, mercy, and compassion. "God's alien works," on the other hand, "are these: to judge, to condemn, and to punish. . . . God is compelled to resort to such 'alien' works and to call them his own because of our pride. By manifesting these works he aims to humble us. . . . For it is his will that, when we have been chastened, we cast ourselves on his mercy" (LW 13, 135). God's proper work is accomplished through his alien work: "For the proper work and nature of God is to save. But when our flesh is so evil that it cannot be saved by God's proper work, it is necessary for it to be saved by his alien work" (LW 16, 233). All of God's work, even his alien work, is salvific, an expression of love. (*See also* **Evil, Problem of.**)

There can be no suggestion, therefore, that these two are somehow equal aspects of the Divine. Luther can even say that God's alien work is "contrary" to his true nature and that he engages in it unwillingly: "his compassion is more abundant [than his wrath] because it is a part of God's nature, since wrath is truly God's alien work, in which he engages contrary to his nature, because he is forced into it by the wickedness of man" (LW 2, 134). His true nature, despite all appearances to the contrary, is love. Seen in this light, the human experience of evil, devastating as it sometimes is, should not end in despair. For "faith in God" is precisely the confidence and trust that goodness and love will have the final word.

Here I have dealt with the most important aspects of Luther's doctrine of God. These various themes may leave the impression that this doctrine is complex. But, as is so often the case with Luther, underneath the apparent complexity lies something of utter simplicity. Thus it is easy to summarize Luther's doctrine of God in a nutshell: God has revealed something about himself to humankind, and he has done this through Jesus Christ. What he has revealed about himself is that he loves us. This, and nothing else, is the kernel, the only thing humans really need to know.

Gospel Luther uses this term to refer to the central core of Christian teaching as he understands it. It can also refer to the New Testament books of Matthew, Mark, Luke, and John. And Luther can use it as well to refer to the entire Word of God, including the law (e.g., LW 51, 20; WA 39:1, 535, 1–5). But this usage is rare. Most often the law is sharply distinguished from the gospel understood in what Luther calls its "proper sense," and accordingly law and gospel are related as demand and gift: "The gospel . . . most beautifully follows the law. The law introduces us to sin and overwhelms us with the knowledge of it. It does this so that we may seek to be freed and desire grace" (LW 32, 226). How then does Luther define what the gospel is? Among the multitude of definitions throughout his writings, the following are representative.

In his early lectures on Romans in 1515–16, Luther defines it simply as the message about Christ: "See there you have it: The Gospel is the message concerning Christ" (LW 25, 148). In 1518 he expanded on this basic definition: "The gospel is a preaching of the incarnate Son of God, given to us without any merit on our part for salvation and peace. It is a word of salvation, a word of grace, a word of comfort, a word of joy" (LW 31, 231). In other words, the gospel is exclusively positive: if a "word" fails to bring us peace, comfort, and joy, that is, if it is not good news, it is not the gospel.

Moreover, the gospel, Luther emphasized in 1521, is exclusively about Christ: it is the Christ story. It can be told in different ways but it is essentially one: "One should realize that there is only one gospel, but that it is described by many apostles. . . . Gospel is and should be nothing else than a discourse or story about Christ" (LW 35, 117). Yet, Luther hastens to add, it is the Christ story rightly understood. Not everything about this story is good news. If, for instance, we understand the many works of Christ as examples for us to follow, despair rather than joy might be the result. Christ as example is, Luther says, "the smallest part of the gospel, on the basis of which it cannot yet even be called gospel. . . . The chief article and foundation of the gospel is that before you take Christ as an example, you accept and recognize him as a gift" (LW 35, 117). It is not the following of the example that makes us righteous, but rather the faith that receives the gift.

Thus the gospel, for Luther, is the proclamation of how faith in Christ makes us righteous. As he explained in 1523, this is the decisive criterion: "those who emphasize most and in the loftiest way how faith in Christ alone makes us righteous are the best evangelists. That is why the Epistles of Paul are more of a gospel than Matthew, Mark, and Luke. For these [latter] describe not much more than the record of the works and miracles of Christ. But the grace that we have through Christ—no one describes this better than St. Paul" (WA 12, 260, 9–15). Luther values the canonical Gospels of course: they are indispensable since they give us what he understands to be the "facts" about Christ. But, strictly speaking, these "facts" are not yet the gospel. For this we need Paul, who interprets the meaning of the entire "Christ event" for us. That is, he explains how faith in Christ makes us righteous. In this sense, the gospel is more readily accessible in Paul's Letters than in the Gospels (LW 35, 365).

Essentially the same position grounds the definition he gave in his *Lectures on Galatians* of 1535: "The proper definition of the gospel is that it is the promise of Christ, which frees us from the terrors of the law, sin, and death, and brings grace, forgiveness of sins, righteousness, and eternal life" (LW 27, 184). The gospel as the "promise of Christ" is of course given to us in the Gospels. Paul's value is that he explains how this promise becomes "saving" for us.

How does this gospel reach us? In his Smalcald Articles of 1537 Luther acknowledges that it can happen in a variety of ways. The gospel can come to us through baptism, for instance, or through the Lord's Supper, or even through penance. But most often and ordinarily, for Luther, it comes through preaching (*BC* 319). Its proper form is the spoken, proclaimed, even shouted word, which is why, he said in 1521, Christ wrote nothing (LW 35, 123; cf. WA 10:1:1, 17, 7–12). Luther's own efforts to proclaim it occupied him throughout his life and absorbed a massive amount of his creative energy, perhaps even more than his polemical writings. It would not be too much to call precisely this Luther's obsession: proclaiming God's unconditional love for humans, and denouncing the perverse human tendency to make it conditional after all.

Grace Luther's personal religious quest has often been described as a "search for a gracious God." This echoes the words Luther himself used in a highly personal letter to his friend Philip Melanchthon from October 27, 1527: "Pray for me, miserable and despised worm that I am. . . . for I seek and thirst only for a gracious God" (WABr 4, nr. 1162, 272, 27–32). Scholars agree that the young Luther absorbed from his religious-social-cultural-familial milieu an image of God as angry, demanding, and punishing. The "gracious God" he was searching for was the opposite—loving, merciful, and giving. And he found this God in the same place Christians always have, revealed in the person of Jesus Christ.

That narrative, however, can be misleading. We should not imagine, for instance, that this religious quest propelled the young Luther into the monastery, that there in his so-called

Reformation breakthrough his searching ended once and for all, and from that time forward his Reformation program progressed smoothly. Quite the contrary, his quest for a gracious God was a lifelong project. Again and again, at every stage of his life, agonizing bouts of what he called *Anfechtungen* caused him to lose sight of this God of grace. And repeatedly, to his unceasing astonishment, "grace and peace" returned to him.

No wonder then that Luther could speak of precisely this as the heart of Christianity: "These two words, 'grace' and 'peace,' contain a summary of all Christianity. Grace contains the forgiveness of sins, a joyful peace, and a quiet conscience. But peace is impossible unless sin has first been forgiven" (LW 26, 26) The lifelong quest and its resolution became for Luther the object of theological reflection. Even more pronounced in Luther is the untiring explaining, preaching, and celebrating of the gospel of God's grace.

It should be clear by now that when we come to the topic of "grace" in Luther, we are not dealing with one concept among many. In a sense it is the only concept—it cannot be singled out and explained in isolation from the rest. It is all-inclusive: in order to explain it fully, one would have to explain everything else fully. Perhaps that is why Luther never wrote a work devoted to this topic. What follows here is nothing more than a brief description of Luther's basic definition. The multiple implications are taken up in other sections of this book (*see*, e.g., **Christology; Creation; Faith; God; Gospel; Holy Spirit; Justification; Resurrection**).

Trained in scholasticism, Luther had a firsthand acquaintance with its elaborate structural development of the doctrine of grace, as well as with the common technical vocabulary used in this area of theology, and with the various schools of thought ranging from Neo-Augustinian to Neo-semi-Pelagian. Already in his first lectures on the Psalms (1513–15), Luther was critical of this tradition. By 1520 his break with it was complete: grace is not a "quality of the soul" (LW 32, 227); it is not an infused power that enables us to prepare ourselves for further grace (LW 34, 305); it is not a habit or a virtue that enables us to fulfill the law in a meritorious way (LW 26, 180). This scholastic way of speaking about grace Luther now rejected in its entirety. In its place he put what he understood to be the "Pauline" way of speaking about grace (LW 32, 229).

Grace, Luther argued, is not a "something," a created reality, in us. Rather it refers to God's way of regarding us. God can be favorably disposed to us, and this is called his "grace." Or he can be unfavorably disposed to us, and this is called his "wrath." Accordingly, as in Paul's Letter to the Romans, "Grace actually means God's favor, or the good will which he himself bears toward us" (LW 35, 369; cf. 32, 227). The gospel, the "good news" that comes to us through Jesus Christ, is that God is not angry and demanding and punishing (i.e., wrathful), but loving and merciful and giving (i.e., gracious). Faith is the mechanism in us that grasps this, and the result, Luther said, is that "the gate to paradise" is opened to us (LW 34, 337).

If we begin to list the forms in which Luther thinks the grace of God comes to us, we quickly become aware that such a list is endless. It comes to us as Christ himself (WA 3, 269, 17; cf. 2, 247, 23; LW 25, 53; 31, 298), as God's presence (WA 7, 571, 5–6), as the Holy Spirit (LW 31, 13; 12, 377–378; 34, 305), as the forgiveness of sins (LW 26, 26; 34, 164; WA 46, 658, 3–6), as God's mercy (WA 3, 226, 10; LW 32, 227), as the imputation of righteousness (LW 25, 258; 35, 370), as eternal life (LW 32, 229), and so forth. In short, God's favor expresses itself in every conceivable way: grace is everything!

Luther asserted that it is God's very essence not to receive but to give (WA 4, 269, 25–26). To say this is to affirm that all reality has the nature of "gift."

Since creation is *ex nihilo* (out of nothing), the universe, nature, our individual existences—all are gifts. And since our redemption is *sola gratia* (by grace alone), that too is pure gift. Luther's last written words, from the day before he died, reflect this profound awareness: "We are beggars. That is true" (LW 54, nr. 5677, 476). A thousand years earlier, Augustine, the "Doctor of Grace," had realized the same thing: "What have I," he asked, "that I have not received?"

Heaven   For Luther, Christian eschatology, specifically the belief in the resurrection and eternal life, is concretely expressed in the concept of heaven. (*See also* **Eschatology; Resurrection**.) Only in the most general and abstract language can we really define what this is. We can say, for instance, that it is eternal happiness with God (WA 37, 151, 8–10). Or we can say that in heaven we will be "perfectly pure and holy people, full of integrity and righteousness, completely freed from sin, death, and all misfortune, living in new, immortal, and glorified bodies" (*BC* 438). But as for concrete specifics, these elude us. Even the particulars found in Scripture should not be taken too literally (LW 51, 253; cf. *BC* 439). An excessive literalism can only lead to awkward questions about matters such as overcrowding or bodily waste in heaven (LW 28, 170–172). The truth is that we really do not know: "As little as babies in their mother's womb know about what awaits them, so little we know about eternal life" (WATR 3, nr. 3339, 276, 26–27). Following Paul (1 Cor. 15:51), Luther insists that we are dealing with a "mystery."

Faced with the mysterious, humans often resort to the language of image and metaphor, and Luther encourages this (LW 28, 176–177). Here imagination comes into play: "we must use pictures with children and simple people" (LW 51, 253). Thus, for his son Hans, Luther could describe heaven as "a pretty, beautiful, and delightful garden

where there are many children wearing little golden coats. They pick up fine apples, pears, cherries, and yellow and blue plums under the trees. They sing, jump, and are merry. They also have nice ponies" (WABr 5, nr. 1595, 377, 5–9). Luther called this "cheerful speculation," and he encouraged it (WATR 2, nr. 2507a, 497, 30–35).

Luther's rule of thumb for such flights of fancy is this: the promise of paradise is the promise that "all our needs and wants will be satisfied" (LW 28, 144). The promise of infinite happiness means that "whatever delights your heart will be yours abundantly" (LW 28, 146). For instance, if the presence of loved ones is essential to your happiness, be assured—they will be there (cf. WABr 5, nr. 1529, 241, 79–82). Luther personally advanced the notion that humans will be able to fly (LW 28, 143–144; 28, 188); that the Elbe River will flow with pearls and precious stones (WA 36, 599); and that we will be strong enough to handle the lions and bears "the way we [now] handle puppies" (WA 42, 48, 1–2); that Cicero will be there (WATR 2, nr. 2412b, 457, 20–21; WATR 4, nr. 3925, 14, 3–4); that creatures that are currently ugly will be "most beautiful"; that creatures that currently stink will have "a wonderful fragrance" (WATR 2, nr. 2652b, 580, 13–15); and so forth.

Luther understood, of course, that such dreams of infinite happiness in the future must never be absolutized. This is because our understanding of what will make us ultimately happy is often mistaken and changeable. What we can count on, Luther thought, is this: heaven is eternal happiness with God (WA 37, 151, 8–10); and God is "the life and the inexhaustible foundation of all good and endless joy" (WA 39, 599, 16–17). Living in his presence will be the ultimate fulfillment of everything humans have ever wanted.

Hell   The term "hell" occurs hundreds of times in Luther's writings.

Sometimes he uses it to vehemently dismiss people he is unhappy with. He says of "the papists," for instance: "Let them go to hell" (LW 34, 366). What he meant by this is precisely what we mean today when we use the phrase.

More often in Luther, "hell" is used in combination with terms like "sin" and "death." Thus the triad "sin, death, and hell" recurs with great frequency: it is Luther's formulaic, shorthand way of referring to all that Christians are "saved" from. "Hell" in this context simply means the negative things about human life.

If we look more closely at other ways in which Luther uses this term, the landscape of his hell acquires sharper features. In his 1535–1545 *Lectures on Genesis* he makes clear that the conventional Roman Catholic view is unacceptable. This tradition, he says, posited "five places after death": a hell of the damned, a hell for unbaptized infants, purgatory, a limbo for the "fathers" of ancient Israel, and heaven. This he dismisses as "foolishness" and "silly ideas" (LW 4, 315). As for unbaptized infants who die, we do not know what happens to them: we simply commend them "to the goodness of God." And as for any kind of "torment by eternal fire," Luther expresses great hesitation. After pointing out some contradictory biblical passages, he concludes by saying that about this "I am making no positive statement" (LW 4, 315). About the damned mentioned in John 5:29 he adds: "I am unable to say positively in what state those are who are condemned in the New Testament. I leave this undecided" (LW 4, 316).

Properly speaking, Luther believed, hell is not a place. In his lectures on Jonah from 1524–26 he is explicit on this: "It is not a specific place, but in Scripture it is nothingness" (WA 13, 232, 19–20). For Luther it is an experience, an experience of nothingness. And nothingness, metaphysically speaking, is the opposite of Being itself, or God. Thus hell is the experience of the absence of God. Or

as Luther puts it, "To be deprived of the vision of God is hell itself" (LW 4, 315).

Essentially, Luther thought, we know nothing about how the absence of God will be experienced after death. But what we do know a great deal about is how the absence of God is experienced in this life, here and now. Thus the only hell we really know about is the one we encounter in our lives. And this is the one Luther speaks about almost exclusively.

Thus he describes the experience of *Anfechtung* as hell. Describing his own "dark night of the soul," he said in 1518, "I myself 'knew a man' [2 Cor. 12:2] who claimed that he had often suffered these punishments, in fact over a brief period of time. Yet they were so great and so much like hell that no tongue could adequately express them" (LW 31, 129). Here "hell" is indeed pain—the ultimate, indescribable, emotional pain.

Hell is also for Luther the terror of death that cripples our lives. In his 1519–21 lectures on the Psalms he said: "I hold that the sorrow of death and of hell are the same thing. Hell is the terror of death, that is, the sense of death, in which the damned have a horrified dread of death and yet cannot escape" (WA 5, 463, 22–25). So too hell can be described as anxiety: "Those who are anxious seem to enter hell, and therefore, when someone finds himself in the most extreme misery of this kind, this experience is also called the most acute hell" (WA 13, 232, 17–19). As a final example, Luther can speak of despair as hell: "The theologian is concerned that man become aware of this nature of his. When this happens, despair follows, casting him into hell" (LW 12, 310–311).

This hell, whether it is the experience of *Anfechtung*, or the fear of death or anxiety or despair—this we humans know a great deal about. In each case it is the experience of the absence of God, and it is very real. The gospel, for Luther, is what rescues us out of hell, not in some future life but now. It counteracts the hellish aspects of our lives by making God—his love, his protection, and his peace—present to us in faith.

Holy Spirit   Luther has distinctly less to say explicitly about the Holy Spirit than about the other two persons of the Trinity, and in this he mirrors the theological tradition he inherited. Yet this does not mean that the Holy Spirit is unimportant in his understanding of Christianity. Rather, this doctrine is indispensable: all talk of God as creator and God as redeemer would be fruitless were it not for this doctrine of God as he is present to us—a presence that makes us holy.

Luther was utterly convinced that the Council of Constantinople (381) had understood the Bible correctly in saying that the Holy Spirit is "true God" and "of one substance with the Father and the Son" (LW 41, 86–93). He proceeds from the Father and the Son and therefore he is identical with the "Spirit of God" and the "Spirit of Christ." To Christ himself he appeared as a dove (Matt. 3:16), and in the early church he manifested himself in tongues of fire and in strange languages (Acts 2:3–4). This he no longer does. Commenting on Galatians 4:6, Luther says that the Spirit is still sent into our hearts, but "[t]his happens without a visible form" (LW 26, 375). Nor is it the work of the Spirit to transmit any new revelations to human beings. "God will not come to you in your little room and speak to you" (WA 17:2, 460, 2–3). God has bound his revelation to the historicity of Jesus Christ.

How is the Holy Spirit present? Luther occasionally speaks of the Holy Spirit as God's presence in all of creation. "[T]he Holy Spirit is among humans in a twofold way. First through a general activity, by which he preserves them as well as God's other creatures. Second, the Holy Spirit is given from Christ to believers" (WA 39:2, 239, 29–31). In the first way he is in his creation, holding it in existence and acting in every act—a concept close

to the medieval scholastic understanding of God's *concursus generalis*. But Luther is much more interested in the second, his presence as Christians experience it. While the first is presupposed, the second is elaborated at some length.

What then is the proper work of the Holy Spirit? Luther describes this in various ways. One way to understand it, and this is found in his sermons, is as the disbursement of a treasure, namely Christ's work of redemption. "[T]he treasure still lies in one pile; it is not yet distributed or applied" (WA 12, 569, 22–25). The Holy Spirit comes "to disburse the treasure" (WA 12, 570, 6–9). His work, in other words, is to apply Christ's saving work to us.

Another way Luther speaks of this is that the Holy Spirit "reveals" Christ to us. Without Christ, Luther says, we would not know the Father except as "an angry and terrible judge. But neither could we know anything of Christ, had it not been revealed by the Holy Spirit" (*BC* 440). Thus the Holy Spirit is the revealer of God's revelation. Luther does not mean that without the Holy Spirit we could not know about the life of Jesus, his teaching, and so forth. But without the Holy Spirit, we could not grasp his meaning for us.

In this sense, the Holy Spirit "brings us to Christ." He makes contemporary for us something that has happened in the past. Luther can say that in a sense creation and redemption are both "behind us, . . . but the Holy Spirit continues his work without ceasing until the Last Day" (*BC* 439). Christ's work "is finished and completed; Christ has acquired and won the treasure for us. . . . But if the work remained hidden so that no one knew of it, it would have been all in vain, all lost. In order that this treasure might not remain buried . . . God has . . . given the Holy Spirit to offer and apply to us this treasure" (*BC* 436). In other words, what happened many centuries ago is made contemporaneous for us by the work of the Holy Spirit.

Perhaps most commonly, Luther describes this work as the act of internalization. The gospel of Jesus Christ can be proclaimed endlessly, but it remains "empty words and prattle" (LW 21, 299) until the Holy Spirit proclaims it to one's heart. Until it reaches the heart, when humans grasp its meaning for them personally, it remains external and does them no good. "It is easy enough," Luther says, "for someone to preach the word to me, but only God [i.e., the Holy Spirit] can put it into my heart" (WA 10:3, 260, 21–22). This work of internalizing in the heart goes way beyond a kind of intellectual convincing. It is more like an immediacy of conviction, an awareness, an acceptance, an existential trust, which in the end is precisely what Luther means by "faith."

In describing this, Luther does not shy away from the term "feeling." "We should, therefore, not believe the gospel because the church has approved it, but rather because we feel [*sentitur*] that it is the Word of God. . . . Everyone may be certain of the gospel when he has the testimony of the Holy Spirit in his own person that this is the gospel" (WA 30:2, 687, 31–688, 4). The term "feeling" is problematic for us because of its associations with Pietism and nineteenth-century liberalism, and because it was "sentimentalized" and trivialized in the twentieth century. What Luther meant by "feeling" in this context was the deepest kind of immediate consciousness or awareness or trust that the redemption accomplished in Christ was "for me." When we have it, Luther believes, we can be sure that it is the work of the Holy Spirit.

What is external to us must be interiorized: this way of approaching the work of the Spirit dominated Luther's debate in the 1520s with Andreas Bodenstein von Karlstadt, Thomas Müntzer, and others—early followers who had turned against Luther and whom Luther now referred to as the "heavenly prophets," "enthusiasts," or "fanatics." "They boast of possessing the Spirit," Luther said in 1525, "more than the Apostles, and yet for more than three years they have now secretly prowled around and flung around their dung" (LW 40, 222). Karlstadt seemed to Luther to have "devoured the Holy Spirit feathers and all" (LW 40, 83). Against them, Luther used the "outer/inner" dynamic to make the point that the inner must remain inseparable from the outer. "Outwardly [God] deals with us through the oral word of the gospel and through material signs, that is baptism and the sacrament of the altar. Inwardly he deals with us through the Holy Spirit, faith, and other gifts. But whatever their measure or order the outward factors should and must precede" (LW 40, 146). In other words, there can be no manifestations of the Spirit that add to or go beyond the external Word as it is present in the church, "through which he [the Holy Spirit] speaks and does all his work" (*BC* 439). The external Word is offered to us in the church's proclamation and sacraments. This word and nothing else is what the Holy Spirit internalizes. In his Smalcald Articles, formulated with great care in 1537, Luther expressed this as follows: "God gives no one his Spirit or grace apart from the external Word which goes before. We say this to protect ourselves from the enthusiasts, that is, the 'spirits,' who boast that they have the Spirit apart from and before contact with the Word" (*BC* 322). This is ultimately what it means to say that the Holy Spirit *is* the Spirit of Christ.

Though he has bound himself to the church, Word, and sacrament, the Holy Spirit yet remains free. "The Holy Spirit breathes where he wills and God justifies whom he wishes. He takes hold of the contrite and justifies him through faith in Christ which he pours into him through the preaching of the gospel" (LW 34, 173). Thus the effect of the preaching of the gospel is not automatic: sometimes it leaves people cold and sometimes it has its effect only ten years later (LW 14, 62). Contrary to what the "enthusiasts" thought, humans cannot induce the Holy Spirit to come to them or even prepare for this: "I am able to do this much: I can go and hear or read or preach the Word so that it enters into my heart. That is the true preparation, which does not lie in human powers and capability but rather in God's power" (WA 12, 497, 3–6). This, and acknowledging our need, is the true "preparation." To anxious and distressed hearts, the Holy Spirit is given as "Comforter" (John 14:26).

When he comes he awakens "the understanding of it [the gospel] in the heart" (BC 436). In this "understanding of the heart," humans grasp God's love and forgiveness, that is, they are "made holy" (BC 435). Thus the primary office of the Holy Spirit is "Sanctifier." The "fruits of the Holy Spirit" follow (love, joy, peace, longsuffering, gentleness, goodness, faith, meekness, temperance—Gal. 5:22–23). In fact "all the duties of Christians—such as loving one's wife, rearing one's children, governing one's family, honoring one's parents, obeying the magistrate, etc., which they [Roman Catholics] regard as secular and fleshly—are fruits of the Spirit" (LW 26, 217), that is, they all now come from a transformed heart. In this sense, those who possess the Spirit are holy. But this does not mean they are perfect. In the life to come, the Holy Spirit "will perfect our holiness and will eternally preserve us in it" (BC 439).

These are the major contours of Luther's doctrine of the Holy Spirit. If Luther has distinctly less to say about the Holy Spirit than about the other persons of the Trinity, it is only because he prefers the language of "grace" and "faith." For what he means by grace is precisely the presence of the Holy Spirit, and what he means by faith is nothing else than the work of the Holy Spirit. Wherever humans experience the presence of grace, wherever they respond in faith, indeed, wherever they experience love, joy, peace, and so on—there the Holy Spirit is present and at work.

Islam/Muslims   Luther's view of Islam (including Muhammad and the Qur'an) was grounded in a combination of fear and fascination. The fear was a widely shared phenomenon in Western Europe in the early sixteenth century: the Muslim Ottoman Turks had captured Constantinople in 1453 and were advancing steadily westward, arriving at the outskirts of Vienna in 1529. Tales of brutality and atrocity circulated widely, giving urgency to new calls for a defensive crusade. But in addition to fear, it was also his boundless intellectual curiosity that drove Luther to take an interest in Islam. Besides Judaism (and the religion of ancient Rome), it was the only non-Christian religion known to him, and its very otherness fascinated him.

To some extent Luther's knowledge of Islam was based on hearsay, though some of the stories circulating were so wild that he discounted them (LW 46, 176). More importantly it was based on a selective reading of the substantial medieval Christian literature on Islam. He knew, for instance, Nicholas of Cusa's Cribratio Alcorani, another fifteenth-century work entitled Libellus de ritu et moribus Turcorum, and the thirteenth-century Confutatio Alcorani by Ricoldo di Monte Croce. In 1542, to his great delight, he finally acquired a Latin translation of the Qur'an and read it apparently in one day (WA 53, 272, 9). These, and no doubt other writings, formed his understanding of Islam.

Luther took up the pen in response to the Turkish Muslim threat for the first time in 1529 in On War Against the Turk (LW 46, 135–205) and then again later that year in Army Sermon Against the Turk (WA 30:2, 149–197). These are part warning, part encouragement, and part call to arms. He also republished the Libellus de ritu et moribus Turcorum in 1530, and his own German translation of Ricoldo's Confutatio Alcorani in 1542 (WA 53, 261–396). Finally, also in 1542, Luther used his influence to have a new and better Latin translation of the

Qur'an published (WABr 10, nr. 3802, 160–163; and Luther's preface in WA 53, 561–572). These tools, Luther thought, would make Christian arguments against Islam more convincing.

The picture of Islam that emerges from these and other minor writings is entirely in accord with the general medieval and early modern Western view: a strange combination of fact, legend, distortion, misunderstanding, rumor, and utter fabrication. The only difference perhaps is that in Luther the vehemence of the denunciation is ratcheted up a notch. Thus Muhammad is depicted by and large as an utterly immoral fraud. Episodes from Hadith dealing with the life of the Prophet are embellished, distorted, and given the worst possible interpretation. As for the Qur'an, which Luther believed was written by Muhammad, it is a book filled with nonsense and self-contradictions. Indeed, Luther finds it astounding that rational human beings could give credence to such a book: how could these multitudes of human beings have been so duped for almost a thousand years? Part of the answer, Luther thought, lies in human stupidity, but part of it also has to do with the "fact" that the Qur'an sanctions the basest human instincts: greed, cruelty, murder, and sexual license.

Almost lost amid the vitriol is Luther's theological critique of Islam. It is a wide-ranging indictment, scattered throughout Luther's later writings, but it is based on four principles. First, it seems clear to Luther that Islam is essentially an extreme version of the ancient Arian heresy: Christ is not God but a creature (LW 38, 310). Second, because Muslims do not see Christ as God's authentic and final revelation, the God they worship is an idol (WA 30:2, 196, 26–31). Third, Islam (like Judaism and Roman Catholicism) is a religion of self-salvation: paradise is the reward for those who pray, give alms, fast, and so forth (LW 26, 396–401). Fourth, robbery, murder, and lechery are "commanded in their law as a good and divine work"

(LW 46, 178). Thus, in the end, the entire social order, including the family, is destroyed (LW 46, 178–182).

In the final analysis then, for Luther Islam is not the antichrist (this title he reserves for the pope), but the devil (WA 30:2, 195, 32–33), the Gog of Daniel 7 (WA 30:2, 171, 8–13), the horrible sixth angel of Revelation 9:13–19 (LW 35, 404). Islam became, in the mind of the older Luther, the point at which all that was alien and terrifying coalesced. In this he was not alone. None of Luther's views on Islam were essentially new, and all of them were widely shared in the sixteenth century. By expressing them anew, Luther helped to ensure that the medieval Catholic demonization of Islam would find its place in Protestantism as well.

Judaism/Jews In describing traditional Christian attitudes toward the Jews, historians conventionally distinguish between religious anti-Judaism and racial anti-Semitism. In the medieval and early modern periods, we are overwhelmingly dealing with the former. Christian dislike, and sometimes hatred, of Jews was based on a commonly held set of theological assumptions. These included the following: The Jews had rejected Christ, God's Messiah, and indeed had killed him. The result was that God's covenant with them was not only broken but abrogated. The Jews were no longer God's chosen people, and their entire religion had been rendered null and void. Divine grace was now available to them only through conversion to Christ. Their role in the providential unfolding of human history had come to an end. Their obstinate blindness prevented them from even understanding their own Scriptures, which speak everywhere of the coming Messiah. These beliefs were the pillars of medieval anti-Judaism, a consensus among theologians, however much they differed on the details. And it was this understanding of the Jews that sixteenth-century thinkers, including Luther, inherited.

I should immediately add that these were not abstract theological ideas: they came, more often than not, weighed down with heavy emotional baggage. "Hatred" is not too strong a word to describe this. The term certainly applied, for instance, to the vehemently anti-Jewish writings of the Counter-Reformation polemicist John Eck. And the greatest of the era's humanists, Desiderius Erasmus, applied it to himself: "If it be Christian to hate Jews," he said, "we are all good Christians." Luther echoed Erasmus's remark (WA 2, 429, 9–12), and even a brief survey of his writings on the Jews confirms that he too was, or became from time to time, a hater of the Jews.

The medieval theological assumptions listed above were present and operative in Luther's work from the outset. One finds them, for instance, expressed here and there in his early *Lectures on the Psalms* (1513–15; e.g., LW 10, 68; 10, 245; 11, 500). So too one finds them all, more or less explicitly, in his *Lectures on Romans* (1515–16; e.g., LW 25, 25–26; 25, 232). And they are unmistakably present in his first writing devoted to the Jewish issue, his 1523 work, *That Jesus Christ Was Born a Jew.*

In this work these assumptions undergirded a relatively benevolent, paternalistic attitude. The Jews, Luther argued, have traditionally been treated like dogs: no wonder Christian efforts to convert them have failed miserably (LW 45, 229). If Christians, guided by "the law of Christian love," dealt kindly with them, it might be possible to instruct them from Scripture (LW 45, 200), proving to them that Jesus was the Messiah (LW 45, 213–229), and thus converting them. Anger and bitterness are largely absent here, and one senses in some of Luther's statements a kind of respect: "We [Christians] are aliens and in-laws [to Jesus]; they [Jews] are blood relatives, cousins and brothers of our Lord" (LW 45, 200–201).

A few years after writing *That Jesus Christ Was Born a Jew*, an incident occurred that may have been pivotal in hardening Luther's attitude. While the details remain vague, he mentioned it at least four times. It seems that after meeting some Jews, debating with them, and helping them in some way, he discovered that they referred to Christ as "a hanged highwayman." Because of this insult against Christ, he said, "I do not wish to have anything more to do with any Jew" (LW 47, 192; cf. WATR 3, nr. 3512, 370, 9–21; WATR 4, nr. 4795, 517, 4–15; nr. 5026, 619, 20–24). He may have despised the Jews after this incident, but he continued to need their linguistic expertise for help in his translation of the Hebrew Scriptures, and he needed their exegetical help, for instance, for his *Lectures on Genesis* (1535–45). In these lectures he relied on their scholarship on occasion (e.g., LW 1, 264; 2, 14; 3, 71), but also excoriated them: beware "the dung of the rabbis." They "have made of the Holy Scripture a sort of privy in which they have deposited their foulness and their exceedingly foolish opinions" (LW 4, 351). While the rabbis knew the language, Luther believed, they could not understand the Old Testament because they had collectively rejected Christ (LW 1, 296 and 303; 3, 358). There is nothing new here in terms of ideas, but there seems to be a new level of bitterness.

On the other hand, we find Luther in 1537 writing a letter to his "friend," Rabbi Josel of Rosheim, claiming to have been betrayed by the Jews, but still asserting his goodwill: "For my opinion was, and still is, that one should treat the Jews in a kindly manner" (WABr 8, nr. 3157, 89, 9–10). The purpose of such kindness, of course, was to convert them; and the larger purpose of Luther's letter was to deny Rosheim the help he was seeking (cf. LW 54, nr. 3597, 239). Overt anger may be absent here, but Luther's "kindness" had its limits.

Anger also seems to be largely absent from his 1538 treatise *Against the Sabbatarians*. This somewhat obscure group advocated Sabbath observance, and reportedly circumcision as well. Luther assumed that these Christian "Judaizers" were the result of Jewish proselytizing, and he attempted in this work to set them straight. His basic argument was that an authentic Judaism, with its law, priesthood, temple worship, and so forth, could be practiced only in Jerusalem. Yet God had effectively exiled the Jews from Jerusalem for fifteen hundred years. For what crime? Rejecting the Messiah (LW 47, 73). "[I]t is evident that he [God] has forsaken them, that they can no longer be God's people" (LW 47, 97). In his elaboration of this argument, Luther repeats all of the medieval theological assumptions listed above. Yet the caustic wrath of some later works is not found here.

It *is* unmistakably present in Luther's *On the Jews and Their Lies*, which appeared early in 1543. Again, no new doctrinal positions are to be found here, but the depth of Luther's anger had clearly reached a new level. The reasons for this cannot be specified with precision. But it is not irrelevant to point out that in 1539 Luther had read a relatively new work by the Jewish convert to Christianity, Anthony Margaritha, entitled *The Whole Jewish Faith*. Then, in late 1542, he had read an older book, Salvagus Porchetus's *Victory over the Godless Hebrews*, as well as a Jewish apologetic pamphlet that cannot be identified. Finally, we know too that in the winter of 1542–43, he had the Margaritha book reread to him over dinner (LW 54, nr. 5504, 436). Steeped in this literature, Luther presented his arguments in *On the Jews and Their Lies* with extraordinary vehemence and vulgarity.

Luther's ultimate fury in this work seems to erupt in relation to three particular charges. Both Margaritha and Porchetus had reported that Jews think Mary was a whore who conceived Jesus during her menstrual period, and that as a result Jesus was born an idiot (LW 47, 267). Those two "Jewish" charges, and a third "Jewish" belief, namely that Chris-

tians are polytheists (LW 47, 290)—these seem to have angered Luther the most.

Provocative as this may have been, it in no way excuses Luther for his notorious list of recommendations for action: the Jews' synagogues and homes should be burned; books like the Talmud should be confiscated; rabbis should be forbidden to teach; Jews should receive no safe-conduct privileges when traveling; usury should be prohibited; their money should be confiscated; they should be given manual labor; and so forth (LW 47, 267–292). In particulars, these recommendations fell slightly short, for instance, of Erasmus's ideal of a Jew-free Europe, or of Pope Julius III's order that *all* Hebrew books be destroyed, or of John Eck's defense of the conventional ritual murder allegations against Jews. (These last accusations Luther had doubts about [LW 47, 217], and Eck, for this reason, accused him of whitewashing the Jews!) Still, when all is said and done, we must conclude that Luther's list amounts to an undeniably vicious program of persecution.

In his preparatory reading for composing *On the Jews and Their Lies*, Luther had come across a medieval Jewish legend to the effect that Jesus had applied kabbalistic numerology to the Tetragrammaton (YHWH), thereby acquiring his miraculous powers. Luther undertook to refute this in another book published in March 1543: *On the Tetragrammaton and on the Genealogy of Christ* (WA 53, 579–648). In the second part he attempted to deal with the problematic genealogies of Jesus in Matthew 1:1–16 and Luke 3:23–37. Whereas they trace Joseph's ancestry, Luther argued that Mary too was a descendant of David, and he set out to harmonize the two genealogies. In this work Luther's massive anti-Jewish prejudice is evident throughout. Yet here the intensity of his hatred seems to have diminished. Abusive, yes—but not on the same scale as *On the Jews and Their Lies*.

The same is true of Luther's final writing against the Jews, a book entitled

On the Last Words of David, completed on August 18, 1543. This work was exegetical, dealing with 2 Samuel 23:1–7. Luther's larger purpose, however, was to defend his unrelentingly christological interpretation of the Old Testament as a whole. Christians are obliged "to interpret the Hebrew Bible, wherever it is feasible, in the direction of the New Testament" (LW 15, 270). It was self-evident to Luther "that the God who led the children of Israel from Egypt . . . is the very same God, and none other than Jesus of Nazareth . . . whom the Jews crucified, and whom they still blaspheme and curse today" (LW 15, 313). Even learned Jews utterly fail to understand their own book, and it is the duty of "our Hebraists to wrest the Old Testament from the rabbis" (LW 15, 343). Again, the old anti-Jewish beliefs and prejudices are present here, but the anger level seems to be ratcheted down.

Standing back from the details and looking at the larger picture, we must confess that it is an ugly one. Luther's theological understanding of the Jews and their role in the history of salvation is in complete continuity with that of the Middle Ages. As a young student, he appropriated this consensus from his scholastic teachers, and he remained true to it to the end of his life. On the other hand, the affective dimension is marked by discontinuity. In his early work of 1523 we do not sense the seething anger and vicious hatred that comes to the fore two decades later. Thus, while Luther's beliefs about the Jews remained constant, his feelings about them vacillated along a spectrum from "dislike" to "hatred."

Today, five hundred years later, we cannot forgive Luther for this, even when we take into account all the mitigating factors. We cannot exculpate Luther, for instance, by simply labeling him "a man of his times." The fact is that he knew better. Even if Erasmus was correct in thinking that all Christians hated Jews, Luther at some level "knew" that hatred is never the Christian way:

he certainly was tireless in proclaiming this. His better instincts prevailed in 1523 when he asserted that the treatment of Jews should be guided by "the law of Christian love" (LW 45, 229). His better instincts prevailed again in 1544 when he refused to simply repeat the age-old accusation that the Jews were "Christ-killers." In that year, he revised an older hymn to be sung as follows:

T'was our great sins and misdeeds gross
Nailed Jesus, God's true son, to the cross.
Thus you, poor Judas, we dare not blame,
Nor the band of Jews; ours is the shame.
(WA 35, 576)

Luther's hatred of the Jews is unforgivable because he knew better. Following the logic of his hymn revision, he knew at some level that "we" nailed Jesus to the cross; and when we hate, we nail him to the cross again.

Justification   For Luther, "justification" refers to the way in which the redemption accomplished in Christ is applied to individual human beings. Assuming the Christian belief in Christ as "savior," the doctrine of justification attempts to say how this "salvation" becomes ours. It explains how the status of a human being is transformed from "sinner" to "righteous."

It would not be much of an exaggeration to say that Luther spent most of his theological career working on it. From at least 1517 (LW 31, 9–16) to the end of his life, he returned to the subject scores of times: justification is a central theme in most of his major writings and at least a minor theme everywhere else. Obviously he thought it was important. "[F]or if this article stands," he said in 1532/33, "the church stands, and if it falls, the church falls" (WA 40:3, 352, 3; cf. 335, 5–10). Decisive as it is for the church, it is also crucial to the theological enterprise itself: Luther opened a 1537 academic disputation by saying, "The article of justification is the master and prince, lord, rector, and judge over all types of doctrine; it preserves and governs all church doctrine. . . . Without this article, the world is sheer death and darkness" (WA 39:1, 205, 2–5). In another disputation from a year earlier, Luther went as far as to say that this doctrine is what makes a theologian a theologian (LW 34, 157). It is in fact a spelling out of the second article of the creed (cf. BC 434–35), Luther's term for what he otherwise calls "the gospel of Jesus Christ."

The intensity of Luther's focus on this one doctrine may be something new in the history of Christian theology. But it is misleading to say, as many have, that the theological tradition had never before made justification a major theme. True, the word "justification" was not much used. But the doctrine itself was taken up by every theologian after Augustine and debated again in every age, most often under the rubric of "nature and grace" or in the context of the sacrament of penance. It was not because previous theologians had ignored it that Luther took it up with such vigor, but rather because, in his opinion, the tradition had developed it in the wrong direction. Specifically, already in his 1517 Disputation Against Scholastic Theology, he accused the scholastics of being "Pelagians" (LW 31, 9–16). However subtle the scholastic argument, Luther thought, it ultimately attributed the decisive cause of salvation to the human person, and thereby made Christ superfluous. Thus, though there are differences, echoes of Augustine's polemic against Pelagius are audible throughout Luther's writings.

What then did "justification" mean for Luther? Besides extended discussions, we also find a good number of attempts at a capsule summary—efforts to capture the heart of it in a sentence or two. Some of these have become famous. For example, there is the Augsburg Confession's attempt from 1530 (actually written by Philip Melanchthon, and approved by Luther) (BC 38); or Luther's summation in the Smalcald Articles of 1537 (BC 325). Best of all, perhaps, is this one from his preface to the 1535 Lectures on Galatians: the doctrine of justification teaches "that we are redeemed from sin, death, and the devil and endowed with eternal life, not through ourselves and certainly not through our works . . . but through the help of another, the only Son of God, Jesus Christ" (LW 27, 145). The problem with such summaries, as Luther well knew, is that they can strike the reader as banal, conventional, inoffensive clichés. Only by unfolding its inner meaning could Luther begin to show how unconventional, how offensive, and even how "earth-shattering" he believed it to be.

Since the doctrine of justification is the answer to a problem, we do well to begin by describing the problem—the human predicament as Luther understood it. His term for this is "sin" or human sinfulness. (See also **Sin**.) We trivialize it entirely if we reduce it to the occasional immoral acts that humans choose. Rather, Luther insists, we "sin" in everything we do (LW 31, 40; 32, 83; etc.), even in our "best" moral actions (LW 32, 86). "Sin" is in fact a comprehensive term for an entire mode of existence characterized by unbelief, idolatry, efforts at self-justification, ingratitude, pride, and egocentricity. Moral effort, no matter how heroic, cannot alter this; we are "enslaved" to it, as Paul said (Rom. 7:15–21) and as Luther explained in his 1525 treatise On the Bondage of the Will (LW 33, 288). To understand this about the human condition is to understand something essential about ourselves. And to understand this about ourselves is to despair (LW 26, 126).

Being overwhelmed by despair prepares a person to "hear" the solution to the human predicament, what Luther calls the gospel of Jesus Christ (LW 32, 226). (See also **Gospel**.) This is quite simply the "good news" that, though we are utterly undeserving of it, God loves us unconditionally. Or, as Luther put it in his 1535 Lectures on Galatians: "The proper definition of the gospel is that it is the promise of Christ, which frees us from the terrors of the law, sin, and death, and brings grace, forgiveness of sins, righteousness, and eternal life" (LW 27, 184). If we are adequately prepared for it, this "news," Luther believed, should be stunning to us, and life-transforming. For it casts all the negativities of human life (i.e., "sin, death, and the devil") in a new perspective, and promises an ultimate triumph over them.

How does all this happen? Luther's one-word answer is: "faith." (*See also* **Faith**.) The slogan, ever-after associated with Luther, is of course, "justification by faith alone." And this is indeed his watchword: "faith alone justifies without our works" (LW 34, 153). "Then we do nothing and work nothing in order to obtain this righteousness? I reply: Nothing at all" (LW 26, 8). But "faith" must not be understood here as mere intellectual assent to a set of propositional truths. Rather it is for Luther something more like an appropriating, or apprehending, or grasping, or accepting of Christ (LW 34, 153). It is an existential receptivity, in other words, to the love of God revealed in Christ, a trusting confidence that I am the object of this love. "This is the faith that alone justifies us" (LW 34, 110). The love that faith receives is transformative.

This brings us to the vexed question of precisely what is changed in the process of justification: is it merely our relationship to God, or is it rather also something in us? Luther's answer is complex and has given rise to considerable controversy. We can summarize the basics as follows.

First, on the foundation of Romans 4:5 ("his faith is reckoned as righteousness"), Luther developed a doctrine of "imputation." By this he meant that God "counts" or "reckons" or "accepts" us as righteous because of our faith: "these three things are joined together: faith, Christ and acceptance or imputation. . . . God accepts you or accounts you righteous only on account of Christ, in whom you believe. . . . A Christian . . . is some-

one to whom, because of his faith in Christ, God does not impute his sin" (LW 26, 132–133; cf. 26, 260). But the question now is, do we really *become* righteous or does God merely *regard* us as righteous? Melanchthon and other later interpreters took the latter point of view, and this became known as a "forensic" doctrine of justification. But Luther is more complex than this, and it seems dubious that his doctrine is "merely" forensic.

For one thing, we must factor in his view that the justified person is at one and the same time righteous and a sinner (*simul iustus et peccator*). At times Luther used this formula to mean that the justified person is completely righteous and completely sinful simultaneously. "For this is true, that by God's reputing we are truly and totally righteous, even if sin is still present. . . . Thus we are also truly and totally sinners" (WA 39:1, 563, 13–564, 4). Considered from the vantage point of God's forgiveness, we are totally righteous; seen as we are in ourselves, we are totally sinful (LW 34, 166). Standing on its own, this "totalistic" formula (*totaliter iusti . . . totaliter peccatores*) would seem to exclude any notion of moral growth or progress in righteousness.

Elsewhere, however, Luther explicitly embraces the concept of the Christian life as growth in holiness. And he explains how the concept of imputation is compatible with such progress: "a man who is justified is not yet a righteous man, but is in the very movement or journey toward righteousness. Therefore, whoever is justified is still a sinner; and yet he is considered fully and perfectly righteous by God who pardons and is merciful" (LW 34, 152–153; cf. 26, 232). Imputation in effect covers the residual sinfulness of the justified person who is nevertheless growing in righteousness. And Christian righteousness is not "merely" forensic but substantial: "[God] begins in reality to cleanse. For he first purifies by imputation, then he gives the Holy Spirit, through whom he purifies even in substance. Faith cleanses through the remission of sins, the Holy Spirit cleanses through the effect" (LW 34, 168).

Yet one senses that Luther made these statements almost as a concession. He could not bring himself to abandon entirely the doctrines of imputed righteousness and forensic justification. For Luther's most fundamental theological instincts told him that we are in grave peril when we begin to speak about "our" righteousness. As he emphasized from beginning to end, "our" righteousness is not ours but a gift. Already in 1517 he was insisting that its origin is in God: "We do not become righteous by doing righteous deeds but, having been made righteous, we do righteous deeds" (LW 31, 12). In 1535 he was still making the same point: "the mercy of God alone is our righteousness, not our own works" (LW 34, 113). In 1536 he specified the way in which God regards "our" righteousness: "our righteousness is dung in the sight of God. Now if God chooses to adorn dung, he can do so. It does not hurt the sun because it sends its rays into the sewer" (LW 34, 184). In the following year he again traced the source of "our righteousness" to God: "faith makes the person, the person does good works, good works neither make the faith nor the person" (WA 39:1, 283, 18–19). And so on. The point is that the doctrines of imputed righteousness and forensic justification function as safeguards against the universal and unending human proclivity to claim "our" righteousness as our own.

It is obvious from the foregoing that for Luther it is of the highest importance to be clear on the relation of justification to human acts, "works." Works do not cause justification, but rather they show that it has happened (LW 34, 161, 165). They are "necessary for salvation" not in the sense that they cause it, but rather in the sense that their absence reveals a "dead" faith (LW 34, 111, 164, 172). "True faith is not idle. We can, therefore, ascertain and recognize those who have true faith from the effect or from what

follows" (LW 34, 183). Good works are not the cause but the inevitable consequence of justification.

To summarize then, Luther's doctrine of justification entails the following: humans are helpless to overcome their condition of sinfulness; the gospel announces that God loves, accepts, and forgives them in spite of this; faith is the human existential realization that we are the objects of that love, as well as the human receptivity to that love; receiving that love is transformative for humans, fulfilling their most fundamental need and freeing them to love spontaneously.

Luther never tired of expounding the theological meaning of this doctrine, working out its implications, and finding new ways to explain it. But it was not merely an academic, theological exercise for him. Rather, he found great personal comfort in it. Besieged as he was by *Anfechtungen* and self-doubt, this doctrine brought peace and certainty. For it emphasized that we will not ultimately be judged by our works or by our achievements. God's love for us is unconditional, given to us entirely as a gift. That is what our destiny depends on, and for that reason it is guaranteed (LW 26, 387).

Law   As Luther understood it, God's Word (or his self-revelation) comes to humans in two forms: law and gospel. Here the first of these is our focus, though the second will eventually come into play as well, since law cannot be fully grasped without reference to gospel. God, Luther assumed, places certain demands on his human creatures, and these are expressed in law. Thus law is the revelation of the divine will. Humans in different times and places have enshrined this law in specific legal codes, like the Mosaic law or Roman law. These codes, in theory at least, are attempts to apply the divine will to specific times, places, and circumstances. In practice, of course, some do this more adequately than others.

For what reason has God given us law? What is its purpose? In answer to this question, Luther speaks of the law as having two "uses," the "civil" and the "theological" (LW 26, 308). By the "civil use of the law" he means its social and political purpose. Society needs law to restrain the wicked, to ward off an otherwise certain descent into chaos: "For the devil reigns in the world. . . . This is why God has ordained magistrates . . . and all civic ordinances" that "bind the hands of the devil and keep him from raging at will" (LW 26, 308–309). Without the civil law, and above all the threat of punishment attached to such law, civilization would cease to exist. "If there were no worldly government . . . each would necessarily devour the other, as irrational beasts devour one another. . . . [I]t is the function and honor of worldly government to make men out of wild beasts and to prevent men from becoming wild beasts" (LW 46, 237). Human nature is such, Luther believed, that were it not for the constraints of the civil law, the law of the jungle would prevail.

How precisely can we understand God as the origin of this civil law? According to Luther, the law that Moses gave to the Jews was not new. Nor was the law that Christ gave. Both were interpretations, clarifications, and "renewals" of a law antecedent to them, a "natural law" (LW 40, 98). And this was implanted in human beings by God: "There is . . . a single law, effective in all ages and known to all men because it is written in everyone's heart. . . . [T]he Spirit never stops speaking this law in the hearts of all men" (LW 27, 355). This "single law," since it comes from God, is the measure by which all positive legal codes must be evaluated. It is the only eternally binding and universally valid law.

Given that this natural law has been interpreted and applied in a multitude of ways in human history, what is its basic, foundational principle or content? It is the "Golden Rule," or principle of reciprocity: "All men have a certain natural knowledge implanted in their minds (Rom. 2:14–15), by which they know naturally that one should do to others what he wants done to himself (Matt. 7:12). This principle and others like it, which we call the law of nature, are the foundation of human law and of all good works" (LW 27, 53). Jesus' demand that we love our neighbor as ourselves (Matt. 19:19; 22:39; Mark 12:31–33; Luke 10:27) means just this, and in making this demand he was only reminding humans of what they already know: "you do not need any book to instruct and admonish you how you should love your neighbor, for you have the loveliest and best of books about all laws right in your heart" (LW 27, 57). All laws governing human affairs, be they social, political or economic, should be built on this foundation (e.g., economic law in LW 45, 307).

Luther emphasizes that in this matter of law—the making of law, its application, its enforcement, and so on—human reason reigns supreme. Reason must be, he says, "the highest law and the master of all administration of law" (LW 45, 119). In legal matters, no appeal to divine authority is necessary: "In temporal human affairs, human reason suffices" (WA 10:1:1, 531, 6–8; cf. LW 26, 88). Here, in government and the courts, "men must act on the basis of reason—wherein the laws have their origin—for God has subjected temporal rule and all of physical life to reason" (LW 46, 242). Reason is thus a great thing, a precious gift of God, and wholly to be trusted in matters having to do with political, social, and material life. Coupled with human free will, which also is operational in such matters (LW 26, 174), it enables humans to achieve true greatness in making the world and society better, more tolerable, and more livable.

Obedience to the civil law is pleasing to God, according to Luther (LW 26, 11–12; 26, 232; 44, 130). It results in "political" or "civil" righteousness. But does such obedience "justify" human beings, that is, does it result in a kind of righteousness that would make them acceptable to God? Here Luther is emphatic: "Not at all" (LW 26, 308; cf. WA 39:1, 459, 16–17). It does indeed "restrain sin," as Luther puts it, and thus such obedience makes the world a better place. But it does not make the person righteous in the sight of God, because such obedience proceeds out of wholly unworthy motives such as a fear of punishment (or hope for reward): "Does this mean then when the [civil] law restrains sins, it justifies? Not at all. When I refrain . . . I do not do this voluntarily or from the love of virtue but because I am afraid of the sword and of the executioner" (LW 26, 308). A moral "goodness" based on fear (or on greed for that matter) may be worth something in the eyes of the world, but in God's eyes it is worthless. The law, though it is and remains God's Word, is not a way to salvation.

With this we come to what is for Luther the second use of the law, its "theological" or "proper" use. It is to help us understand the depth of our own sinfulness: "the proper use and aim of the Law is to make guilty those who are smug and at peace, so that they may see that they are in danger of sin, wrath, and death, so that they may be terrified and despairing, blanching and quaking at the rustling of a leaf" (LW 26, 148). The law, at its most basic level, demands that we always act out of love for God and out of love for our neighbor. But because humans always act out of love for themselves, they can never do this. The divine demand exceeds the human capacity to fulfill it, and consequently humans experience the demand as oppressive: "the law is a word of destruction, a word of wrath, a word of sadness, a word of grief, a voice of the judge and the defendant, a word of restlessness, a word of curse. . . . Through the law we have nothing except an evil conscience, a restless heart, a troubled breast because of our sins, which the law points out but does not take away. And we ourselves cannot take it away" (LW 31, 231). As the Word of God, the

law reveals the demanding, just, wrathful God who seems to be our enemy (WA 39:1, 370, 13–16). In short, the theological purpose of the law is to drive us to despair, not to despair as such, but to despair of ourselves. For in driving us to despair, Luther thinks, it drives us to Christ (WA 39:1, 456, 7–8; cf. LW 26, 329). In other words, if humans were capable of doing God's will, what need would they have for a savior?

Here already we have broached the crucial theme of the relation of law and gospel. Being able to distinguish between them, Luther said over and over again, is what makes a "real theologian" (LW 26, 115; WA 7, 502, 34–35; WA 39:1, 361, 1–6). To begin with, it must be understood that for Luther, the law/gospel dichotomy is not parallel to the Old Testament/New Testament dichotomy. For one finds plenty of gospel in the Old (e.g., in the covenants) and plenty of law in the New (e.g., in the Sermon on the Mount). Nor is the relation of the two to be understood in a sequential, salvation-historical way as Augustine seems to have understood it: the gospel does not supersede the law. Rather Luther conceives of the law and the gospel as being in a dialectical relationship: they are constantly in tension, and one makes no sense apart from the other. They must be distinguished, but they "neither can nor should be separated. . . . One cannot understand forgiveness of sins unless one first understands what sin is" (WA 39:1, 416, 8–14).

In Luther law and gospel are related as humility is to exaltation, as fear is to hope, as wrath is to mercy (LW 31, 51). Sometimes they are explained with the analogy of illness and medicine. In his 1535 *Lectures on Galatians*, his explanation centers around the categories of "demand" and "gift": "for the law is a taskmaster; it demands that we work. . . . The Gospel, on the contrary, does not demand; it grants freely. . . . Now demanding and granting are exact opposites and cannot exist together. . . . Therefore, if the Gospel is a gift and offers a gift, it does not demand anything. On the other hand, the law does not grant anything; it makes demands on us, and impossible ones at that" (LW 26, 208–209). We might summarize as follows: without the gospel humans would have no knowledge of a savior; and without the law they would not realize that they needed one. Or, we might say, acquittal makes no sense in the absence of accusation.

Luther's disciple Philip Melanchthon, as well as later Lutherans, added to this a "third use of the law": the law, they held, plays an educational and accusatory role also in the lives of the justified. Though Luther himself did not put it in these terms, he clearly envisioned a continuing function of the law in the lives of believers. In the first of the Ninety-five Theses in 1517, he had asserted that the entire life of the believer is to be "one of repentance" (LW 31, 83). Here the young Luther was taking for granted the law's continuing accusatory function in the lives of Christians. In 1538 the older Luther had not changed his view on this: "Insofar as Christ is made alive in us, we are to that extent without the law, sin, and death. Insofar as he is not made alive in us, we are to that extent still under the law, sin, and death" (WA 39:1, 356, 15–18). Christians, insofar as they are "at the same time righteous and sinners" (simul iustus et peccator), remain under the law.

Moreover, Luther held that the law teaches the justified how to live. The law works, he said, "to order that sort of new life which those who have become saints and new persons ought to enter upon" (WA 39:1, 542, 14–15; cf. 39:1, 485, 16–20; even if Melanchthon's heavy editorial hand is present in some of these statements, they still express Luther's sentiment). The law, "given to me for my life," can become "precious and good" (LW 22, 144). Whether or not we call this a "third use of the law," what is clear is that for Luther it has a continuing relevance for the lives of Christians.

From Luther's point of view there are two ways that the Christian understanding of the law can be distorted. The first is in the direction of legalism, and Luther spent virtually his entire career struggling against this. To his mind, this was the error of Roman Catholicism. In this tradition, Christianity had been transformed into a religion of law: it revolved entirely around the following of rules. Rightly understood, Luther thought, the gospel of Jesus Christ frees us from all such oppressive legal structures (the classical statement of this is his 1520 treatise, On The Freedom of a Christian, LW 31, 333–377).

In taking this position, Luther was already planting the seeds of a second distortion, one on the other end of the theological spectrum—antinomianism. Beginning already in 1527, and continuing more pointedly in the years 1537–40, some of Luther's followers took the position that the law has been abrogated in its entirety, that it has no function for Christians, that it need not be preached. As Luther put it, these antinomians (mostly John Agricola) "dare to expel the law of God or the Ten Commandments from the church and assign them to city hall" (LW 47, 107). The Decalogue may be a fine guideline for civic virtue, but it has nothing to do with Christianity.

These antinomians claimed to derive their position from Luther himself. As he now took up the pen against them, Luther conceded that there was some truth to this: his early struggle had been directed against Roman Catholic legalism and for this reason he had one-sidedly emphasized the gospel as the end of the law: "To the consciences of men so oppressed, terrified, miserable, anxious, and afflicted, there was no need to inculcate the law. Now, however," he continued, "when the times are very dissimilar from those under the pope," that is, when people are smug and self-righteous, the law must be preached (LW 47, 104–105). "Our view hitherto has been and ought to be this salutary one—if you see the afflicted and contrite, preach grace as much as you can. But not to the secure, the slothful, the harlots, the adulterers, and blasphemers" (LW 47, 105). The context, in other words, must determine one's emphasis.

Theology, if it could be done in a vacuum, would find the perfect *via media*: between legalism and antinomianism; between optimism and pessimism about human nature; between emphasizing God's demanding justice and his loving mercy; between encouraging "unbelieving workers" and "workless believers" (LW 24, 249). In characterizing Luther's theology, one does not immediately think of adjectives such as "balanced." But it may have been precisely that, had he not been doing it in the real world.

Lord's Supper The Lord's Supper, or eucharist, played a central role in Luther's personal religious life and in his theology. His lifelong conviction was that in it, the divine mysteriously becomes present to us. First as a friar and then as a young priest, Luther experienced this as troubling, indeed terrifying. Later, by the 1520s, and then to the end of his life, the Lord's Supper became for him an indispensable source of strength, peace, consolation, and comfort. Given this experiential dimension, it is not surprising that Luther invested major effort in trying to understand what precisely it is and how it works.

His starting point was the medieval inheritance: building on the Augustinian foundation, the scholastics from Peter Lombard to Thomas Aquinas, John Duns Scotus, and others had constructed an elaborate and intricate eucharistic theological tradition. This had been summarized in all its complexity in Gabriel Biel's massive *Exposition of the Canon of the Mass* (1488), a work that Luther read assiduously as a student. Besides this theological tradition, Luther was also familiar with the church hierarchy's official pronouncements: for example, Pope Nicholas II's repudiation in 1059 of Berengar of Tours' "spiritualist" understanding of Christ's presence; the 1215 decree of the Fourth Lateran

Council with its application of the language of sacrifice to the mass; the 1439 decree of the Council of Florence with its repeated stress on worthy reception of the sacrament; and so forth. Luther's immersion in this tradition of eucharistic theology and dogma obviously shaped what he had to say on the subject, in both positive and negative ways.

Luther's appropriation of this inheritance remained largely uncritical up to 1519. Late that year he published a sermon entitled *The Blessed Sacrament of the Holy and True Body of Christ, and the Brotherhoods* (LW 35, 49–73). This work makes clear that he had been thinking critically about the subject for some time. In many particulars the tradition is affirmed, but on at least two fronts Luther appears to be groping toward something significantly new. First, in attempting to define what a sacrament is, Luther designates faith as one of its constitutive elements (LW 35, 60), a point that he will make again with much greater clarity. Second, and related to this, Luther rejects the scholastic axiom that sacraments have their effect *ex opere operato* (the sheer performance of the act brings about the effect, the infusion of grace). This Luther repudiates, not because he sides with the Donatist position (that the personal worthiness of the minister of the sacrament has something to do with its validity), but rather because he thinks the axiom excludes the faith of the recipient (LW 35, 63–64).

What is new, though inchoate and somewhat confused, in this 1519 sermon reemerges with greater clarity in a 1520 work entitled *A Treatise on the New Testament, that is, the Holy Mass* (LW 35, 79–111). Here the basic interpretive category is "testament": the eucharist originated as a bequest of forgiveness from Christ, made when he was about to die (LW 35, 84). It is composed of six elements: the testator (Christ), the heirs (Christians), the testament (the words of Christ at the Last Supper), the seal or sign (the bread and wine, under which are Christ's body and blood), the blessing bequeathed (forgiveness of sins and eternal life), and the duty (the acceptance of faith) (LW 35, 86–87). As a testament, the Lord's Supper is the promise of a gift, signified by bread and wine, and received by faith.

On the basis of this definition, Luther argues, one can easily deduce which eucharistic practices are in fact abuses. Luther gives his readers an extended list:

1. When the words of consecration are spoken quietly or in Latin, Christians cannot hear the testament or accept it (LW 35, 90–92).
2. Whenever the mass is made into a "work," its meaning is lost: "a testament is not a *beneficium acceptum, sed datum*; it does not take benefit from us but brings benefit to us" (LW 35, 93).
3. Whenever the mass is understood as a sacrifice, its character as testament and gift is lost (LW 35, 97).
4. Masses said for souls in purgatory or for the dead imply that the mass is something humans give to God, the opposite of what it really is (LW 35, 102).
5. Mass "in one kind" is wrong, "though this does not matter much, since the word is more important than the sign" (LW 35, 106).
6. When the mass is made into "a kind of magic" for warding off evil or for healing and so forth, it is seriously misunderstood (LW 35, 107).
7. When the mass is used for raising money, it is abused.
8. The opinion that some masses are more powerful than others is based on a misunderstanding (LW 35, 107–108).
9. Private masses and endowed masses contradict the true meaning of the Lord's Supper (LW 35, 108).

This was Luther's earliest listing of abuses connected with the eucharist. In subsequent writings he was to repeat the list, amplify and illustrate it, and even write entire treatises on one or the other. What remained constant to the end of his life was his insistence on one error as the most fundamental of all: it is the view of the mass as something we give to God, a "work" (see above, no. 2). This mistake is a disastrous one. Indeed, the opposite is true: it is something God promises to give to us.

Luther achieved an even greater clarity in another 1520 work, *The Babylonian Captivity of the Church*, written shortly after *A Treatise on the New Testament*. Here we find, first, a shift in emphasis: Luther now launches a major polemic against communion in one kind (LW 36, 19–28). We also find in this work something new, namely an attack on transubstantiation. This doctrine, Luther argues, "rests neither on the Scriptures nor on reason" (LW 36, 31). It makes more sense to hold that the bread and body of Christ, and the wine and blood of Christ, are there simultaneously (LW 36, 35). But Luther's point is that this should not be dogmatized—made into an article of faith. Such theological understandings are optional: "I permit other men to follow the other opinion" (LW 36, 35). Third, this work leaves no room for doubt about what Luther sees as the place where the tradition went astray: the "worst captivity" is the understanding of the mass as a "work" or sacrifice. From this, all manner of abuses have followed (LW 36, 35–36).

This newfound analytic clarity manifests itself in a work from the following year, *The Misuse of the Mass*: "To make a sacrifice of the sacrament is . . . to change completely its nature and character. . . . [S]acrifice and promise are further apart than sunrise and sunset" (LW 36, 168–169). What is new in this work is Luther's attempt to relate misunderstandings of the eucharist to misunderstandings of the priesthood. If all Christians are priests equally (*see* **Universal Priesthood**), then the "papal priesthood" is a fraud (LW 36, 139, 142). Priests have "invented" the mass to enhance their "own greed and honor," to control and dominate the laity (LW 36, 154 and 159). All of them should quit (LW 36, 144). The true task of a "priest" is not to sacrifice but to preach (LW 36, 148).

Late in 1521 Andreas Bodenstein von Karlstadt and others began insisting on reforms in the administration of the Lord's Supper in Wittenberg. By April of 1522 Luther had published *On Receiving Both Kinds in the Sacrament*. In this work, while he took nothing back, he advocated a slower, more gradual introduction of reforms for the sake of simple believers with weak consciences. In all external practices, Christian liberty ought to be the watchword: "so long as we are Christians, we are lords over such human commandments, so far as our consciences are involved. And we are in duty bound to risk our necks for it and not to give up our liberty" (LW 36, 243). What precisely are these "externals" that are optional? Again, the list is substantial: for example, laypeople receiving communion with the hands (LW 36, 244), chanting and vestments, liturgy in Latin, receiving communion in one kind or both (254–55), frequency of celebration, requirement of private confession (258), married priests (260), the eucharistic fast (261). On all these questions and more, Luther had his own opinion. But the point here is that rules should not be made about such things. Rather we should err on the side of Christian liberty (LW 36, 343; 350).

The question of venerating the consecrated elements was a case in point, and Luther addressed himself to this in his 1523 essay *The Adoration of the Sacrament*. His personal preference was to avoid it. But nobody can make rules: "Free, free it must be, according as one is disposed in his heart and has opportunity" (LW 36, 295).

If redefining the sacrament and correcting abuses dominate in Luther's writings up to this point, his focus shifted in the next years (1523–26) to more strictly liturgical considerations. In the spring of 1523 he announced that the daily mass in Wittenberg had been

discontinued, actually replaced by daily services of readings and preaching, "for the Word is important and not the mass" (LW 53, 12–13). Later that year Luther produced his own first liturgy, *An Order of Mass and Communion for the Church at Wittenberg* (LW 53, 19–40). It retained many traditional elements, most notably Latin—only the hymns and the sermon were to be in German. As for the rest, it was somewhat shortened and simplified, with all the references to sacrifice deleted. Again, Luther emphasized freedom: on these liturgical issues, very little should be made obligatory (LW 53, 30).

Luther issued his most extended critique of the traditional "canon" of the mass in a 1525 work, *The Abomination of the Secret Mass* (LW 36, 311–328). Here he focused above all on two features that he insisted were *not* optional. The first was the practice of whispering the words of consecration, words that were supposedly too holy for the laity to hear. The second was the language of sacrifice. Both, Luther insisted, must be abandoned.

Finally, in 1526, Luther issued his own *German Mass and Order of Service* (LW 53, 61–90). A German mass (produced by others) had been celebrated at Wittenberg since 1521. Here now was Luther's version. It was not a repudiation of the Latin mass: Latin, Luther said, is very good for people who understand it, that is, university people (LW 53, 62–63). But the vernacular is obviously better for "the unlearned lay folk" (LW 53, 63). And, Luther reminds his readers, preaching—not the liturgy of the Lord's Supper—is "the most important part of divine service" (LW 53, 68). Nevertheless, it was this German liturgy that became the hallmark of the Reformation as it spread from town to town in the German-speaking territories.

In the years after 1526, liturgical issues fade in Luther's writings, and a major theological issue moves to the fore: the doctrine of the "real presence." Opponents of all kinds had been pressing Luther in this regard for some time: between 1524 and 1527 there appeared at least twenty-four printed attacks on his view of the Lord's Supper. More and more, they focused on the issue of the real presence. Beginning in 1526, and continuing until 1528, Luther responded in three major writings.

The first, directed against Karlstadt, Huldrych Zwingli, and John Oecolampadius, was his 1526 work *The Sacrament of the Body and Blood of Christ—Against the Fanatics*. Luther defines the question succinctly: these people say "that Christ's body and blood are not present in the bread and wine" (LW 36, 335). They attack the traditional doctrine of the real presence as irrational, "not fitting" (LW 36, 228). Luther's answer is clear from the outset: they understand this belief (that Christ's body is really present) literally, and thus they make nonsense out of it. "Just as he [Christ] enters the heart without breaking a hole in it, but is comprehended only through the word and hearing, so also he enters into the bread without needing to make any hole in it" (LW 36, 341). The analogy is revealing: Christ is present in the bread in the way he is present in the human heart—really but not literally. In fact, Luther insists, Christ is actually present everywhere. (This doctrine of Christ's ubiquity was further developed by Luther in the following years.) But he wants humans to find him in his word: "He [Christ] is present everywhere, but he does not wish that you grope for him everywhere. Grope rather where the word is and you will lay hold of him in the right way" (LW 36, 342). But if this is the case, if Christ is present in the preaching of the gospel, what then is the need for his presence in the sacrament? Luther's answer: "although the same thing is present in the sermon as in the sacrament, here there is the advantage that it is directed at definite individuals" (LW 36, 348). Christ's presence is individualized and particularized in the sacrament. Here he becomes present—really, bodily (though not literally)—for me.

The second important work from this period is the much lengthier 1527 treatise *That These Words of Christ, "This Is My Body," etc., Still Stand Firm Against the Fanatics*. The issue is the same, though here Luther is fixated on the Gospels' account of Jesus' words at the Last Supper, "This is my body" (Matt. 26:26; Mark 14:22). For Zwingli, the word "is" means "represents," while for Oecolampadius it means "is a sign of" (LW 37, 28, and 34). Both are crude literalists, basing their argument on the doctrine of the ascension. Since Christ "ascended into heaven and is seated at the right hand of the Father," his body can be nowhere else (LW 37, 46). Luther contends, on the other hand, that the ascension and sitting at the right hand of the Father is by no means to be taken literally (LW 37, 55–57). (*See also* **Ascension**.) In fact, Christ is present everywhere, but not in a literal way: for example, he is not present in the bread in the way that bread is present in a basket, but rather in the way that God is present in our hearts (LW 37, 65). The "fanatics" speak of the body of Christ "no differently than if it were perishable, digestible, masticable meat, such as one buys in a butcher shop and cooks in the kitchen" (LW 37, 124). This is *not* what the doctrine of the real presence means. Christ is present everywhere, Luther argues, but in the sacramental bread he is "present for you" (LW 37, 67–68). We eat the body and bread together, the body spiritually with the heart, the bread physically with the mouth (LW 37, 85, and 93).

The third major work in which Luther addressed this issue was in his *Confession Concerning Christ's Supper* (1528). Lengthy and disorganized, wordy and abusive, this work repeated much of what he had said before. What is new here is a further development of the doctrine of the ubiquity (omnipresence) of Christ. For this, Luther falls back on his scholastic past, in particular the work of William of Ockham and Biel. Because Christ's human and divine natures are inseparable, Luther argues, his humanity is present wherever his divinity is present. In the ascension, both became ubiquitous. Thus "Christ's body is everywhere because it is at the right hand of God which is everywhere, although we do not know how that occurs" (LW 37, 214). In the sacrament, Christ's ubiquitous body is united with the bread "for us." Avoiding the language of "substance" (e.g., transubstantiation, consubstantiation), Luther's term for this is a "sacramental union" (*unio sacramentalis*; LW 37, 299–301).

The controversy came to an end, or better, reached a stalemate, in 1529. From October 1 to 4, Luther and some supporters met with Zwingli and his colleagues at Marburg. Seven different observers wrote accounts of the proceedings, and all agree that no consensus was reached. Luther formulated certain "Marburg Articles" and Zwingli signed. Most notable among them was the following:

> [W]e all believe and hold . . . that the sacrament of the altar is a sacrament of the true body and blood of Jesus Christ and that the spiritual partaking of the same body and blood is especially necessary for every Christian. . . . And although at this time, we have not reached an agreement as to whether the true body and blood of Christ are bodily present in the bread and the wine, each side should show Christian love to the other side insofar as conscience will permit. (LW 38, 88)

(Two years previously Luther had advised his followers *not* to "practice Christian unity with them and extend Christian love to them"; LW 37, 27.)

With this, the development of Luther's views on the Lord's Supper was essentially complete. He did not, however, suspend his writing on the subject. Some of these later writings on the topic are of great value. For instance, his 1529 catechisms included the clearest of summaries, largely devoid of polemic (BC 362–64, 467–76). In 1530 there appeared a primarily devotional work on the subject (LW 38, 97–137).

On the other hand, angry polemical works continued to appear as well. In 1533 *The Private Mass and the Consecration of Priests* (LW 38, 147–214) stressed the communal nature of the Lord's Supper. In fact, private masses are no sacraments at all. In 1535, in his *Disputation Theses Against the Council of Constance*, Luther utterly abandoned his soft position on communion in both kinds: a church that condemns what Christ commands is an "abomination of the antichrist and furious whore of the devil" (WA 39:1, 16, 20–24). In 1537 the Smalcald Articles drew the starkest distinction between the "terrible abomination" of the Roman mass and "the sacrament administered according to Christ's institution" (BC 301–2). Luther's last substantial work on the subject was his 1544 *Brief Confession Concerning the Holy Supper* (LW 38, 287–319), an attack on Caspar Schwenckfeld, denier of the real presence, "a stupid fool, who is possessed by the devil, has no understanding and doesn't know what he is mumbling about" (LW 38, 282).

The ugly, violently abusive language of the older Luther with regard to the Lord's Supper may well strike the modern reader as inappropriate, if not downright anomalous. After all, he is writing about the rite though which Christians receive "forgiveness of sin, life, and salvation," as he said in his Small Catechism (BC 362). How can this be reconciled with the language of hate? Perhaps in the final analysis it cannot be; no excuses should be made for Luther in this regard. At the same time, we need to understand why Luther felt so strongly about this. If we deny that Christ becomes present in this rite, or if we transform the rite into an instrument of power, control, and domination, then it no longer mediates "forgiveness of sin, life, and salvation." Thus, from his point of view, everything is at stake here.

Marriage If we are to understand Luther, we must remember that many of his assumptions, widely shared by his sixteenth-century contemporaries, differ dramatically from our own. Three in particular bear on the topic of marriage: first, women are in important ways inferior to men; second, wives are to be submissive to husbands; and third, marriage has the twofold purpose of generating offspring and fostering love in a covenant of fidelity. These were foundational to Luther's worldview, and he held to them from beginning to end.

On other issues surrounding marriage, Luther's thought underwent a dramatic development between 1519 and the time of his own marriage in 1525. This development closely parallels changes in his understanding of human sexuality and his escalating critique of the celibate lifestyle.

He first expressed himself at length on the subject in his 1519 *Sermon on the Estate of Marriage* (LW 44, 3–14). The view Luther expresses here falls entirely within the medieval tradition of male, celibate, clerical thinking on marriage. The institution was established by God and therefore it must be affirmed as good. The fall, however, distorted human sexuality and thereby also corrupted marriage. Sex, here referred to as "the wicked lust of the flesh" (LW 44, 10), is the disease; and marriage, Luther says, "may be likened to a hospital for incurables which prevents inmates from falling into a graver sin" (LW 44, 9). In other words, marriage after the fall exists for the sake of those who cannot abstain from sex. Its function is to control the dangers of sex, and, to some extent, to sanitize its filth.

We can witness the beginning of Luther's break with this view in his *Babylonian Captivity of the Church* (1520). Here, in the name of Christian liberty, he rejects the vast panoply of canon law concerning marriage: "Does the pope set up laws? Let him set them up for himself, and keep hands off my liberty" (LW 36, 102). We can notice too in this work that the tone in which he

speaks of sexuality has changed: here terms like "natural emotions" replace "wicked lust of the flesh" (LW 36, 104). Most importantly, Luther here rejects the sacramental status of matrimony. It was not instituted by Christ, nor does it confer grace. Rather it was instituted by God in creation, and it exists everywhere, even outside the church (LW 36, 92–95). For Luther, as we shall see, the denial of marriage's sacramentality is by no means a devaluation of marriage but the opposite.

By 1522 we find in Luther a new emphasis on sexual feelings as natural, necessary, and created by God (LW 39, 297; 45, 18). In *The Estate of Marriage* Luther makes the point that God instructed Adam and Eve to "be fruitful and multiply": sexual desire, therefore, is not "wicked lust" but is God's ordinance "implanted in us." Almost all humans are incapable of resisting this "ordinance of God within them," and indeed, why should they? (LW 45, 19, and 21). In certain particular circumstances, Luther thinks, celibacy may be preferable to marriage: "In itself, however, the celibate life is far inferior" (LW 45, 47). Marriage still functions here as a safeguard against sexuality's destructive power, but Luther has come a long way from marriage understood as a "hospital for incurables."

In response to Luther's arguments, increasing numbers of nuns, monks, friars, and priests were now getting married. In Luther himself, now that the intellectual obstacles to marriage had been overcome, one senses a progressive breakdown of the personal, emotional barriers. In 1522 he said that not "one in a thousand" can remain celibate (WA 10:2, 279, 19–21), and in 1523 he made that one in a hundred thousand (WA 12, 115, 20–21). In 1524 he gave considerable thought to the role of one's parents in marriage matters (LW 45, 385–393). And in March of 1525 he again argued that sexual desire and passion is "God's word and work" (WA 18, 275, 19–28). How perverse then that the effect of the Roman system was to attach shame to the married state: being ashamed of marriage, he argued, is really being ashamed of one's sexuality, and this in turn is being ashamed of our humanity. "[I]t is the god of the world, the devil, who so slanders the marital state and has made it shameful. . . . [I]t would be better to marry in order to spite him" (WA 18, 277, 32–36). His advice then to those who are dithering is: "Put the doubts out of your mind and take the plunge. Your body demands it. God wills it and drives you to it" (WA 18, 276, 34–277, 1).

One senses that he was speaking to himself, for a few months later, on June 13, he married Katherine von Bora, a former nun. They had six children, two of whom died at a young age, and had nieces, students, and others living in their home almost continually. Katherine, who was perhaps as strong-willed as Luther, seems to have ruled all aspects of home and family life. An abundance of surviving letters and recorded table talk all point toward a happy marriage, with plenty of good humor, gentle teasing, and disagreements tempered by genuine affection.

From this point on, Luther's praise of married life is continual and extravagant. An example of this is found in his Large Catechism. Here, in opposition to the denigration of marriage implicit in a celibate ecclesiastical culture, Luther insists that marriage is the noblest and most richly blessed of all walks of life: "it is not a walk of life to be placed on the same level with all the others, but it is before and above them all, whether those of emperor, princes, bishops, or any other" (BC 414). It can be difficult, Luther admits: "there is no kind of life which, once undertaken, isn't a matter of regret at times" (LW 54, nr. 3508, 218). As for himself, he said, "If I ever have to get married again, I will hew myself an obedient one [wife] out of stone" (WATR 2, nr. 2034, 300, 9–11). Still, marriage is vastly superior to any other lifestyle.

On the matter of the goodness of sexuality within marriage, one can find in the later Luther statements that sound regressive. Thus in his late Lectures on Genesis (1535–45), the traditional language of shame and filth surfaces from time to time (e.g., LW 5, 37–38). Far more typical, however, is a resounding affirmation of its goodness. For example, Luther was apparently often approached with the question of whether it is legitimate to marry for reasons of sexual desire. In 1532 he responded, "This is ridiculous, a question that contradicts both Scripture and nature." The sexual union of marriage partners, he added, "is also most pleasing to him [God]." The desire for one's spouse is from God, and it should continue as long as possible. Loss of desire for one's spouse, sexual boredom, is the work of the devil (LW 21, 89). This perspective is what dominates.

Along with it, one finds in Luther the highest praise for marital fidelity. True love, he thinks, implies a spontaneous, wholehearted faithfulness to one's spouse (BC 415). On seeing another beautiful woman, Luther says, a man should think thus: "In my wife at home I have a lovelier adornment . . . even though she may not have a beautiful body or may have other failings. . . . This is the one whom God has granted to me and put into my arms. . . . Then why should I despise this precious gift of God and take up with someone else?" (LW 21, 87). Adultery is wrong because it harms one's spouse (BC 413) and both parties involved (LW 45, 43).

Though Luther wrote an Order of Marriage for Common Pastors in 1529 (LW 53, 111–115), and a 1530 work dealing mainly with the problem of engagements (LW 46, 259–319), he was convinced that marriage was a largely secular matter. It was important, and ordained by God, but it should not be regulated by the church. "For marriage is a rather secular and outward thing, having to do with . . . matters that belong to the realm of the government, all of which have been completely subjected to reason" (LW 21, 93). Pastors may pronounce a blessing over a marriage in church, marriage bans may be published in church, and so forth, but the church's role is not indispensable. Its business is not to make rules and laws about marriage but rather to advise and comfort troubled consciences (LW 46, 317). In this way too Luther's view of marriage was a departure from that of the medieval church.

Mary Woven into the rich tapestry of late medieval religious life were certain Marian strands—some liturgical, some devotional, some theological. For instance, there was the relatively new devotion to St. Anne, Mary's mother (according to legend). The rosary was much older, but experiencing an unprecedented surge in popularity. New titles such as *Mater Dolorosa* (Mother of Sorrows) accompanied new meditations such as the one focused on the cosuffering of Mary at the cross. New Marian feasts found their way onto the liturgical calendar, as Mary was not only prayed to but held up as the supreme exemplar of Christian virtue. Preachers explained how Mary's mercy offsets the stern justice that will be meted out by her son on judgment day. Theologians argued vehemently over doctrinal issues like the immaculate conception and the assumption. While largely agreeing on her role as intercessor on behalf of poor sinners, theologians debated the appropriateness of titles like "mediatrix" and even "co-redemptrix."

This tapestry, with all these Marian strands and many more, Luther made his own, first as a child and then as a novice monk and theological student. Later, as a reformer, Luther dealt with these Marian issues in a differentiated way. Some of the threads, he thought, had no place in the tapestry whatsoever, and he rudely yanked them out. Others he was less sure about and he left them basically untouched. Still others he carefully altered, adjusting their place in the tapestry. Finally, some he enthusiastically celebrated and cultivated to the end of his life.

Mary's virginal status before the birth of Jesus (*ante partum*) was not an open question: Christians had always affirmed this on the basis of the New Testament and the creeds, and so too did Luther. Gradually, however, in addition to this, the tradition had come to embrace two further affirmations in this regard: Mary's virginity remained intact in the birth process (*in partu*), and to the end of her life (*post partum*). Thus the devotional title "Mary, ever virgin," became possible. Luther appears to have embraced this traditional belief and never abandoned it. In a sermon from 1522, he spoke favorably of virginity *in partu*: Mary "gave birth without sin, without shame, without pain, and without injury, as she also conceived without sin" (WA 10:1:1, 67, 6–9). Then in the following year, in his treatise *That Jesus Christ Was Born a Jew*, he noted Scripture's silence on the question of virginity *post partum* (LW 45, 205), and concluded: "we should be satisfied simply to hold that she remained a virgin after the birth of Christ because Scripture does not state or indicate that she lost her virginity" (LW 45, 206; cf. 45, 212). Nothing in the later Luther suggests that he changed his mind about this. Indeed, a table talk recorded in 1539 seems to support this (WATR 4, nr. 4435, 311, 17–22). Even more clearly, he endorses virginity *post partum* in two sermons from 1540 (WA 49, 174, 4–6; 49, 182, 6–14).

Luther weighed in, though less clearly, on another theological issue, the immaculate conception. The point in question was whether Mary had inherited original sin: for two centuries Dominicans had argued in the affirmative against the Franciscans, who said she was conceived "immaculately," that is, without original sin. Initially, in his 1521 *Commentary on the Magnificat*, Luther hinted that he supported the "immaculatist" position (LW 21, 327). He took the issue up again, in a more thorough way, in a sermon in 1527. Here he acknowledged that "there is not a single letter about it [the immaculate conception] in the Gospels or elsewhere in the Scriptures" (WA 17:2, 280, 19–20). His view rested on the then current theory of human conception as being twofold: the "first conception," it was thought, involves the physical alone and takes place in the sex act, while the "second conception" takes place later and involves God infusing a soul into the physical body, the beginning of "human life." Thus Luther says that Mary "was cleansed from original sin" (WA 17:2, 288, 11), referring to the "first conception." And he also says: "from the first moment that she began to live, she was without any sin" (WA 17:2, 288, 13–14), referring to the "second conception." Did Luther then subscribe to a belief in the immaculate conception? No simple answer is possible. We can say that at this stage he did not repudiate it. But he added (in the same passage) that since Scripture is silent, this belief cannot be required of Christians. To that must be added only one more fleeting reference from a sermon in 1540: "Mary was born of parents in sin just like other human beings" (WA 49, 173, 9–10). Despite Luther's ambiguity here, we should not lose sight of the following: perhaps on the immaculate conception issue, and certainly on the virginity *post partem* issue, Luther endorsed beliefs that he knew were not to be found in Scripture. This must be factored into our understanding of his *sola scriptura* principle.

The assumption, Mary's ascension into heaven at the end of her life, was not an official church teaching, but it was marked by a feast day on the liturgical calendar. Luther preached an Assumption Day sermon for the last time in 1522: we must believe that Mary is in heaven, he said, but as to how she got there, we must confess that we do not know (WA 10:3, 269, 18–20). His view is expressed again, with great clarity, in a sermon from 1544: "The feast of the ascension of Mary is completely papist, that is, full of blasphemy and established without any grounding in Scripture" (WA 52, 681, 6–7).

Like the vast majority of late medieval Christians, the young Luther assumed that the invocation of the saints, and therefore also of Mary, was proper and efficacious. In a 1519 sermon we find Luther commending this practice, above all for Christians on their deathbeds: they should "invoke all the holy angels and especially their [guardian] angel and the mother of God" (WA 2, 696, 24–25). In 1521, in his *Commentary on the Magnificat*, we find a more qualified endorsement: "We ought to call upon her, that for her sake God may grant and do what we request. Thus also all other saints are to be invoked" (LW 21, 329). But, Luther repeatedly insists, she cannot actually give, or do, anything. God alone gives all and does all (LW 21, 328–329). Shortly thereafter, in 1523, Luther suggested that the *Ave Maria* should be "laid aside" because it is commonly misunderstood as a prayer (WA 11, 60, 37–61, 1). By the time he formulated the Smalcald Articles in 1537, he could reject invocation of the saints (and of Mary) as "one of the abuses of the Antichrist" (BC 305).

For Luther, the issue was not whether Mary or the saints in heaven pray for us. He concluded his 1521 *Commentary on the Magnificat* with a positive reference to Mary's intercession (LW 21, 355), and even in his 1537 Smalcald Articles he conceded that "perhaps" the saints in heaven pray for us (BC 305). The problem rather is that our prayers to Mary make her into a mediator between us and her son: Mary is then understood as merciful and Christ as the angry judge. And Mary can convince her son to be merciful to us. This scenario was exemplified, in Luther's opinion, by Bernard of Clairvaux's famous vision of Mary baring her breasts to the adult Christ, as though to remind him of his obligation to her (WA 21, 65, 29–34). This view is what Luther firmly rejected, at least from 1521 on (WA 7, 568, 27–32; 10:3, 325, 37).

To elevate Mary from the ordinariness of the human situation to intercessor, then mediator, and sometimes even co-redemptrix, Luther argued, was to detract from Christ and diminish his role (LW 21, 322). If Mary mediates in some way, Christ is no longer the sole mediator, and if Mary is co-redemptrix, Christ is no longer the sole redeemer. In the final analysis, Luther argued, this kind of thinking is idolatrous: Marian devotees have elevated Mary so high that they have made a goddess out of her (WA 10:3, 315, 8–13; cf. LW 21, 323–324; BC 306).

What Luther retained and promoted from among the various features of late medieval Marian piety was the depiction of Mary as exemplar of Christian virtue. One finds this already in his deeply devotional Commentary on the Magnificat (1521). Here Luther focused on Mary's lowliness, her humility. Not that this made Mary in some way worthy or meritorious; rather it points in every way to the perfectly gratuitous nature of God's favor (LW 21, 298; 21, 322). In later works, above all in sermons, Luther came back to the theme repeatedly. Only as fully human, he argued, can Mary function as an example for us. Thus we see that she was not perfect: when her son was missing, she looked in the wrong place for him (WA 12, 413, 36–414, 3); and at the Cana wedding she got rather too assertive with her son (WA 21, 63, 37–64, 1). "Mother of God"—yes, but human, all too human, nevertheless (Luther affirmed the theotokos title throughout his life). Besides humility, Mary was an example for us of faith (WA 15, 478, 23–25), obedience (WA 52, 150, 4–9), chastity and modesty (WA 52, 682, 33–683, 3), and so forth.

Ministerial/Pastoral Office

Luther's understanding of the office of minister or pastor has its foundation in his 1520 classic, The Babylonian Captivity of the Church. Here is where he first developed the concept of "universal priesthood": all believers are "priests" by virtue of their baptism. At the same time, he insisted, "no one may make use of this power except by the consent of the community or by the call of a superior" (LW 36, 116). In theory all Christians could function as ministers or pastors, but in practice they should not, without being called.

This basic concept was developed by Luther in two works from 1523, first in Concerning the Ministry. Here Luther makes the small point that the name of the office should be "servant" or "minister" rather than "priest" (LW 40, 35). More importantly, he emphasizes that this office exists for the sake of order. One person "shall be chosen or approved who, in the name of all with these rights, shall perform these functions publicly. Otherwise there might be shameful confusion among the people of God" (LW 40, 34). The second work is entitled That a Christian Assembly or Congregation Has the Right and Power to Judge All Teaching and to Call, Appoint, and Dismiss Teachers, Established and Proven by Scripture. In this work Luther emphasizes the biblical foundation of his universal priesthood doctrine, and points out some of its implications. For instance, it empowers Christians to contradict, even defy, bishops or scholars or councils (LW 39, 306). And it is because of the universal priesthood that Christians are qualified and authorized to call their own pastors, as well as pass judgment on them. The ministerial/pastoral office—the "office of preaching"—is "the highest office in Christendom" (LW 39, 314). Congregations call individuals to it (LW 39, 310), and bishops should ordain only those who have been called in this way (LW 39, 311).

What we find in the mid–1520s and later in Luther is not so much development on this issue as shifts in emphasis. These were largely due to his encounter with the Reformation's "left wing": the

Zwickau Prophets, Andreas Boden-stein von Karlstadt, Thomas Müntzer, the Anabaptists, "spiritualists," and so forth. In one way or another, these devalued (or seemed to Luther to devalue) the church's institutional/structural/organizational aspect. In response to this challenge, Luther's later teaching on the office of minister or pastor centers on five emphases.

First, the call is crucial. Those who preach without one are denounced in the strongest terms (e.g., in his 1532 *Commentary on Psalm 82*; LW 13, 63–65). And in our age the call does not come as a private revelation from God. Rather it is mediated, as Luther explained in his 1535 *Lectures on Galatians*: "God calls in two ways, either by means or without means. Today he calls all of us into the ministry of the word by a mediated call, that is, one that comes through means, namely, through man. But the apostles were called immediately by Christ himself" (LW 26, 17). And because it is mediated, it is verifiable. Self-appointed ministers are unacceptable.

Second, Luther emphasizes that although the call is mediated through humans, it comes ultimately from God. Thus he is explicit in naming this calling "divine" (LW 26, 17). Ephesians 4:11 makes clear, according to Luther, that the ministerial/pastoral office is instituted by God (LW 37, 364).

Third, it follows from this that pastors or ministers have authority in the church. Luther can go so far as to say that "the mouth of every pastor is the mouth of Christ" (in a sermon of 1534; WA 37, 381, 13–14). This is of course not an absolute authority. And Luther's assertion is not a retraction of his universal priesthood doctrine, which makes all Christians spiritual equals. Rather, for Luther, pastors have authority because, and insofar as, it is conceded to them by other Christians (see LW 41, 154, quoted below).

Fourth, the office of minister or pastor is one of the "marks" of the church (*see* **Church**). Though Luther enumer-

ated these marks differently at different stages of his career, the later Luther includes this (along with the Word of God, baptism, the Lord's Supper, and penance): "the church is recognized externally by the fact that it consecrates or calls ministers, or has offices that it is to administer. There must be bishops, pastors, or preachers, who publicly and privately give, administer, and use the aforementioned four things or holy possessions in behalf of and in the name of the church, or rather by reason of their institution by Christ" (LW 41, 154; cf. 41, 196). Where this office is missing, the church lacks one of its essential, constitutive features.

Finally, all of this is for the sake of order and the avoidance of chaos.

> There must be bishops, pastors, or preachers. . . . The people as a whole cannot do these things, but must entrust or have them entrusted to one person. Otherwise, what would happen if everyone wanted to speak or administer, and no one wanted to give way to the other? It must be entrusted to one person, and he alone should be allowed to preach, to baptize, to absolve, and to administer the sacraments. The others should be content with this arrangement and should agree to it. (LW 41, 154)

Ministers or pastors lead because they are called. And they do their task with an authority that comes from a divine calling mediated through human consensus.

See also **Ordination; Universal Priesthood**

Monasticism Monasticism was a major feature on the religious landscape of Western Europe in the early sixteenth century, one of the long-standing pillars of the ecclesiastical establishment. On July 2, 1505, a close call with a thunderbolt, a vow to St. Anne, and an abrupt career change put the young Luther into the center of it. This nineteen-year-old student of philosophy and law became a monk, entering the monastery of the Order of Augustinian Hermits in Erfurt on July 17, and taking the traditional vows of poverty, chastity, and obedience a year later. It was a momentous turning point for him, as well as for the institution.

Luther was a monk for the next fifteen (or twenty?) years of his life. We know a good deal about his experience in the monastery, largely from his later reminiscences. For instance, we know that he had difficulties with his spiritual life (LW 54, nr. 518, 94–95), above all with the sacrament of penance (LW 54, nr. 119, 15). He had a distanced but troubled relationship with his father (LW 54, nr. 623, 109). He was terrified by his first celebration of the mass, after he was ordained to the priesthood in 1507 (LW 54, nr. 1558, 156). He observed the "Rule" of his order strictly (LW 54, nr. 495, 85), going to the greatest excess in fasting (LW 54, nr. 4422, 339). He found the vow of chastity the easiest to fulfill (LW 54, nr. 121, 15). This and much more he tells us in his Table Talk. Even if we allow for the exaggerations, distortions, and inaccuracies common to this material, we cannot doubt that he embraced the monastic life with utter sincerity and considerable enthusiasm.

A second "thunderbolt," as he called it, struck the young monk sometime between 1513 and 1518, namely his so-called tower experience (LW 54, nr. 4007, 308–309; cf. 54, nr. 3232c, 193–194). As he explained it, the "righteousness of God" that Paul wrote about (Rom. 1:17) is terrifying until one realizes that it is "by the righteousness of God that we are justified and saved through Christ" (LW 54, nr. 3232c, 194). This personal breakthrough, sometimes referred to as Luther's Reformation "discovery," was the dawning in his consciousness of what was henceforth to be his signature doctrine—justification by grace alone through faith alone. (*See also Justification*.)

Luther worked out the full implications of this teaching in a highly com-

plex process that extended to the end of his life. Early on he came to see its obvious ramifications for the practice of indulgences. Later, often in the heat of controversy, he developed its implications for the church, the sacraments, authority, the Christian life, the priesthood, and so forth. So too with monasticism: Luther came to see that his "new" understanding of justification had momentous consequences for his chosen lifestyle.

His realization that the monastic life was at odds with his doctrine of justification came to him like a "thunderbolt" (he uses the term again: LW 44, 254). Precisely when this happened is uncertain, but already in his *To the Christian Nobility of the German Nation*, which appeared on August 18, 1520, he was complaining that there were too many monasteries and warning of the danger that faith in Christ is eclipsed by monastic works (LW 44, 172–173). By October 6 of that year, when *The Babylonian Captivity of the Church* was published, his critique had intensified. Now he called for the complete abolition of all monastic vows because they are abused by monks, and misunderstood by "the unthinking masses who are almost always led by the glitter of works to make shipwreck of their faith" (LW 36, 74–75). As for monks, they need to understand that their works "do not differ one whit in the sight of God from the works of the rustic laborer in the field or the woman going about her household tasks" (LW 36, 78). How many would choose this life if they really believed that?

Luther's thinking along these lines reached its full development in the following year, 1521. Increasing numbers of monks and nuns were abandoning the monasteries and convents; it was at least in part for them that Luther now set out to clarify and publicize his opinion. In September he outlined his position in two sets of "themes" on the subject, both published in October (WA 8, 323–329 and 330–335). Then in ten days in November, he composed *The*

Judgment of Martin Luther on Monastic Vows (LW 44, 251–400). A personal letter from November 21 dedicated the book to his father: here Luther announced that "Christ has absolved me from the monastic vow" (LW 48, 336).

In the book, Luther argued at considerable length that monastic vows are contrary to "God's Word," to faith, to Christian freedom, to the first commandment, and to common sense and reason. Along the way, Luther had much to say about many aspects of monastic life. But he gave only one fundamental reason for rejecting it. This can be summarized as follows: Almost everyone (LW 44, 295) living under monastic vows understands this lifestyle as an alternative path to forgiveness, holiness, salvation, and eternal life. Yet the only way is faith in Christ: "Faith in Christ cannot tolerate grace and justification coming from our own works or the works of others, for faith knows and confesses continually that grace and justification come from Christ alone" (LW 44, 286). Poverty, chastity, and obedience are good, but monks take these vows and practice these virtues for the wrong reason. It happens, though rarely, that one's motivation can be correct: "Sometimes vows are made through Christ working in us in the spirit of freedom . . . when neither satisfaction for sins is claimed by them, nor righteousness and salvation sought through them" (LW 44, 303). Then, and then alone, are vows pleasing to God. Luther's own vows had not been of that sort, nor, he was convinced, were the vows of the vast majority, "scarcely one in a thousand," as he later put it (WA 11, 397, 24).

At first sight, it may seem that Luther's 1521 break with monasticism was decisive and unwavering. But this is not the case. In the dedicatory letter to his father, he seemed to suggest a continuing emotional attachment: "I am still a monk and yet not a monk" (LW 48, 335). He continued living in the Wittenberg monastery, though almost no monks remained after 1522. It was

not until October 9, 1524, that he laid aside his monastic cowl, a step that he later described as "painful and difficult" (LW 54, nr. 4414, 338). And it was not until June of 1525 that he got married, though by then most former monks and nuns had married. Clearly his fifteen (or twenty?) years as a monk, despite all theological convictions, were not easy to leave behind. One senses this lingering emotional attachment even in his Table Talk, stemming from a much later period in his life (post–1531). In this informal setting among friends, Luther raised the topic with surprising frequency. Sometimes these references are merely hyperbole for the sake of humor, for example, when he suggests that monks masturbate "almost the whole day long" (LW 54, nr. 3921, 295). But other more serious references are anecdotes and memories unmistakably tinged with nostalgia.

Intellectually, however, Luther never wavered from the position he elaborated in 1521. Of course he had more to say. In 1523 he wrote a short work encouraging nuns to leave their convents and urging their families to help them (WA 11, 387–400). In 1526 he composed an answer to exegetical questions surrounding the taking of monastic vows (LW 46, 145–154). The Smalcald Articles from 1537 repeat the essence of the stance he took in 1521: monasticism is "contrary to the first and chief article concerning redemption in Jesus Christ" (BC 306). To trust in one's own moral and religious acts—"This is known as denying Christ" (BC 325). Monasticism, therefore, is a fundamentally mistaken form of the Christian life.

Nature   This term, in Luther's usage, refers to all the nonhuman realities God has created. The sixteenth century witnessed highly progressive, even revolutionary, thinking about nature in figures such as Nicolaus Copernicus and Giordano Bruno. Luther's views on nature may be of some interest, but on the whole he did not contribute in any direct way to the birth of modern science.

Luther believed, of course, that "[e]verything that is, was created by God" (LW 1, 7). Human beings are the pinnacle of God's creating, and in fact all of nature was created for the sake of humans (LW 1, 58; 8, 90; *see* **Creation**). For specifics on how God created, Luther relied on the creation account in Genesis 1 and 2; like all theologians of his time, he took this to be historical. Accordingly, Luther held that God created things by speaking them into existence: he simply spoke the names of things and they became realities (LW 1, 21–22). "Therefore, any bird whatever and any fish whatever are nothing but nouns in the divine grammar" (WA 42, 37, 6–7).

Because nature is created by God, Luther believed, God is in some way present in nature. We can discover something about God by studying nature. The simplest thing, like a leaf of a tree, reveals something about God's power (WA 23, 132, 26–30). Then too, since nature is created by God, and since it is intended specifically for humans, it must be regarded as a gift, one that should move us to gratitude (BC 433).

The gift of the natural world should also evoke in us a sense of wonder and awe. Throughout Luther's writings, and especially in his Table Talk, one finds heartfelt expressions of amazement about the utterly commonplace: the leaf of a tree, for instance (as mentioned); or an egg and the life that emerges from it (LW 54, nr. 3390b, 200); or the seed: "If you really examined a kernel of grain thoroughly, you would die of wonderment" (WA 19, 496, 11). "We possess such beautiful creatures; but we pay little attention to them, because they are so common" (WATR 5, nr. 5539, 224, 38–39). Observing nature can even strengthen faith: if God can create all this, "could he not also defend my body against enemies and Satan or, after it has been placed in the grave, revive it for

a new life?" (LW 1, 49). Nature stands ready to astonish and edify those who set aside their dullness and ingratitude, and begin to really see.

Among Luther's occasional remarks on scientific subjects, perhaps the best known are those on astronomy. For one, he was very skeptical about astrology and directly, if jokingly, critical of Philip Melanchthon's excessive interest in the subject: Melanchthon, he said, pursues astrology "as I take a drink of strong beer when I am troubled with grievous thoughts" (WATR 1, nr. 17, 7, 9–10). More seriously, Luther was aware of Copernicus's heliocentric proposal, and he rejected it (LW 54, nr. 4638, 358–359). We should note, however, that this is expressed in a single statement in the Table Talk, and that Luther's tone is more one of annoyance than outrage. Then too it is important to realize that a disciple of Copernicus and advocate of heliocentric theory taught as Luther's colleague at the University of Wittenberg, apparently without a negative reaction from Luther. In other words, Luther was not a dogmatic opponent of scientific progress.

Elsewhere Luther warned theologians against making pronouncements on subjects such as astronomy: "the astronomers are the experts from whom it is most convenient to get what may be discussed about these subjects" (LW 1, 41). Just as theologians have their own technical language, so too do astronomers and other scientists. A mutual respect among the disciplines is in order (LW 1, 47).

When it comes to the natural world, Luther was very much a person of his time. He shared its prevailing assumptions; he did not make inferences that to us, in the twenty-first century, seem almost self-evident. For instance, from the basic principle that nonhuman nature is created by God, he did *not* draw the conclusion that it has an intrinsic value of its own, independent of humans. And, from the basic principle that nonhuman nature is a gift, he did *not* draw the conclusion that it ought not to be defaced and squandered. For that, however, Luther cannot be blamed.

Ordination

Ordained to the priesthood in 1507, Luther carried out his priestly functions for about twelve years before beginning to question the whole concept of ordination as a sacrament. In 1519 we find him doing this, albeit privately, in a letter to his friend George Spalatin (WABr 1, nr. 231, 594–595, 19–24). By 1520 he had clarified his thinking on this issue and was ready to go public.

This he did, first and foremost in his *Babylonian Captivity of the Church*. The sacrament of ordination is, he declared, "an invention of the church of the pope" (LW 36, 106). So too is the fiction of "sacramental character," the teaching that certain sacraments, this one included, imprint an indelible and ineradicable mark on the soul (LW 36, 111). This, together with the practice of celibacy, has been used to create distance between clergy and laity (LW 36, 114), giving the clergy an aura of holiness (LW 36, 115). This entire complex of ideas is a particularly pernicious fiction because, Luther says, it has turned "servants into tyrants": "Here, indeed, are the roots of that detestable tyranny of the clergy over the laity.... [The clergy] not only exalt themselves above the rest of the lay Christians ... but regard them almost as dogs and unworthy to be included with themselves in the church.... In short, the sacrament of ordination has been and still is an admirable device for establishing all the horrible things that have been done hitherto in the church" (LW 36, 112).

On Luther's analysis, this sacrament functions in the church by contributing to the power differential between clergy and laity. In other words, it helps the clergy to dominate, tyrannize, and oppress the laity. Because it thus contributes to the erosion of our Christian freedom, it is of the highest importance:

"if this sacrament and this fiction ever fell to the ground, the papacy with its 'characters' will scarcely survive. Then our joyous liberty will be restored to us; we shall realize that we are all equal by every right" (LW 36, 117).

Ordination is not a sacrament for Luther, but at the same time he is not in favor of utterly abolishing the rite as such (LW 36, 107). To understand his position, one must take into account his teaching on the universal priesthood of the baptized (*see* **Universal Priesthood**). In this treatise he summarizes it as follows: "we are all equally priests, that is to say, we have the same power in respect to the word and the sacraments" (LW 36, 116). (In another 1520 work, *To the Christian Nobility*, he explained it much more fully. See LW 44, 127–129.) Yet, Luther recognized, chaos would result if all Christians exercised these powers. Some, not all, are called to this ministry of Word and sacrament. Ordination is the rite by which such persons are appointed to this office. Luther put it this way: "Therefore, when a bishop consecrates it is nothing else than that in the place and stead of the whole community, all of whom have like power, he takes a person and charges him to exercise this power on behalf of the others" (LW 44, 128). Thus ordination is nothing more than the conferring of the ministerial/pastoral office. This conferral is radically demystified. It is not accompanied by an exalted power, status, holiness, or dignity. What is conferred is only the authorization to use a power that all Christians possess.

Since many of the early leaders in Luther's movement were former Roman Catholic priests, there was no urgency to compose a new liturgical rite of ordination. Nor was Luther very interested in the exact form such a liturgy should take. The first "evangelical" ordination apparently occurred in Wittenberg in 1525. From 1537 we have an eyewitness account of Luther ordaining one Benedict Schumann (WATR 5, Nr. 5376, 112; tr. in LW 53, 123, n.1). In 1539 Luther finally composed a rite which was then universally accepted among his followers (LW 53, 124–126).

See also **Ministerial/Pastoral Office**

Papacy It sometimes seemed to Luther late in his life, as he looked back over his career, that his supreme cause had been his struggle against the papacy. Those who today casually survey his work could be forgiven for drawing the same conclusion. For after 1520 this issue comes up in almost every one of his writings, and a good number of these writings are devoted entirely to it. Yet such a picture of Luther would be a serious distortion. As he said many times, what he cared most about was quite another issue, namely his understanding of the human predicament and the way out, what he referred to in shorthand as "the gospel." The issue of the papacy was secondary: it was important insofar as this institution obscured and contradicted "the gospel."

It was only in 1520 and 1521 that Luther's view on this matter hardened into an unshakable conviction. Before that one finds in his writings a gradual evolution in this direction. Prior to his youthful trip to Rome in the winter of 1510–11, he gave no hint of a critical attitude. In Rome he observed and heard about abuses and immorality, but it certainly did not occur to him to denounce the papacy for this reason. Even as late as 1516 one finds Luther arguing for the necessity of the church's hierarchy (WA 1, 69, 11–13). By 1517 there are indications of ambivalence: the Ninety-five Theses (LW 31, 25–33) include a good number of propositions with an antipapal edge to them (e.g., theses 48, 51, 81–89). At the same time Luther repeatedly gives the pope (Leo X) the benefit of the doubt (e.g., theses 9, 38, 42, 50, 55, 74, 91). Accused by traditionalist opponents of being blatantly antipapal, Luther published a defense of his theses in August of 1518 (LW 31, 77–252). To this he added a letter of submission addressed to the pope: "Most blessed Father, I prostrate myself at your blessed feet with all that I am and have. Raise me up or slay me, call me or dismiss me, approve me or reprove me as you please. I will listen to your voice as the voice of Christ reigning and speaking in you" (WA 1, 529, 22–25).

By 1520, however, humble submission had given way to direct confrontation. Many complex factors contributed to this evolution. On October 12–14, 1518, Luther met with Cardinal Cajetan in Augsburg. On November 9 of that year, Pope Leo X issued the bull *Cum postquam*, reaffirming the conventional practice of indulgences. In 1519, from July 4 to 14, Luther debated these issues with John Eck in Leipzig, for the first time questioning papal primacy and the teaching that the papacy existed *de iure divino*, "by divine right" (i.e., that it was divinely ordained; WA 2, 161, 35–38). Besides all this, literary attacks on Luther proliferated (Tetzel, Wimpina, Eck, Cajetan, Prierias, Alveld, etc.).

All of this propelled Luther to a new level of criticism in 1520. In late June of that year, he published a reply to one of his many attackers, *On the Papacy in Rome: Against the Most Celebrated Papist in Leipzig* (LW 39, 49–104). The papacy, he argued, is not divinely instituted (LW 39, 57), and the pope is not the "vicar of Christ" (LW 39, 72). Yet God in his providence has allowed the papacy to evolve, perhaps as a punishment for Christendom. Be this as it may, the pope must abandon his claim to inerrancy and submit to the authority of Scripture. "If these two things are granted," Luther concludes, "I will let the pope be" (LW 39, 101–102).

Scarcely two months later, Luther's *To the Christian Nobility of the German Nation* appeared (LW 44, 115–217). Here he appears to have abandoned whatever hope he had left for the pope to initiate a genuine reform. Since the distinction between the "spiritual" and "temporal" estate is a fraud, he argues, there is a fundamental equality among all Christians. The German nobility therefore can and should take matters into their own hands (LW 44, 127–132). And what precisely should be reformed? Luther offers twenty-seven suggestions, eighteen of which center on the papacy (LW 44, 156–216). To be sure, they dramatically rein in papal power, but they do not call for the abolition of the papacy.

On September 6, Luther penned a letter to Pope Leo X, dedicating to him his latest writing, *The Freedom of a Christian* (LW 31, 334–343). This letter, obviously written with great care, is a masterpiece of ambiguity. On the surface, Luther is utterly subservient. He insists that he has never attacked Leo personally, but rather only the "curia," the bureaucracy of advisers and assistants appointed by the pope (LW 31, 334–335). Luther warns Leo that he sits "as a lamb in the midst of these wolves" (LW 31, 336). They are Leo's enemies, Luther suggests, because they are his flatterers: they tell him he is inerrant, that he is superior to a council, that he is head of the universal church, and so forth (LW 31, 340, and 342). Luther's advice: Don't listen to them! Is Luther subtly suggesting here that Leo is none of these things? Yes. Luther's surface humility echoes that of Leo's obsequious flatterers. But beneath it is a biting, defiant, perhaps even mocking critique.

A month later, on October 11, a copy of Leo X's bull *Exsurge Domine* arrived in Wittenberg. Luther knew it was coming, of course. But it now became official: forty-one statements, all supposedly mined from his writings, were condemned as "heretical, scandalous, erroneous, offensive to pious ears, misleading to simple minds, and contradictory to Catholic teaching." Luther studied the list with great interest, and then, on December 10, consigned it to the flames, along with some "papal books" (books of canon law, papal decretals, and scholastic theology).

Luther's explanation followed in late December: *Why the Books of the Pope and His Disciples Were Burned* (LW 31, 383–395). They were burned, he explains, quite simply because they were full of errors, and he gives thirty examples. What is noteworthy is that here all ambivalence and subtlety has evaporated. Luther uses the term "Antichrist" throughout, referring directly to the pope. He issues his critique categorically and decisively. The error underlying all others is, "*No one on earth can judge the pope. Also, no one can judge his decision. Rather, he is supposed to judge all people on earth*. This is the main article. . . . If this article stands, then Christ and his Word are defeated. . . . This is the article from which all misfortune has come into all the world" (LW 31, 386–388). It is not known when, or if, Leo X ever read this. In any case, within a matter of days (on January 3, 1521), he promulgated the bull *Decet romanum pontificem*, officially excommunicating Luther.

Here was a turning point. For the remaining twenty-five years of his life, Luther was not "under the pope." He had much more to say about the papacy, but there is little in it that one could see as a substantive development in his view. What we find in these subsequent writings on the pope are a few clarifications, and an escalation in the level of vehemence with which he denounces the papacy.

The first such clarification occurs in Luther's 1521 *Defense and Explanation of All the Articles* (i.e., the articles condemned in *Exsurge Domine*). Here Luther emphasizes that he is not merely repudiating popes, but the institution itself: "even if St. Peter would preside at Rome today, I would deny that the Roman bishop is the pope. The pope is a fictitious thing in this world; he never was, nor is, nor will be; he is only fabricated. Hence I deny the very seat of the beast and I care not at all whether he who occupies it is good or evil. In the church there is no seat which would be above the others by divine right. All are equal" (LW 32, 82). Though the later Luther catalogues endlessly the immorality of popes and their abuses of office, this is not for him the main issue. It is the office itself that contradicts the gospel.

Two statements on the issue from Luther in mid-career can be noted briefly. The first came in 1528, in Luther's *Confession Concerning Christ's Supper*. This work is notable since Luther wrote it as a final and definitive statement so that no one in the future could possibly misunderstand his position. Here he repeats: "the papacy is assuredly the true realm of Antichrist," a worse "abomination" than the Turks (LW 37, 368). The second is found in his 1530 treatise on *The Keys*. In this work Luther argues at length against the papacy's long-standing custom of claiming the "power of the keys" (Matt. 16:19) for itself (LW 40, 353–359).

On the basis of what we have seen so far, it is tempting to conclude that by mid-career Luther's rejection of the papal office was absolute. A 1535 statement from his *Lectures on Galatians* should serve as a caution: "It is not because we want to assert sovereignty over the pope [that we condemn him]. . . . All we aim for is that the glory of God be preserved and that the righteousness of faith remain pure and sound. Once this has been established, namely that God alone justifies us solely by his grace through Christ, we are willing not only to bear the pope aloft on our hands but also to kiss his feet" (LW 26, 99). In other words, Luther suggests, if the pope confesses "the gospel," he can remain pope. Does this statement represent Luther in a moment of weakness, regressing to an earlier stage in his understanding? Or was he thinking that since this condition would never be met, he would never have to recognize the pope as pope? Or did he mean that if popes ever confessed "the gospel," they would so utterly transform the office that it would be virtually unrecognizable? Despite everything he had said earlier, was his rejection of the papacy still not absolute at this stage?

By 1537 this question appears to be resolved. From that year we take note

of another writing that Luther intended as final and definitive, his "last testament," the Smalcald Articles (*BC* 297–328). In this "confession," the antipapal language has grown harsher: terms like "tyranny" (298) and "Antichrist" (309) are standard. He is not pope, but "only bishop, a pastor, of the church of Rome." When he claims papal power, he "corrupts the entire holy Christian church . . . and negates the first, chief article on redemption by Jesus Christ" (307). In Luther's mind, papal power and the gospel are incompatible. Only by giving up his power would it even be possible for the pope to confess the gospel. But in that case he would no longer be pope. Here the logic of Luther's view leads to an exclusion of the papacy that is absolute.

A final milestone, painful for almost everyone, which we cannot ignore, is one of Luther's last works, *Against the Roman Papacy, an Institution of the Devil* of 1545 (LW 41, 263–376). Experts often regard this as Luther's most bitter, indeed hateful, writing. Theologically speaking, one finds nothing new in it: the pope (Paul III at the time) is not the "vicar of Christ" but a "vicar of the devil" (LW 41, 357). Old arguments attacking papal primacy and inerrancy are repeated. Most of Luther's attention, however, is lavished on the very frequent outbursts of obscenity, tirades against the pope laced with scatological references and accusations of what Luther saw as sexual deviance. For example, the pope is referred to as "Madame Pope Paula III" (LW 41, 273), and members of his curia are accused of being "in their front parts men, in their back parts women" (LW 41, 282). This "sodomy slur" is the ultimate weapon in Luther's arsenal of abuse.

Old, sick, tired, besieged by opponents on every side, fearful that his life's work would come to nothing—all these factors together threw Luther off balance, emotionally speaking. If a reading of *Against the Roman Papacy* leaves any doubt about this, one need only glance at the vulgar, violently obscene woodcuts he commissioned from Lucas Cranach to accompany his text (for descriptions see WA 54, 348–373). Even some of Luther's ardent followers cringed when they saw them. And so have many of his admirers ever since. To say that Luther was emotionally unbalanced in his waning years is not to exonerate him: the historical record is not thereby erased. It reminds us that the truth about Luther is more complicated than either his admirers or detractors think.

See also **Church; Councils**

Penance   Penance, and the complex issues surrounding it, were at the heart of Luther's personal and theological development. His central question from the outset had been, "How do I find a gracious God?" He could just as well have asked "How do I find forgiveness?" for it comes to the same thing. In Luther's time, penance was the locus, both theological and existential, of forgiveness.

As a person of deep piety, the young Luther found himself immersed in the rather elaborate late medieval penitential system. The standard features of this system can only be outlined here. The Fourth Lateran Council in 1215 had mandated a once-annual private confession to a priest for all Christians, and by Luther's time this minimum requirement had become the standard practice. Contrition, a "sufficient" sorrow for one's sins, was held to be a prerequisite. Recounting all one's "mortal" sins to a priest then followed, and this confession could be valid or invalid depending on an extensive set of conditions (in addition to contrition). The priest then pronounced absolution, "I absolve you . . . ," and prescribed some works of "penitence" or "satisfaction." The validity of the absolution (or forgiveness itself) depended on the validity of the confession. This, in its basic contours, was the way in which the sacrament of penance was understood. In practice it was much

more complex, no doubt varying considerably depending on the confessor.

The purpose of the system as a whole, objectively speaking, was to be the institutional conduit that mediated divine forgiveness to human beings. Seen from its subjective side, its purpose was to inculcate in Christians a sense of their personal sinfulness, that is, to induce guilt feelings, and then to alleviate that guilt when certain conditions were met. Already as a young monk in the Augustinian order, Luther experienced the system as dysfunctional: he felt an enormous burden of guilt that no amount of confession and absolution could alleviate. Looking back on this "scrupulosity" from a later vantage point (1531), he described it as torment:

> When I was a monk, I made a great effort to live according to the requirements of the monastic rule. I made a practice of confessing and reciting all my sins, but always with prior contrition; I went to confession frequently, and I performed the assigned penance faithfully. Nevertheless my conscience could never achieve certainty but was always in doubt and said "You have not done this correctly. You are not contrite enough. You omitted this in your confession." Therefore the longer I tried to heal my uncertain, weak, and troubled conscience with human traditions, the more uncertain, weak, and troubled I continually made it. (*LW* 27, 13; cf. 43, 336–337)

For Luther, the system did not work, and plenty of evidence suggests that a good many other Christians at the time experienced something similar. Indeed, one of the few things all the Protestant reformers could agree on was that this system had to go.

Yet Luther's critique did not begin until 1517, and even then only in a relatively oblique way. In his Ninety-five Theses (LW 31, 25–33) he attacked the sale of indulgences—a relatively recent addition to the penitential system. This attack was motivated by a pastoral concern for people's troubled consciences (e.g., thesis 10) and by a theological concern for preserving the credibility of church teaching (theses 81–90). He in no way explicitly attacked penance itself (thesis 7). Yet in his reinterpretation of the traditional scriptural grounding of the sacrament (theses 1 and 2), and in his reigning in of the more extravagant papal claims (e.g., theses 5 and 6), there are intimations of the critique to come.

A significant escalation can already be discerned in 1518 when Luther published his *Explanations of the Ninety-five Theses* (LW 31, 83–252). Here the tone is bolder, in its call for a reform of the church itself (LW 31, 250), in the doubts expressed regarding purgatory (LW 31, 135), papal power (LW 31, 172), and so forth. More importantly, Luther now asserted, "It is not the sacrament, but faith in the sacrament that justifies" (LW 31, 107). Clearly a rethinking of the entire penitential system was under way.

By 1519 several new themes were dominating Luther's analysis, all of them evident in his instructive sermon entitled *The Sacrament of Penance* (LW 35, 9–22). First, he now saw the issue of power as being central. The penitential system was used by the church, he thought, to control and dominate: "by means of the keys [Luther's term for the penitential system] the clergy should be serving not themselves but only us. . . . They [the priests] create nothing but tyranny out of this lovely and comforting authority [of the keys], as if Christ were thinking only of the will and dominion of the priests when he instituted the keys" (LW 35, 17).

As the system then functioned, according to Luther, it served the "dominion of the priests": to use today's language, it operated as an instrument of social control. And Luther set about undermining this by dismantling important elements in the system. He argued, for instance, that one need not worry about fulfilling the conditions for a "valid" confession, nor about the adequacy of one's contrition: "For the faith of the sacrament makes all the crooked straight and fills up all the uneven

ground" (LW 35, 20). Nor, he argued, does one have to confess all sins; rather one should confess only those sins "which at the time are oppressing and frightening the conscience" (LW 35, 20). Most dramatically, he contended that laypersons can administer the sacrament and give absolution (LW 35, 12 and 21). With such innovations, the "dominion of the priests" would be decisively curtailed.

Besides the issue of power, Luther was also concerned in this same treatise with the excessive burdening of consciences, a "torture" he himself had experienced. The existing system recommended "calming the heart" by good works and pious practices such as indulgences, pilgrimages, and asceticism (LW 35, 10f). But this, Luther now argued, only makes matters worse; for it means trusting in oneself, and this "issues finally in despair and eternal damnation" (LW 35, 15). The true method of easing the burdened conscience is faith, which accepts the forgiveness offered in absolution (LW 35, 11). Everything depends on faith, or, as Luther defines it here, "receptivity" (LW 35, 18): "For as you believe, so it is done for you" (LW 35, 11). Here the heart of the sacrament is redefined. Its principal parts are no longer confession, absolution, and satisfaction but rather absolution, faith, and peace (LW 35, 19).

This understanding was carried over by Luther into his famous 1520 treatise, *The Babylonian Captivity of the Church*. Some of the themes lightly touched on in the preceding year are here heavily emphasized. For instance, the power issue is highlighted: terms like "tyranny," "despotism," and "extortion" are sprinkled through the section on penance (LW 36, 81, 83, and 86). The impossibility of enumerating all sins and having contrition for each is highlighted: after all every work, even our "good" ones, are tainted by sin (LW 36, 84–85). The gross misunderstanding of "works of satisfaction" as making reparation to God for our sins comes under withering criticism (LW 36, 89–90). Alongside these reiterated themes we also find a new theme, namely repentance understood as a return to our baptism (LW 36, 59). This is in turn integrated into the decisive development—the rejection of penance as a sacrament. While he heartily endorses confession and absolution (LW 36, 86, and 88), Luther, at the very end of the treatise, raises the question of its sacramental nature: "it has seemed proper to restrict the name of sacrament to those promises which have signs attached to them. The remainder, not being bound to signs, are bare promises. Hence there are, strictly speaking, but two sacraments in the church of God—baptism and the bread. For only in these two do we find both the divinely instituted sign and the promise" (LW 36, 124). Whereas in 1519 Luther appeared to be intent on rescuing the sacrament from abuses and distortions, by 1520 he was intent on deleting penance from the list of "sacraments." But this did not mean it was unimportant.

Also in 1520 Luther wrote *A Discussion of How Confession Should Be Made*, a work important for Luther's pastoral/ psychological insight. Again here he inveighs against the Roman Catholic use of penance to control and tyrannize the people (LW 39, 32, 36, 40). But he is particularly critical of the disposition required of the penitent for the confession to be valid, namely a "violent hatred of [one's] sins." That anyone claimed to have this, Luther suggested, was a "profound pretense" and a "miserable fiction." To see this, the penitent need only ask "what he would feel and what he would do if there were no punishment, no God, no commandment, etc." (LW 39, 30). This gets us closer to the truth: "there is no one whose intention is as good as it should be." Rather than even trying to work up a "violent hatred of sin" in ourselves, we should simply say, "O Lord God, I do not have what I should have, and I cannot do it. Grant what you command and com-

mand what you will" (LW 39, 31). For those plagued by a scrupulous conscience Luther advised: whereas the Roman Catholic requirement had been that one must go to confession before receiving communion, such a person should sometimes receive communion without confessing, for example after a night of excessive drinking. Just as some consciences need to be sensitized, others need to be desensitized (LW 39, 40).

The following year, 1521, saw several more writings on the subject coming from Luther's pen. Sixteen of the forty "errors" censured by Pope Leo X's bull of condemnation *Exsurge Domine* had to do with penance, and thus Luther's reply dealt at length with the issue (LW 32, 7–99). (Here, incidentally, Luther again calls penance a "sacrament" [LW 32, 51]. This may have been inadvertent, or perhaps a sign of wavering.) He expressed himself at surprising length on the theme in *On Confession, Whether the Pope Has the Power to Require It* (WA 8, 129–185, 204). Here he rejected the allegorical interpretation of the story of Jesus and the lepers (Luke 17:11–19)—a traditional grounding of the requirement (WA 8, 154, 1–4). And he says that people should have no more regard for this papal law than they would "for a clod of dung in the street." He also wrote in 1521 *An Instruction to Penitents Concerning the Forbidden Books of Dr. M Luther* (LW 44, 219–229)—an attack on the Catholic practice of withholding absolution from those who refuse to conform to the rules. Obviously penance, and its function in the power relations between clergy and laity, was a burning issue for him at this stage of his career.

By the time his two catechisms appeared in 1529 his views on penance had long since crystallized. The Large Catechism included "A Brief Exhortation to Confession" (BC 476–80). In short, Luther said, "If you are poor and miserable, then go and make use of the healing medicine" (479). And in the section on baptism he explained that since penance is a return to one's baptism, the sacrament of baptism subsumes penance (465–66). The Small Catechism featured a section on "How simple people are to be taught to confess" (360–62). These writings, like the Augsburg Confession of 1530, emphasized the importance of a kind of private confession intended to be liberating rather than oppressive (BC 44).

Again in 1530 Luther renewed his attack on the Roman penitential system, this time in a work called The Keys (LW 40, 321–378). The traditional understanding, based on Matthew 16:19, was that the church had been given two keys, one to "bind" and one to "loose." The first convinces people of their sinfulness (inculcating guilt feelings), the second grants absolution (alleviating guilt). The problem, Luther argued in this work, is that the pope "uses only the key which binds." Why? For reasons having to do with power: "The key which looses would work too great havoc. It would deprive the papists, of as much power, honors, possessions as the key which binds brings to them" (LW 40, 336). Using the "loosing" key, the purpose of which is to "console a truly frightened sinful conscience" (LW 40, 373)—in other words, to alleviate people's guilt—would undermine the honor accorded to the clergy, dry up financial contributions, and generally disempower the clergy. This is why, Luther thinks, they do not use the second key.

Since Christ gave both to the church, they must both be used (LW 40, 376). The first, when used alone, produces only "a troubled conscience, a fearful heart, despair, and the beginning of the pangs of hell" (LW 40, 376–377). It is what Luther calls "law," and its very purpose is to drive us to the second key, absolution or "the gospel," where consolation, peace, and joy are to be found. Here too, in this "loosing" key, is to be found a true freedom over and against spiritual leaders who oppress us.

Luther made his last major statement on penance in the Smalcald Articles (1537). Here he reiterated much that he had said before, emphasizing again that "law" must be accompanied by "gospel": if it is not, the ultimate result is the kind of despair that drove Judas to his suicide (BC 313). The "papist" system is again criticized: under it no one could be sure his or her contrition was sufficient; people could not be sure their confession was complete; and no one knew how much "satisfaction" was enough (BC 314–315). Thus consciences were left wallowing in uncertainty. But the more basic problem, Luther suggests here, is that the "papists" have failed to understand what "sin" is. They think of it as discrete, individual acts of evil, infractions of this or that item on a list of prohibitions. In fact, Luther argues, "sin" is a condition that encompasses the whole person (BC 318): all our acts, even our best ones, are tainted by who we are, namely sinful human beings. This, in the final analysis, is what must be confessed. And absolution, precisely because it depends not on us (our disposition or satisfaction) but on God, is utterly certain (BC 318).

Luther himself continued to practice private confession till the end of his life. As a youth in the monastery, it had caused him the most acute torment. But with his redefinition, it became for him the most exquisite consolation and source of peace. To receive absolution from one's fellow Christian is to accept the promise of the gospel. It is, he said, "a cure without equal for distressed consciences" (LW 36, 86).

Prayer

Luther devoted extraordinary amounts of time and energy to praying. He also invested time and energy—though far less—in critical reflection on prayer: what it is and what it is not; why it matters; how one should do it; and so forth. Here as elsewhere in Luther, personal practice and theology coexisted in a mutually enriching symbiosis: life and thought were for him ultimately inseparable. In the following summary I focus on his understanding of prayer, but in doing this, I cannot leave his practice untouched.

From a very young age and throughout his youth, prayer was an integral part of Luther's life. If his home was at all typical, he probably learned there at least the "Our Father" and "Hail Mary." The schools he attended as a child in Mansfeld, Magdeburg, and Eisenach no doubt drilled him in the catechetical basics: the "Our Father," the creeds, and the Decalogue. Mandatory weekly attendance at mass familiarized him with the prayers of the liturgy. Above all, in the Augustinian monastery at Erfurt, the "canonical hours" or "divine office" involved praying the Psalms incessantly, until he had them memorized in their entirety. As a university professor, his religious order gave him the right to defer the daily scheduled prayers for the sake of other duties and to catch up on weekends. By 1520 Luther found himself three months in arrears. After a final, grueling attempt to catch up, he quit (LW 54, nr. 495, 85; WATR 2, nr. 1253, 11, 5–11; 4, nr. 5094, 654, 11–14; 5, nr. 6077, 474, 29–475, 17).

Throughout this early period of his life, Luther's understanding of prayer was, as he later came to think, markedly sub-Christian. The first prayer from him that we know of was flat-out deal making: caught in a violent thunderstorm, he promised to become a monk if rescued. Then, in the monastery, he clearly operated on the assumption that God rewards faithful completion of the divine office. And in 1519 he was still recommending prayer as mantra or incantation: the common practice of reading the Gospels to the crops, he explained, purifies the air of devils and makes the crops grow better (LW 42, 91). He gradually came to see with a stunning clarity the inadequacy of such prayers. They imply a God who is somehow susceptible to human manipulation; and that, to use the traditional word, is idolatry. He finally broke through, in other words, to an understanding of prayer purged of these grosser magical elements.

Already as early as 1516 Luther had criticized the monastic regimen of prayer as all too often deteriorating into mindless repetition (WA 7, 733, 36–37). In the following years this critique escalated and expanded. Thus in his 1519 *Exposition of the Lord's Prayer for Simple Laymen*, Luther denounced rote repetition, whether it was of the canonical hours (LW 42, 23–24), or of the rosary and other such prayers (LW 42, 21–22). These, he said, "are to be valued only insofar as they spur and move the soul to reflect on the meaning and the desires conveyed by the words" (LW 42, 20–21). The more that such reflection takes place, the fewer the words, and "[t]he fewer the words, the better the prayer" (LW 42, 19). As beginners, "we should cling to the words and with their help soar upward, until our feathers grow and we can fly without the help of words" (LW 42, 25)

This critique of Roman Catholic and especially monastic prayer as being too wordy receded somewhat in succeeding years, and a new emphasis rose to the fore. In Luther's *Personal Prayer Book* of 1522, for instance, one finds an attack on prayer understood as a "work," as something humans offer to God, as a meritorious act (LW 43, 12). He was now convinced that in the monasteries above all, this is what prayer had become. And in his view, real prayer was precisely the opposite: it had nothing to do with us offering something to God; rather it was our acknowledgment that we have nothing to offer, that we are the needy ones. "True prayer," as Luther later put it, "has to do with receiving, not giving" (BC 444)

By 1522 the contours of Luther's mature theology of prayer were in place. Yet he never wrote a systematic treatise on the subject. Thus his views must be pieced together from a few pastorally oriented writings on the subject and from innumerable scattered references in his sermons, lectures, and so forth.

Sifting through this material, one sees immediately that Luther uses the term "prayer" in two ways. In the broadest, most general sense, "the lifting up of the heart [to God] constitutes the essence and nature of prayer" (LW 42, 25). Accordingly prayer can take a huge variety of forms. For example, one can "pray" by reciting the Decalogue (LW 43, 200) or the creed (LW 43, 209), by a kind of meditative thinking (LW 43, 201), by reading/reciting Scripture passages (WATR 5, nr. 5517, 209, 21–24), or even by working faithfully (LW 43, 194). The wordless sigh can be a more authentic prayer than all the "bellowing and babbling," the "howling and growling" of the canonical hours in the monasteries (WATR 3, nr. 2918, 79, 1–4; BC 441, 443). As Luther put it in a sermon of 1522, "By 'prayer' is understood not oral prayer alone, but rather all that the soul does in connection to God's Word: to hear, to speak, to create poetry, to contemplate" (WA 10:1:1, 435, 8–10). In its most general sense, "prayer" means all of this.

In its more particular and proper meaning, Luther essentially restricts prayer to petition. Without this, he says, "it cannot be called a prayer" (BC 443). To pray, in other words, means to express one's deepest needs and longings. Already in 1519 this is what Luther most often meant by prayer: "spiritual and sincere prayer reflects the heart's innermost desires, its sighing and yearning" (LW 42, 20). And this narrower understanding of prayer dominates in his later works on the subject, in particular the Large and Small Catechisms of 1529 (BC 345–480) and the 1535 pamphlet entitled A Simple Way to Pray (LW 43, 189–211).

To whom then does Luther think we should pray? Not to Mary, though there is value in reciting the "Hail Mary" as a meditation (LW 43, 39–41). Nor to the saints (WA 30:2, 644, 5–10; BC 59), though it may be that they pray for us (BC 305). Rather, pray to God alone—or to any person in the Trinity. Since "the

one, undivided divine essence is in all and in each person," the other two will not be jealous (WA 54, 69, 5–10).

More important for Luther is the question of why we should pray. The most basic reason, he thinks, is because God has commanded us to do so. Where? In the second commandment of the Decalogue, "You shall not make wrongful use of the name of the LORD your God." Every negative commandment, Luther held, carried implicitly within it a positive one. Thus the commandment not to misuse God's name mandates us to use it correctly, and we do this by calling on God, expressing our need, and imploring his help (BC 352, 441; WA 6, 223, 13–15; LW 14, 61). In doing so, we acknowledge him precisely as God, that is, as the only one who can, in the final analysis, fulfill our need. Thus in praying we obey the second commandment, and in the first petition of the Lord's Prayer ("hallowed be your name") we ask that the world will too (BC 445–446).

We have already seen that for Luther the essence of prayer, properly understood, is the attempt to formulate and express our deepest desires and needs. And humans, he believed, need help in doing this (LW 44, 59). Until the end of his life he regarded the Psalms as one of the most superb and precious models for prayer (LW 35, 253–257; WATR 1, nr. 421, 183, 8–12). Yet the Lord's Prayer, he said in 1535, is "even better than the Psalter, which is so very dear to me" (LW 43, 200). In this prayer Jesus himself taught us what to ask for, and Christians who use it cannot go wrong. It is finally the only prayer necessary (LW 43, 12). Here "God takes the initiative and puts into our mouths the very words and approach we are to use" (BC 443).

Of the various commentaries Luther wrote on the Lord's Prayer, his 1529 catechisms are the classics. Here Luther's theology of prayer reached its highest development. Several major features stand out in these works.

First, Luther forcefully emphasizes that our prayers do not bring about any change in God. We do not persuade him to change his mind. "What we pray for concerns only ourselves in that . . . we ask that what otherwise must be done without us [i.e., what *will* be done in any case] may also be done in us" (*BC* 449). God's will, his intention, will be carried out, whether we pray for it (in the third petition) or not. God's kingdom will come regardless. He does all these things we ask for, Luther repeatedly says, "without our prayer" (*BC* 356–358).

Why then should we pray for them? After all, Luther says, God knows our needs long before we express them (*BC* 444). His answer is that prayer changes not God but us: "God therefore wants you to lament and express your needs and concerns, not because he is unaware of them, but in order that you may kindle your heart to stronger and greater desires and open and spread your apron wide to receive many things" (ibid.). In other words prayer transforms and intensifies our desires and prepares us for their fulfillment. Our prayers change not God's mind but ours.

The petition for our daily bread Luther understands as comprehensive, pertaining to "all kinds of earthly matters." Even without our prayers, God gives these things "even to the godless and rogues, yet he wishes us to ask for them so that we may realize that we have received them from his hand and may recognize in them his fatherly goodness toward us" (*BC* 451). Prayer alters our awareness, making us grateful. Even the petition to "forgive us our debts" does not bring about a change in God: "Not that he does not forgive sins even apart from and before our praying; for before we prayed for it or even thought about it, he gave us the gospel, in which there is nothing but forgiveness. But the point here is for us to recognize and accept this forgiveness" (452). Praying this petition changes us by bringing "a confident and joyful heart" (*BC* 453). The last petition, "rescue us from the evil one," is constantly granted by God without our

prayer, but it too changes us (and here we see, incidentally, how for Luther "the devil" personifies the entire negative side of human existence): "this petition includes all the evil that may befall us under the devil's kingdom: poverty, disgrace, death, and, in short, all the tragic misery and heartache, of which there is so incalculably much on earth" (455). This petition teaches us "to seek and expect help from no one but him [God]" (*BC* 456).

In the end, the summation of all prayer for Luther seems to be: "Your will be done" (*BC* 444). And this will is fulfilled even without our prayer. The point of our prayer, then, is to align our will with God's will, to "submit to the will of God" (*BC* 449). This is what James 1:6 means when it says we are to "ask in faith." Faith means trust, and trust is nothing but the submission of our will to God's. Thus "faith makes the prayer . . . acceptable" (LW 44, 58). Faith makes prayer "true prayer," and God "hears" it (*BC* 456).

But what can it possibly mean, in this context, to say that God "hears" our prayers? Does he answer them? This was a theological question for Luther, but one that also carried a burning existential urgency. Anguished pleading with God in a desperate situation was not foreign to him: as he aged he endured excruciatingly painful illnesses with increasing frequency; even worse, as a parent he had knelt at the bedside of his dying daughter. He knew the meaning of the prayer, "Let this cup pass from me." And as in the Gethsemane story, he experienced the terrifying silence that seemed to be the answer.

The theme of persisting in prayer and delayed answers comes up often in the later Luther (e.g., LW 4, 361–362; 7, 174–175). Abraham, Isaac, Joseph, Rebekah, and Rachel are the prime biblical examples, and Monica—Augustine's mother—is the favorite postbiblical exemplar of waiting for answers to prayer (e.g., LW 3, 159–160). In a somewhat troubling analogy to human fatherhood,

Luther speaks of God "playing" with us by temporarily withholding what we ask for (LW 4, 326). But none of this directly answers the question: Does God answer our prayers?

There is no sidestepping here: the older Luther took up this issue with remarkable frequency, boldness, and consistency, particularly in his late sermons and lectures, and informally in the Table Talk. The following statement summarizes his answer: "If what we ask for will hallow his name, increase his kingdom, and happen according to his will, then he [God] assuredly hears us. But if we pray for anything contrary to these things, we are not heard; for God does nothing contrary to his name, kingdom, and will" (WATR 1, nr. 1212, 604, 6–9; cf. 604, 22–25). In other words, God answers our prayers if, and only if, what we pray for is in accordance with his will.

Very often we as humans do not know what God's will is: "God's will is clear when it pertains to his glory and our salvation. But when temporal affairs are concerned, God's will is not so clear. . . . Therefore we should submit our will to his and not doubt in the least that he will certainly grant our petition if it results in his glory and our salvation" (WA 52, 118, 28–119, 4). We do not even know, in many cases, what is good for us or for those we love: "the granting of our prayer is to be defined thus: God does not always do what we want but he does what is good for us. For since God is good, he can do nothing except what is good. But we often ask for our children or our friends or ourselves not what is good but what seems to us to be good. In such cases God also answers our prayer by not doing what we ask" (WA 40:3, 26, 30–35; cf. LW 44, 58). Much of what we ask God for is foolish, Luther said in a sermon in 1537: "God must often say: If I gave you what you asked for, I would be a fool like you. . . . But then our dear Lord is so kind and good as not to blame us for our foolishness" (WA 47, 366, 5–9).

This is why, Luther thought, the Lord's Prayer was the ideal prayer: there are no foolish petitions here. We can be sure that all are God's will, and that he will answer all of them (BC 358). When we make up our own wish lists, we cannot be sure. Because it expresses our deepest needs, the Lord's Prayer "is without a doubt the most sublime, the loftiest, and the most excellent" of all prayers (LW 42, 21).

In another sense, we could say that the most authentic prayer for Luther is Jesus' prayer in Gethsemane. An elderly, sickly, and tired Luther preached on this a year before he died. The prayer begins with an anguished plea: "let this cup pass from me" (Matt. 26:39). The silence that Jesus heard in reply we too often hear: "God often finds it necessary to let us remain under our cross and in trouble. Now since God alone knows what is good for us and needful to us, we should grant his will precedence over ours and show our obedience in patience" (WA 52, 741, 20–23; cf. LW 42, 75). Thus the prayer that begins with an anguished plea ends in the will's transformation— its submission to God's will: "Your will be done" (LW 42, 45). This was true for Jesus, Luther says, and so too it must be for us (LW 42, 183).

To summarize then, prayer as Luther understands it is our attempt to express our deepest needs and profoundest desires, a process that results in a better alignment of these needs and desires with God's will. Or to say it another way, it is a process that brings about the submission of our wills to God's will. In arriving at clarity on this, Luther broke free of his earlier magical/superstitious view: prayer is not a mantra or incantation, and it can in no way involve a bargaining, deal making, cajoling, bribing, or manipulating of the Divine. When it slides in this direction, as it all too often does, it descends into idolatry.

Predestination   For at least a thousand years before Luther, most Western theologians embraced some form of the doctrine of predestination. Within this tradition, the current most influenced by Augustine was the most overtly and aggressively predestinarian. The young Luther, a member of the Augustinian Order and educated in scholasticism, was steeped in this inheritance.

Though he paid scant attention to the doctrine in his earliest lectures on the Psalms (1513–15), one finds him treating the issue at length in his lectures on Romans (1515–16). Here, with regard to Romans 9–11, Luther affirmed an absolute, double predestination. While all of humanity is part of the "mass of perdition," God in his mercy chooses some for salvation (LW 25, 391). As for the rest, God "hardens" their hearts, that is, reprobates them. "[G]race alone distinguishes the redeemed from the condemned" (LW 25, 394), and no human knows whether she or he is predestined to eternal life or to damnation (LW 25, 387). Along with certain representatives of the mystical tradition, Luther identified the "resignation to hell"—the willingness to be damned for the glory of God—as the most exalted human response to the divine will (LW 25, 382; 25, 384).

This basic teaching did not change substantially in the later Luther. In 1522, in his preface to Paul's letter to the Romans, he reaffirmed double predestination—both to salvation and to damnation—"in order that our salvation may be taken entirely out of our hands and put in the hands of God alone" (LW 35, 378). In his 1525 rejoinder to Erasmus, *On the Bondage of the Will*, he elaborated at much greater length, but the fundamentals remained the same. He quotes Paul: "[God] has mercy . . . upon whom he wills, and whom he wills he hardens. It depends not upon man's willing or running, but upon God's mercy [Rom. 9:16]" (LW 33, 186; cf. 33, 146). And, following Augustine, Luther affirmed that God saves few and damns many (LW 33, 62). What is new here, however, is that this whole

complex of ideas is treated in relation to his concept of the *Deus absconditus*—the hidden God. In some respects, Luther argued, "God hides himself and wills to be unknown to us. . . . [I]n this regard we have nothing to do with him. . . . But we have something to do with him insofar as he is clothed and set forth in his Word [*Deus revelatus*]" (LW 33, 139). Predestination has to do with this hidden God: "This will is not to be inquired into, but reverently adored, as by far the most awe-inspiring secret of the Divine Majesty" (LW 33, 139). Even much later in his career, for instance in his *Lectures on Genesis* from 1535 to 1545, Luther did not change the general contours of this doctrine (LW 5, 42–50).

Yet there is another dimension to this, an experiential one, which Luther felt acutely. Late in his life Luther recalled that as a young monk, this issue drove him to the extremity of fear, doubt, and despair, "to the brink of eternal death," as he put it (WABr 6, nr. 1811, 86, 5–6). This was one form which his so-called *Anfechtungen* took (*see* **Anfechtung**). Of great help to him was his mentor in the Augustinian Order, John von Staupitz, who wrote a book on the subject in 1517 (*Libellus de executione eterne predestinationis*). When driven to despair by the fear of reprobation, Staupitz had advised, look only to the wounds of the suffering Christ. Those wounds, suffered "for you," will erase all fear and doubt (as Luther reports in his *Lectures on Genesis*, 1535–1545; LW 5, 47). This had worked for the young Luther. Only two years later, in his 1519 *Sermon on Preparing to Die*, Luther gave roughly the same advice: dying people should force all thoughts of predestination out of their minds by focusing their gaze on Christ alone (LW 42, 105).

The distinction Luther developed in 1525 between the *Deus absconditus* and *Deus revelatus* served a similar pastoral function. The issue of predestination is buried in God's inscrutable eternal will, and he forbids us to inquire into it. Humans are to focus on what God has revealed about himself in Jesus Christ, and that is, first and foremost, that he loves us. Trust in this, or what Luther calls "faith"—this is the overcoming of all doubt and fear and despair (LW 33, 140). Here we have the foundation of Luther's pastoral advice on the issue, advice repeated with great frequency in different contexts.

One finds it, for instance, in his personal letters of comfort to friends and acquaintances looking for help. For example, in 1531 he wrote to a certain Barbara Lisskirchen about her distress with regard to predestination. In the letter Luther recalls his own similar experience and then suggests: "the highest of all God's commands is this, that we hold up before our eyes the image of his dear Son, our Lord Jesus Christ . . . our excellent mirror wherein we behold how much God loves us" (WABr 6, nr. 1811, 87, 41–44). If we look only at Christ, we see only God's love for us, a love that conquers fear.

We find very similar words of consolation throughout the Table Talk, material from the 1530s to his death in 1546 (e.g., WATR 2, nr. 2631b, 562, 7–19; WATR 5, nr. 5658a, 293–296). Here Luther's advice is often accompanied by warnings: discussing and debating predestination is dangerous. It can become an obsession driving people to despair (WATR 2, nr. 2631b, 562, 7–9). So too we find the same approach in sermons, for instance, in those on the Gospel of John, delivered in 1537 or 1538: "if I want to know how God is disposed toward me and what his plans are for me, I must listen to none other than my Lord's voice. There . . . I hear sheer fatherly, cordial promise and consolation" (LW 24, 70). One finds the same thing, finally, in Luther's lectures. For example, in his course of lectures on Genesis, lasting from 1535 to 1545, predestination is approached from the angle of certainty: "Christ came into this world to make us completely certain" (LW 5, 43). "[I]f you cling to the revealed God with a firm faith . . . then you are most assuredly predestined" (LW 5, 46).

In summary, Luther believed that God predestines human beings unconditionally, some to eternal life and some to damnation. Yet we know next to nothing about this, basically because God has not seen fit to reveal much about this. Far more important for us is what God *has* revealed, what he wants us to know and focus on, namely that he loves us. Opening ourselves up to this love—what Luther calls "faith"—makes all our fear, doubt, and despair evaporate. Being the object of an eternal, omnipotent love makes everything else fade into insignificance.

See also **Faith; Free Will**

Reason   Unlike many of the scholastic theologians of the Middle Ages, Luther did not leave us with a careful and comprehensive statement on the place and function of reason in relation to Christian belief. Nevertheless, he had strong opinions on the matter, and these are scattered in scores of passages throughout his writings. Only by carefully piecing them together, and by observing the way in which reason actually functions in his theology, can we arrive at the following kind of systematic statement.

What we can dismiss out of hand is the view that reason has no place at all in Luther's theology. This accusation, often called "fideism," is an old one, and is based on no serious reading of Luther whatsoever. Rather its watchword is Luther's most famous outburst on the subject: "reason is the devil's whore" (LW 40, 175; 51, 374). Endlessly repeated, this dictum was all too frequently taken as Luther's final word on the matter, absolving scholars of all obligation to investigate further. But Luther has much more to say on the subject. And no great insight is required to see how empty the accusation of fideism is. For on the basis of a strict fideism, no theology is possible—only an endless repetition of the articles of faith. Obviously, that does not apply to Luther.

Humans, Luther believed, were created with reason, "the power to understand and judge" (WA 42, 93, 37; cf. LW 1, 124). Indeed, reason is itself the image of God with which Adam was created (LW 1, 63). Humans share this with the angels, and it is what differentiates them from the animals (LW 1, 112). Rationality is the essence of what it means to be human. And humans did not lose this when Adam sinned: "After the fall of Adam, God did not take away this majesty of reason, but rather confirmed it" (LW 34, 137).

This noble gift of God is celebrated in a virtual paean to reason penned by Luther in 1536: "it is certainly true that reason is the most important and the highest in rank among all things and, in comparison with other things of this life, the best and something divine. It is the inventor and mentor of all the arts, medicine, laws, and of whatever wisdom, power, virtue, and glory men possess in this life. . . . It is a sun and a kind of god appointed to administer these things [earthly affairs] in this life" (LW 34, 137).

All human matters, all things having to do with human life in this world, fall under the jurisdiction of reason, and reason is competent to administer them. In a sermon of 1522, Luther explained: "In temporal, human affairs human judgment suffices. For these things we need no light but that of reason. Hence God does not in the Scriptures teach us how to build houses, to make clothing, to marry, to wage war, to navigate the seas, and so on. For these our natural light is sufficient" (WA 10:1:1, 531, 6–11). One such "human affair," Luther argued in 1539, is the institutional structure of the church. The Holy Spirit has not revealed anything about this because he "does not dabble in such matters as are subject to reason" (LW 41, 60). When it comes to all such mundane matters, Luther has high confidence in the power of rationality, if only humans would use it.

Natural human reason can not only lead us to a knowledge of the moral law (LW 52, 84; 22, 150–151), but it can bring in addition a certain knowledge of God himself, as Luther insisted in the Jonah lectures of 1526: "Such a light and such a perception [natural knowledge of God] is innate in the hearts of all men; and this light cannot be subdued or extinguished" (LW 19, 53; cf. WA 56, 176, 15–32). Furthermore, a person can even reason a way to some of the divine attributes: that God is creator, that he is just (LW 26, 399), and so forth. "That is as far as the natural light of reason sheds its rays—it regards God as kind, gracious, merciful, and benevolent. And that is indeed a bright light" (LW 19, 54). All this humans can know about God prior to any revelation on his part.

Alongside such statements affirming the high competence of reason, one can also find in Luther statements like the following: God "is wholly incomprehensible and inaccessible to human reason" (LW 33, 290). Or take Luther's insistence in a 1522 sermon that human reason "yields only darkness" (WA 10:1:1, 527, 11–14). Are we dealing here with a flat contradiction?

In answering this question, we come to the heart of Luther's position. Again and again, in various ways, he calls for a crucial distinction to be made. In his 1535 Galatians lectures he put it this way: "There is a twofold knowledge of God: the general and the particular. All men have the general knowledge, namely, that God is, that he created heaven and earth, that he is great, that he punishes the wicked, etc. But what God thinks of us, what he wants to give and do to deliver us from sin and death and to save us—which is the particular and the true knowledge of God— this men do not know" (LW 26, 399). General knowledge of God, in other words, comes to us through reason. The "particular" or "true" knowledge of God—about this reason is "stone-blind": it must be revealed to us. In a 1539 disputation Luther explicitly correlates these two realms—reason and revelation—with philosophy and theology:

the first deals with "visible" matters, the latter with "invisible" ones (LW 38, 249). "Philosophy deals with things that can be known, at least in part [by reason], but theology has to do with things that are to be believed. This is the difference" (LW 38, 272). The two realms are even more concretely delineated: "it is one thing to believe in the Son of God, to possess and to expect eternal life, and something else again to be chaste, to marry, to live honestly in the world, to be liberal, meek, obedient, kind, and peaceable" (LW 38, 249). In short, reason yields a basic knowledge, it reigns in philosophical matters, and it even suffices for the virtuous life. What is disastrous, according to Luther, is when reason oversteps its bounds and attempts to be the supreme judge in matters of faith.

When it comes to these things, reason is defective in various ways. First it is insufficient; it fails to give humans what they need to know: "reason does admittedly believe that God is able and competent to help and to bestow; but reason does not know whether he is willing to do this also for us" (LW 19, 54). In fact, on the basis of bitter human experience, reason often draws the opposite conclusion, namely that God does not love us. That is its first defect.

The second is that when reason attempts to specify what God is like, it inevitably falls into error: "Reason is unable to identify God properly.... It knows that there is a God, but it does not know who or which is the true God.... [I]t rushes in clumsily and assigns the name God and ascribes divine honor to its own idea of God.... Nature knows the former—it is inscribed in everybody's heart; the latter is taught only by the Holy Spirit" (LW 19, 55–56). In trying to specify what God is like, reason overreaches its competence and inevitably ends up with an idol of its own making.

The third defect of reason is that it can give us no sure guidance in the human quest for "salvation":

[A]sk [natural reason] what is necessary to please God and to be saved, and it replies: 'You must build churches, cast bells, endow masses, hold vigils, make chalices, monstrances, pictures and ornaments; burn candles, pray this much, fast for St. Catherine, become a priest or a monk, walk to Rome or St. James Compostella, wear a hair shirt, torture yourself, and so on. These are good works, the right way and path to salvation.... [I]t is impossible for us to please God thus. (WA 10:1:1, 532, 1–12)

What reason tells us to do gets us nowhere. On all these properly theological issues—the path to salvation, the true nature of God, God's attitude toward us—reason is blind. This kind of knowledge can come to us only through revelation. And what comes to us through revelation cannot be made subject to reason. When reason sets itself up as the final arbiter of truth in such matters, it trespasses onto foreign territory.

From the beginning to the end of his career, Luther criticized his theological predecessors for allowing precisely this to happen. This is what he meant in his 1517 *Disputation Against Scholastic Theology*, when he said: "Briefly, the whole Aristotle is to theology as darkness is to light" (LW 31, 12) And the same point was the dominant theme of his 1539 *Disputation Concerning the Passage: "The Word Was Made Flesh" (John 1:14)* (LW 38, 239–277). Here he attacked the scholastics ("men of the Sorbonne") for making "the articles of faith subject to the judgment of human reason" (LW 38, 239). They "allow such things as the forgiveness of sins and the mystery of the incarnation and eternal life to be deduced by logic" (LW 38, 248). The "cardinal point," Luther says, is "that God is not subject to reason and syllogisms" (LW 38, 244). "Therefore in articles of faith one must have recourse to another dialectic and philosophy, which is called the word of God and faith" (LW 38, 241). That which God reveals, according to Luther, is "epistemologically privileged"—reason cannot trump it.

Luther's position, then, is that what God reveals and what we apprehend by faith transcends reason. He speaks of "the lofty character and majesty of the matter [articles of faith] which cannot be enclosed in the narrow confines of reason or syllogisms" (LW 38, 241). Such things as "[t]heology, the incarnation, and justification are above and beyond reason and philosophy" (ibid.). But does reason contradict the articles of faith?

At times Luther can say that it does. In fact, reason considers all the articles of faith to be foolishness, Luther said in his 1532 Psalms lectures. "[F]lesh and reason," he said, "fight in our members against the word and faith" (WA 40:3, 46, 12–13). And reason, he said in 1536, "despises faith. . . . It is up to God alone to give faith contrary to nature, and ability to believe contrary to reason" (LW 34, 160). In such statements, reason and revelation seem to be at war with one another. Yet we must recall that when reason contradicts faith, it is overstepping its proper jurisdiction. When it does this it becomes faulty, erroneous, sinful reason, "reason that is under the devil's control" (LW 54, nr. 439, 71), the "devil's whore" (LW 40, 175).

Right reason, on the other hand, does not stand in opposition to revealed truth. Indeed, Luther insists, how could it? For, we recall, reason is God's image in us, and hence it could not contradict truth revealed by God. "Although the Gospel is a higher gift and wisdom than human reason, it does not alter or nullify the intelligence of reason which God himself planted in us" (WA 22, 108, 12–15). Though the two may seem to us to be at odds, this cannot actually be the case: "If anything is really contrary to reason, it is certainly much more against God also. For how can anything not be in conflict with heavenly truth when it is in conflict with earthly truth" (LW 44, 336). Luther's fundamental position is this: what is of God is rational, and

what is rational is of God. This is what Luther meant when he said at the Diet of Worms in 1521: "Unless I am convinced by the testimony of the Scriptures or by clear reasons [*ratio evidens*] . . . my conscience is captive to the word of God" (LW 32, 112). What contradicts "clear reason" contradicts God's Word, and vice versa.

Thus in Luther sinful reason and faithful reason are sharply distinguished. The latter is authentic or right reason, which he sometimes calls "theological reason" (LW 34, 144). Most often, though, he uses the terms "illuminated" or "enlightened" reason. In 1533, over a meal, he

> was asked whether . . . reason has any value at all for Christians. He replied, "Prior to faith and knowledge of God, reason is darkness, but in believers it's an excellent instrument. . . . Faith is now furthered by reason, speech, and eloquence, whereas these were only impediments prior to faith. Enlightened reason, taken captive by faith, receives life from faith. . . . [S]o our reason is different in believers than it was before, for it doesn't fight against faith but promotes it." (LW 54, nr. 2938b, 183)

On another occasion that same year Luther was asked about the role of reason in theology. Once again the distinction is crucial in his answer: "I make a distinction. Reason that is under the devil's control is harmful. . . . We see this in the case of learned men who on the basis of their reason disagree with the Word. On the other hand, when illuminated by the Holy Spirit, reason helps to interpret the Holy Scriptures. . . . [R]eason, when illuminated, helps faith by reflecting on something. . . . [R]eason that's illuminated takes all its thoughts from the Word" (LW 54, nr. 439, 71). Notice too, in the above quotations, that enlightened reason serves faith in various ways. It "furthers" and "promotes" faith, presumably by developing arguments in its favor. It helps us interpret Scripture properly. It reflects on matters of faith, presumably in the interest of making them to some extent understandable.

In summary, reduced to its bare bones, Luther's view of reason is as follows. Reason is God's greatest gift to humanity. Its proper jurisdiction and competence extends to all human affairs. When it claims supremacy in matters of faith, however, it becomes the "devil's whore," for these things transcend reason. By submitting to revelation, granting revealed truth a privileged epistemic primacy, it becomes "enlightened reason." Reason in this sense, kept within its proper bounds, "serves" faith and is obviously indispensable to theology.

Resurrection   The Christian belief in the resurrection was not directly in dispute in the Protestant Reformation. Luther, along with all sixteenth-century Christians, accepted what all three of the historic creeds asserted: that Christ rose from the dead and that humans too will one day rise from death. Luther likewise took for granted the common understanding of the tradition that these two resurrections—Christ's and ours—are inseparably linked, so closely that we can say, "Christ's resurrection is our resurrection" (LW 28, 202; cf. 28, 94). They can be, and indeed must be, treated together. On these basics, the tradition spoke with one voice, and Luther did not contradict it.

This means that Luther wrote relatively little on the resurrection. We recall that much of his agenda as a theologian was set for him by his opponents. Thus it is not surprising that he wrote far more on the papacy, or on the Lord's Supper, than he did on the resurrection. To begin to see then how he understood this doctrine, we must turn to his sermons—Easter sermons, funeral sermons, and most importantly, a series of seventeen sermons on 1 Corinthians 15, preached mostly on Sunday after-

noons from 1532 to 1533. This last series, while it was edited by Luther's disciple Caspar Cruciger, is the most accurate and highly developed treatment of the resurrection to be found in Luther's writings. What follows here is based on these sources.

While Luther did not write much about the resurrection, it would be a serious mistake to conclude that it is unimportant in his theology. Time and again, throughout his career, Luther asserts the opposite. In 1526 he called it "the chief article of our faith" (WA 21, 214, 23). Without this, he said in 1532, the whole point of Christ's advent, life, and death is lost (LW 28, 60). Nor is there, without this, any salvation for us (WA 37, 72, 7–9). And in 1544 he emphasized again that a Christianity without the resurrection would be entirely pointless: "this article [of faith] on the resurrection is the chief one upon which our salvation is finally based, and without which all others would be useless and altogether fruitless" (WA 21, 214, 10–12). The purpose of Christ's coming, his life, and his death is his resurrection. And the purpose of his resurrection is our resurrection. Christianity, since it is a religion of "salvation," is unthinkable without this.

Yet the resurrection was problematic for Luther, both at the level of his personal experience and at the theological level. This is because "reason" contradicts the resurrection—it tells us there is no such thing. This was already the problem Paul was facing among Christians at Corinth: some had applied reason to the resurrection belief and had "perverted this article into tomfoolery" (LW 28, 59). Reason, Luther held, makes nonsense out of the resurrection (LW 28, 170).

Before going further, we do well to pay careful attention to what Luther means by "reason" (Lat. *ratio;* Ger. *Vernunft*) here. As is often the case, Luther gives us no concise definition: only from a careful scrutiny of the context and of his actual usage of the term can we infer what precisely he is referring to. First, "reason" obviously does not refer to every rational thought process, since the text itself leads one through a certain thought process. The "reason" he is referring to is a faculty that makes judgments on the basis of sense perception, feeling, and experience (LW 28, 70). It "does no more than merely to observe the facts as they appear to the eye" (LW 28, 69). Rather than looking beneath the surface of things, it "cannot but say that bread is bread and water is water" (LW 28, 70). Luther calls it "Master Epicurus" (LW 28, 69). It is a vulgar, literalistic positivism—a "swinish" refusal to acknowledge a depth dimension to reality (LW 28, 148). People who function only on this level "are and remain pigs, believe like pigs, and die like pigs" (LW 28, 147). In short, what Luther means by "reason" in this context seems to be very close to what we in our time would call "common sense."

What does "reason," understood in this way, tell us about the resurrection? Reason/common sense tells us only "that one person dies after another, remains dead, decomposes, and crumbles to dust in the grave" (LW 28, 69). Reason/common sense tells us that our lives end in the worst stench in the world, that of the rotting human corpse (WA 49, 729, 13–14). Our feelings, our eyes, our senses, and our heart (LW 28, 70) all point to the conclusion that belief in a resurrection is "ridiculous," "absurd," "silly" (LW 28, 115), in short, "preposterous" (LW 28, 117). This is what Paul was struggling against in Corinth, and this is what Luther is struggling against.

Luther argues to the effect that on matters such as the resurrection, reliance on reason/common sense is inappropriate, "for reason knows nothing and can comprehend nothing of such sublime matters" (LW 28, 63). It is out of place here because "this is called an article of faith, not one of your reason" (LW 28, 70). Faith accepts what is contrary to common sense (LW

28, 71). It looks beyond this: "For to believe firmly that . . . I will live eternally, endowed with a beautiful, glorious body, although I lie under the sod . . . that requires a . . . wisdom which is not governed by any feeling or perceiving, but which can look beyond that" (LW 28, 72). Experience, sense perception, and so forth, contradict the resurrection. They must be ignored (LW 28, 98).

(Luther has a relatively pessimistic view of human experience. It almost always tells us, for instance, that death is the end. But once in a while experience gives us hints that this is not necessarily so. Thus in springtime, some of us notice that "[l]ife is emerging from death everywhere" [LW 28, 179]. Gardens in themselves point to the same thing [WA 49, 72, 9–10]. But these are exceptions—intimations that flicker briefly in our consciousness before they are doused by life's harsher realities.)

Since the resurrection is a matter of faith, Luther argues, the language of common sense must be left behind; people of faith must learn a new language (LW 28, 180; 28, 208). "This is not human, earthly speech, but a divine, celestial speech." To the literalist (Master Epicurus), it is "strange and obscure" (LW 28, 178): "this world is not conversant with such speech and does not understand it" (LW 28, 179). It is a language that speaks of "the resurrection of the flesh," "death swallowed up in victory," "eternal life," "a new spiritual body," and so forth. All of this is gibberish to those who only know the language of reason/common sense.

Elsewhere Luther expresses the same thing with the help of another image, an ocular one. What one sees through the eyes of reason and through the eyes of faith differs dramatically: "if you see a Christian dying and being buried, lying there like nothing more than a dead corpse, dead to both your eyes and your ears, nevertheless, through faith you see another picture instead of that picture of death. You see not a grave, nor a dead corpse. You see only life and a beautiful, thriving garden or a green meadow, and in it only young, living, happy people" (WA 37, 68, 15–20). The eyes of reason/common sense allow us to see only death: "outward, physical perspectives of the flesh . . . place death alone before our eyes" (WA 37, 69, 24–25). But in faith "you get another point of view, which can see through this death into the resurrection. . . . It makes for a new way of thinking and understanding of things" (WA 37, 69, 33–36). Notice again, in this last statement, that Luther's critique of reason is not an abandonment of rationality as such. It is rather a statement about the limitations of commonsense rationality and the need for a different kind of reason, a "reason of faith," if you will.

Whether we think of faith as a new language or as a new way of seeing, what specifically does it allow us to say or to "know" about the resurrection? Here Luther thought caution was in order: we are dealing with what Paul called a "mystery" (1 Cor. 15:51). Our starting point then must be a respectful agnosticism. "As little as babies in their mother's womb know about what awaits them, so little we know about eternal life" (WATR 3, nr. 3339, 276, 26–27). It cannot be logically demonstrated (LW 28, 97). It will not happen "in a manner that might be intelligible to you" (LW 28, 201). Even after it has occurred, we will not know how: "For just as a man who falls asleep and sleeps soundly until morning does not know what has happened to him when he wakes up, so we shall suddenly rise on the last day; and we shall not know how we died or how we came through death" (WA 17:2, 235, 17–20). Almost all of the many questions people have about the resurrection must be answered with, "We don't know."

One more caution in approaching this mystery of faith is in order, from Luther's perspective. Our language about it must avoid an excessive literalism. To be sure, Luther believed that the resurrection of Christ was physical:

he attacked the view that it occurred "only spiritually" (LW 28, 122; cf. 28, 76). But we must immediately add that this risen physical body was not an ordinary physical body: it was different (LW 28, 150), "changed and glorified" (LW 28, 151), with no need of food (LW 28, 142), and so forth. Here we are speaking about a "bodily" resurrection, but with a difference. So too with the resurrection of human beings: Christians believe in the resurrection "of the flesh," but this is not to be taken literally. When Germans hear this phrase, they immediately think of the butcher shop (BC 439). Or people start wondering about overcrowding in heaven, or how the elimination of bodily waste will occur (LW 28, 170–172). To think like this is to take "resurrection of the flesh" literally, to regress into the language of reason/common sense. This is a mistake: what we are talking about is "a wholly different, more beautiful, and perfect existence" (LW 28, 172). More appropriate for this language of faith is image and metaphor (LW 28, 176–177). Paul himself described the resurrection as a "trumpet sounding" and "meeting the Lord in the air" (1 Thess. 4:16–18). But in Luther's view, "These words are purely allegorical. He [Paul] was trying to paint a picture, as we must use pictures with children and simple people" (LW 51, 253). Thus even imagination plays a role in the language of faith. And this is appropriate, as long as we understand that these are weak human attempts to penetrate the mystery and are not to be taken literally.

It is crucial to keep this in mind in order to understand Luther when he speaks in utterly concrete terms, and about himself (he had a gift for this). For example, in a 1533 sermon on the resurrection, he said, "we will sleep until he comes and knocks on the grave and says, 'Dr. Martin, get up.' Then I will arise in a moment and be eternally happy with him" (WA 37, 151, 8–10). The literalist will worry: will it be Paul's "trumpet" or Luther's "knocking on the grave" that will awaken us? But in thinking this way, one will miss the point.

What then is the point? What is the fundamental truth that Christians, with all their images and metaphors, are struggling to express? One way in which Luther formulated it is this: "The whole world dreads nothing more than death and desires nothing more than life. And this treasure we are to have in him without measure and without end" (LW 28, 146). The ultimate problem that plagues all of human life is the prospect of death followed by eternal nothingness—the final negation—the great No. To believe in the resurrection means to affirm that precisely here, hidden beneath this No, a Yes is to be found. Here, Luther says, we will meet God himself, "who is the life and the inexhaustible foundation of all good and of endless joy" (WA 36, 599, 16–17). Eternal life—not eternal nothingness—awaits us. In abstract terms, resurrection means the final negation of the negation.

But Luther prefers a more concrete way of speaking. The resurrection is the solution to life's ultimate problem, yes, but it also is the fulfillment of all lesser human desires as well: "wherever God is, all good things that one may wish for must be present" (LW 28, 146). This means that in the state we call "eternal life," "whatever delights your heart shall be yours abundantly" (ibid.). "[I]n him [God] all our needs and wants will be satisfied" (LW 28, 144). Here again Luther thinks the imagination should be set free. He personally thought that we will be given the ability to fly! (He mentions this often enough for us to surmise that this may have been one of his fantasies; LW 28, 143; 28, 144; 28, 188) And why not? If flying is essential to perfect human happiness, then our future ability to fly is assured. Ultimately, though, Luther concedes, God himself will be the satisfaction of all human wants; in Paul's words, he will be "everything to every one" (1 Cor. 15:28; LW 28, 141–142).

What then does Luther mean by this belief in the resurrection? To put it in his (and Paul's) favorite language, it means to believe that God will eventually bring all his enemies into subjection to himself (1 Cor. 15:25–27; LW 28, 128–141). Or, to translate, to believe in the resurrection means to live with the confidence that someday, despite all appearances to the contrary, life will triumph over death, joy over sorrow, love over hatred, beauty over ugliness.

See also **Death; Eschatology**

Sacraments (General) The sacramental system of the late medieval church was an integral part of the young Luther's life. As a child he received the sacraments administered to all Christian children. As a theological student, he became thoroughly acquainted with the church's official teaching on the subject, above all the decrees of the Fourth Lateran Council (1215) and the Council of Florence (1439). He studied assiduously the tradition of sacramental theology, in all its complexity and ambiguity, reaching back to Augustine in the fifth century and forward to Peter Lombard in the twelfth, culminating for Luther at least in Gabriel Biel's massive *Exposition of the Canon of the Mass* (1488). At twenty-four he was ordained to the priesthood and expected now to preside over these rites. This entire edifice was grounded on one fundamental theological assumption: it is by way of the sacraments that God gives his grace to human beings. Here was the bedrock of the sacramental worldview Luther inherited.

Yet, already at a very young age, it was precisely the sacraments that caused him acute personal/spiritual distress. Penance was a torture for him as a young friar, and his early celebrations of the eucharist as a young priest left him in anguish. Something was clearly amiss. Personal problems, along with the perception of widespread abuses, eventually evolved into a wholesale critique: before long Luther was challenging the system as in some ways mistaken, in many cases dysfunctional, and more often than not oppressive.

Already in October of 1517, Luther's attack on indulgences bore within it an implicit critique of the sacrament of penance. In the months following, he achieved a progressively greater clarity, not only in regard to penance but on the sacraments in general. By August of 1518, in his *Explanations of the Ninety-five Theses*, he could assert, "It is a heresy to hold that the sacraments . . . give grace to those who place no obstacle in the way. . . . [I]t is not the sacrament, but faith in the sacrament, that justifies" (LW 31, 106–107). To thus place faith at the center of one's definition of the sacrament was a novelty, if not a heresy, at least in the opinions of Cardinal Cajetan (LW 31, 261) and Pope Leo X (*Exsurge Domine*, no. 1).

Luther solidified and developed this redefinition in three sermons on the sacraments in November and December of 1519: penance (LW 35, 9–22), baptism (LW 35, 29–43), and the Lord's Supper (LW 35, 49–73). The operative definition in each sermon is this: a sacrament is a concrete representation of a divine promise received by faith (LW 35, 11; 35, 30; 35, 49). Why no sermons on the other four sacraments? Luther explained in a letter to George Spalatin on December 18, 1519: "Neither you nor anyone else should hope for or expect any sermon from me on the other sacraments. . . . [T]here is no sacrament except where a divine promise is expressly given, which calls forth faith, since God has no dealings with us without his word of promise and the faith which receives it" (WABr 1, nr. 231, 594–595, 19–24). Already some of the implications of his new definition were becoming clear to him.

In 1520 Luther finalized the basic contours of his sacramental theology. In his *Babylonian Captivity of the Church*, which appeared in October, he launched his full-blown assault on the traditional sacramental system. Three things, he argued, are needed for a real sacrament. First, there must be a divinely instituted

sign or symbol, attested to in Scripture. The second thing is what the sign points to or represents, and this is the divine promise. Third, there is the faith that receives the promise (LW 36, 65; 36, 92; 36, 124). These are the essentials: where they are, there is a true sacrament.

One of the ramifications of this, already worked out in this treatise, was a drastic downsizing of the sacramental system. When all was said and done, only two of the traditional seven remained. Penance was more problematic for Luther than the rest. Early on in *The Babylonian Captivity of the Church*, one finds him still affirming penance as a sacrament (LW 36, 18). But as the writing of this work progressed, Luther seems to have arrived at greater clarity. "[I]t has seemed proper to restrict the name of sacrament to those promises which have signs attached to them [in Scripture]. . . . Hence there are, strictly speaking, but two sacraments in the church of God—baptism and the bread. . . . The sacrament of penance . . . lacks the divinely instituted visible sign" (LW 36, 124). The others—confirmation, marriage, extreme unction, and ordination—are all lacking one or another of the requisite components.

Here then in basic outline is Luther's mature understanding of the sacraments. To be sure, many details were yet to be worked out in the years after 1520. So too we find shifts in emphasis in the later Luther, often owing to the polemical context he found himself in. But the main lines of his sacramental theology, laid down in 1520, held steady to the end.

One issue that had yet to be clarified after 1520 was the relationship of "Word" and sacrament. What precisely were the divine promises symbolized in baptism and in the Lord's Supper? In short, they were for Luther one and the same, namely, the promise of the forgiveness of sin. Just as there are no distinct "graces" attached to various sacraments, so too there are no distinct "words of promise." There is one grace, one promise, one gospel. When this comes to us in the divinely instituted sign, and when humans open themselves up to it in faith—there is a true sacrament.

But cannot this same promise of forgiveness also confront us in other ways, in preaching for instance? Luther's answer is yes. In no way, however, does this devalue the sacrament or make it superfluous. By 1526 Luther could explain it this way: "for although the same thing is present in the sermon as in the sacrament, here [in the sacrament] there is the advantage that it is directed to definite individuals" (LW 36, 348). The sacrament personalizes, particularizes, and makes tangible the gospel, the divine promise of forgiveness.

All of this had far-reaching implications. For many of Luther's contemporaries, one burning question had to do with the necessity of the sacraments for salvation. Already in *The Babylonian Captivity* (1520) Luther placed the greatest emphasis not on the sign, but on the faith that receives the sign. Accordingly, he argued, it is faith—not the sign—that is necessary: "faith is such a necessary part of the sacrament that it can save even without the sacrament" (LW 36, 67). In 1521 he took up the issue again, this time in connection with the classic Pauline statements on faith and righteousness (Rom. 1:17; 10:10): "He [Paul] does not say that the righteous shall live by the sacraments, but by his faith, for not the sacraments, but faith, together with the sacraments, gives life and righteousness. . . . [Y]ou can become righteous by faith without the bodily reception of the sacraments (so long as you do not despise them)" (LW 32, 14–15). A 1522 sermon applies this explicitly to baptism: "baptism is nothing more than an external sign that reminds us of the divine promise. . . . Nobody should despise it. . . . But if one could not receive it, he is not thereby damned, if he now believes the gospel" (WA 10:3, 142, 18–25). To be sure, at a later stage Luther had cause to rethink this and

to speak more cautiously, especially in light of "spiritualist" challenges. Against these opponents he emphasized, in 1529 for instance, that "[w]hat God institutes and commands cannot be useless" (BC 457). But he never abandoned the basic position he took in 1520. As he put it in 1533, "the sacrament cannot exist without the word, but the word can exist without the sacrament. And in case of necessity, a person can be saved without the sacrament but not without the word" (WA 38, 231, 9–11). The sacraments, Luther held, are not superfluous or unimportant. But neither are they, in any absolute sense, necessary for salvation.

Another issue, one that assumed increasing importance as the Reformation grew and spread and fragmented, had to do with the minister of the sacrament. Early on, certainly by the time of his 1519 sermons on the sacraments, Luther had abandoned the view that priests, at the moment of their ordination, receive an infusion of supernatural power that enables them to perform these rites (*see* **Ministerial/Pastoral Office; Ordination; Universal Priesthood**). Still assuming that penance was a sacrament, Luther argued that it is part of a priest's job to give absolution. But "where there is no priest, each individual Christian, even a woman or a child, does as much" (LW 35, 12). In the following year, Luther developed his new understanding of vocation and extended its application to the minister of the Lord's Supper: "suppose a group of earnest Christian laymen were taken prisoner and set down in a desert without an episcopally ordained priest among them. And suppose they were to come to a common mind there and then in the desert and elect one of their number . . . to say mass. . . . Such a man would be as truly a priest as though he had been ordained by all the bishops and popes in the world" (LW 44, 128). All Christians are able to administer the sacraments, though only priests are called to do so.

To thus demystify the sacraments, to democratize their administration (potentially at least), is to take a major step in the direction of dismantling the medieval sacramental system. In doing all this, the question of power was never far from Luther's mind. In the world he inherited, priests exercised enormous sway over the hearts and minds of the laity. Luther thought that by controlling the sacramental system, priests were attempting to control access to God's grace. Here was the most basic reason why, from time to time, an angry anticlericalism surfaces in Luther's writings on the subject.

See also Baptism; Confirmation; Extreme Unction; Lord's Supper; Marriage; Ordination; Penance

Sexuality   Luther's view of human sexuality must be understood in the context of the medieval intellectual culture from which it emerged. For a thousand years before Luther, theologians and church leaders had viewed sexuality through a lens heavily tinted by Augustinianism and monasticism. In its main contours, the dominant view included the following features: God created the male of the species first, then the female to help him with reproduction (and, some said, for companionship). Thus, insofar as sex was part of God's original intent in creation, it had to be affirmed as good. Yet the sin of the first parents (initiated by the woman) threw the intended order of creation into chaos, and thus sexuality too became "disordered," subrational, and governed by passion. Through this disordered act, the sin of the first parents was passed down to every generation and thus to us. Christ alone was not a product of the sex act and therefore was born "without sin." In the sex act, the human being becomes less than the "rational animal" he or she was created to be, and descends into irrationality, which is by definition evil. Thus the sex act always involves sinfulness, though

this may be somewhat mitigated by certain things like the sacrament of matrimony, the desire for offspring, and so on. Medieval theology produced endless versions of this schema, but despite the various presentations, the basic themes remained relatively constant. In addition the pastoral literature of the period, which translated academic theology into practice, presupposed this foundation. In astonishing numbers, writers of this pastoral literature (all celibate males) produced scores of works dealing with almost every conceivable aspect of sexuality, and revealing at every stage what has been called a "horrified fascination" with the subject. In the view of some experts, Christianity thus became, by the close of the Middle Ages, a sex-hating religion.

This rather monolithic perspective on sexuality was bequeathed to Luther: he was highly trained in its literature, both academic and pastoral. There is no doubt that he failed to move beyond it in his earliest writings. For instance, it heavily influenced his first programmatic reflections on the subject, his *Sermon on the Estate of Marriage* in 1519. Here he echoed the Augustinian view that sexuality was corrupted by the fall, and that therefore even within marriage it is not free from sin (LW 44, 9). The language of desire as "the wicked lust of the flesh" (LW 44, 10) is wholly traditional.

The language of shame and revulsion, along with its medieval Augustinian underpinnings, more or less disappeared for a time in Luther's writings, as we shall see. Curiously, it then seems to have reemerged with a vengeance in his late *Lectures on Genesis* (1535–1545). Here sex within marriage, though excusable, is "shameful and unclean" (LW 5, 37–38). Before the fall, procreation would have occurred "without any depravity," whereas now it is corrupted by the "awful hideousness of lust" (LW 1, 104). And in this "bestial desire and lust" all humans can recognize the consequences of original sin in themselves (LW 1, 115). Clearly the perspective here is firmly grounded in the medieval paradigm. In assessing this, we do well to take into account the fact that the authenticity of these late lectures on Genesis has been seriously questioned (for details see the introduction to the lectures in LW 1, 1–3).

The Genesis lectures appear all the more anomalous in this regard when we see the rather dramatic ways in which Luther broke out of the medieval sexual paradigm after 1519. Here I want to briefly describe three such departures.

First, one finds in Luther after 1519 a wholesale revaluation of sexual feelings as such. To put it briefly: irrational, vehement, and unruly as these feelings may be, God has planted them in us. Already in 1522 Luther emphasizes that such feelings are instinctual and natural: "For it is not a matter of free choice or decision but a natural and necessary thing, that whatever is a man must have a woman and whatever is a woman must have a man" (LW 45, 18). Abstaining from sex has negative health effects (LW 45, 45). In fact, the need for sex "is as deeply rooted in nature as eating and drinking" (LW 39, 297; cf. LW 52, 273). To be ashamed of one's sexuality is to be ashamed of one's humanity (WA 18, 277, 26–36). God created sexuality before the fall in telling Adam and Eve to be fruitful; thus the "passionate, natural inclination" of sexual desire "is God's word and work" (WA 18, 275, 19–28). Sexual feelings, he said, are the ordinance of God implanted in us; few humans can resist these feelings, and why should they? (LW 45, 19 and 21). Indeed, such desire ought to continue as long as possible. When sexual boredom sets in, this, he said, is the work of the devil (LW 21, 89). Luther has come a long way here from the medieval perspective, and his position is difficult to reconcile with language about the "awful hideousness of lust."

A second departure from the medieval past has to do with Luther's view of the power of the feelings God has implanted in us. In fact, he thought, they are so powerful that they are utterly unmanageable outside marriage. "Where nature functions as God implanted it," he said in 1529, "it is not possible to remain chaste outside of marriage . . . for natural inclinations and stimulations proceed unrestrained and unimpeded" (BC 415). Marriage channels the power of sexual desire and protects people from sexuality's potentially destructive power (LW 45, 43–45). Except in the rarest of instances, vows of celibacy are a mistake: one can of course abstain from the sex act, but sexual desire continues and cannot be repressed by any amount of willpower. In his *Lectures on Galatians* of 1535 Luther recalled his own experience and that of John von Staupitz in the monastery. Countless times they resolved to banish sexual thoughts from their minds, and countless times they failed (LW 27, 73). Already in 1521/22 he had dealt in a sermon with one of the consequences of celibacy that was of substantial concern to medieval authors: wet dreams. (Like medieval ecclesiastical writers, Luther showed little reticence in discussing such topics.) "Where men and women do not come together," he said, "nature will nevertheless take its course . . . so it would be better that men and women lay with one another, in accordance with God's creation and nature's demands" (LW 52, 259; cf. 52, 268). In taking this position on the superiority of marriage over celibacy, Luther was of course distancing himself from the entire Roman clerical establishment.

A third way in which Luther moved decisively beyond the existing consensus was his abandonment of all legalism in matters of human sexuality. Medieval church authorities had developed a vast panoply of laws attempting to regulate this aspect of the lives of the laity. This Luther rejected in its entirety, for reasons having to do with his most basic Reformation concern. To prevent social chaos, civil authorities must make and enforce laws. But church authorities, when they do so, attempt to bind consciences and thus try to take away our Christian liberty. The "gospel" in every case is the proclamation that we are set free from all such laws. The gospel frees us from moral codes, not for the sake of sexual license in this case, but precisely so that we can act out of love.

Love, if it is really love, needs no laws. When "husband and wife live together in love and harmony, cherishing each other wholeheartedly . . . [c]hastity [i.e., fidelity] always follows spontaneously without any command" (*BC* 415). But human love, Luther knew, is not perfect; relationships in the real world are flawed and complex, so much so that no legalistic framework can fit. Thus, in certain circumstances, love may require that we ignore the "rules," and sometimes a lesser evil may be accepted to avoid a greater one.

This antilegalistic approach to issues of human sexuality was widely misunderstood by Luther's sixteenth-century opponents as an endorsement of permissive sexual behavior. In part this misunderstanding may have been a willful one, calculated to morally discredit the movement. But we must also acknowledge that to some extent Luther's extremely blunt and public rhetoric on such issues fed these misunderstandings.

Even his followers winced at some of the conclusions he drew in applying these principles to concrete issues and situations. A few examples, all of them complex, can only be listed here. First, he held, among those who commit adultery, there is a difference between some who do it "intentionally" and others who do it "because of weakness" (LW 27, 80). Second, "cross-dressing," while it is condemned in the Hebrew Scriptures, is not sinful if done in the context of play (LW 9, 219). Third, premarital sex is not equally sinful in every case (LW 46, 293). Fourth, there are circumstances in which the wife of an impotent husband should seek sexual fulfillment with another man (LW 36, 103–104; 45,

19). Fifth, there are circumstances in which a secret bigamy would be preferable to divorce (LW 36, 104; 45, 19; 50, 33; 54, nr. 5038, 379; nr. 5046, 382; nr. 5096, 387–389). In the context of Luther's time, such conclusions were provocative to say the least. The important thing to see, however, is what Luther was trying to insist on: the gospel, in freeing us from the law, has consequences for all of human life, even sexuality. Ultimately, he thought, it frees us from all legalism for the sake of love.

Sin   Luther took it for granted that at the very heart of Christian theology there is a fundamental correlation between sin and salvation. Or to put it another way, Christianity is about salvation, and for this to make any sense at all, there must be something to be saved from. This something is what Christians mean by "sin." And in Luther's view, when we speak theologically, sinfulness is the very essence of what it means to be human. He explained in his 1532 lectures on Psalm 51: philosophers understand the human person as a "rational animal"; lawyers look at humans as property owners, and so forth; physicians regard people as either healthy or sick. "But a theologian discusses man as a sinner. In theology, this is the essence of man. The theologian is concerned that man become aware of this nature of his, corrupted by sins" (LW 12, 310–311). In other words, theologians look at the human as she or he stands in relation to God: seen in this way, "sinful" is the most basic characterization. The Gospel statement, "Those who are well have no need of a physician" (Matt. 9:12), is self-evident and yet too easily forgotten. A cure makes no sense without a disease.

The Catholic Church on the eve of the Reformation also emphasized that humans are sinners. One of the notable features of late medieval piety was what we might call the proliferation of sins. Catechetical literature, for instance, listed sins against the five commandments of the church, the seven deadly sins and their "daughters," the nine "alien" sins, the "mute" sins, six sins against the Holy Spirit, sins of the tongue, and so forth. Most extensive of all was the enumeration of sins against the Ten Commandments, sometimes amounting to several hundred. Lay-people, so the teaching church held, must be made aware of all the various ways in which they sin. In other words, their consciences must be "formed" or sensitized by such teaching. This heavy pedagogy of sins, there is no doubt, had its impact on the young Luther.

At first sight, it appears that Luther extended this tradition of listing sins. Thus he wrote at least eight separate commentaries on the Ten Command-ments (*see* **Decalogue**). In one of these, his 1522 *Personal Prayer Book*, he did pre-cisely what the late medieval literature had done, giving an extensive listing of the various sins against each command-ment (LW 43, 14–24). But there is also something unmistakably different about Luther's approach to the topic. Far from shortening the list of sins, he extended it dramatically: we do not "sin" only when we commit one of these several hundred acts. Rather, he insisted, we sin in every-thing we do (LW 31, 40; 32, 83; etc.).

If that is true, then listing discrete human acts and calling them sins makes little sense. Luther occasionally does this, but only for pedagogical reasons. Theologically, such lists are of no inter-est. For if we do sin in all our actions, even our very best ones (LW 32, 86), then the important question is not about human acts but about human nature: what kind of beings are we to act in this way so consistently? In other words, Luther shifted the focus from "sins" to "sinfulness," from committing sins to being sinful. From a theological point of view, it is more important to see the for-est than the trees.

To understand this mode of existence that Luther calls "sin," we must explore what was traditionally called "original sin." In a sermon from the early 1520s, he

explained why: "Hereditary sin or natu-ral sin or personal sin is the truly chief sin. If this sin did not exist, there would also be no actual sin. This sin is not com-mitted, as are all other sins; rather it is. It lives and commits all sins and is the real essential sin which does not sin for an hour or for a while; rather no matter where or how long a person lives, this sin is there also" (LW 52, 152). In other words, the doctrine of original sin *is* the Christian assertion of human sinfulness, together with the universality and per-during nature of this sinfulness.

The doctrine traditionally rests on a story—the narrative of "the fall" in Gen-esis 3. Luther's late *Lectures on Genesis* (1535–45) make clear that he understood the story as an "historical event" (LW 1, 144), as did all sixteenth-century theolo-gians. Adam and Eve were real people, who lived in a state of original righ-teousness: "it was Adam's [and Eve's] nature to love God, to believe God, to know God, etc." (LW 1, 165). As for the snake, "there is no doubt that it was a real serpent in which Satan was," albeit "a most beautiful little beast" at the time (LW 1, 151–152). Had he tempted Adam first, he would no doubt have been told to "Shut up!" (LW 1, 151). But Eve was first and she succumbed and induced Adam to follow suit.

The result was catastrophic, an utter transformation of human existence. Snakes became ugly, human procreation became shameful, childbirth became painful (LW 1, 186). In fact Luther com-piles a large catalogue of all the nega-tive aspects of human life and attributes them all to the fall (LW 1, 203–219)—a catalogue reminiscent of the medi-eval literary genre *De miseria humanae conditionis* (*On the Misery of the Human Condition*). Most importantly, Luther says that after the fall "man not only does not love God any longer but flees from Him, hates Him, and desires to be and live without Him" (LW 1, 165). Thus human nature is damaged, and in this damaged form it is inherited by all. How is it transmitted from one generation to the next? Though he does not emphasize it, Luther basically concurs with Augustine and a large part of the medieval theological tradition in affirming that this fault is transmitted through the sex act (LW 12, 347–348). (He agrees too with the tradition that a virginal conception results in a sinless child; WA 12, 403, 29–32.) In fact, Luther's entire understanding of this story never strays outside the medieval consensus.

His theological originality begins to assert itself, however, when he broaches the question of just what this great first sin was. Astonishingly, we find in his writings at least six answers to this question.

First, we must set aside the view of the "Epicureans," who reduced it all to a "fairy tale" by focusing on "the bite of the apple" (LW 1, 162). Rather, Luther thought, the serpent tempted Eve to disbelieve God when he told her, "you will not die" (Gen. 3:4; LW 1, 146). Here was the ultimate temptation, and it led to the ultimate sin: "Truly, therefore, this temptation is the sum of all temptations; it brings with it the overthrow or the violation of the entire Decalog. Unbelief is the source of all sins; when Satan brought about this unbelief by driving out or corrupting the Word, the rest was easy for him" (LW 1, 147). Luther's word for this first and greatest sin is *Unglaube*. It is often translated as "unbelief" or "disbelief," but a better translation would be "lack of faith." It means to turn away from God and to ground one's existence on something other than God. This "lack of faith" is the source of all sin, just as faith is the source of all righteousness: "the root and source of sin is unbelief and turning away from God, just as, on the other hand, the source and root of righteousness is faith" (LW 1, 162).

Second, lack of faith is the violation of the first commandment of the Decalogue. "You are to have no other gods" means to fear, love, and trust God alone (*BC* 351). This is what "faith" means.

Fearing, loving, or trusting anything more than God—this is the lack of faith (WA 31:1, 148, 1). And this is also idolatry. Idols, the "new and recent gods, whom our fathers did not worship" (Deut. 32:17), Luther thinks, are born in *Unglaube* (LW 1, 148; cf. 1, 49). Worshiping them is the basic sin.

Third, as humans refuse to live by faith, they put their trust in false gods, above all, themselves. Thus, in the end, they "transfer the glory of God to [their own] works" (LW 1, 149), they attempt to justify themselves (WA 17:1, 233, 1–3). The fundamental sin is the human attempt at self-justification.

Fourth, the pathology in our lives, Luther can sometimes say, stems from ingratitude. He understands this as follows: God freely gives us the ultimate gift of his love. Faith is our receptivity to this gift. To refuse it, to close ourselves off from this love, is a lack of faith and the ultimate ingratitude. This sin is therefore "the most shameful vice and the greatest dishonor we can do to God" (WA 31:1, 76, 16). Ingratitude is robbery of God (LW 25, 10). What greater sin could there be (WA 39:1, 580, 13–14)?

Fifth, Luther speaks of the focal point of human sinfulness as pride. "[For] we seek not the glory of God, but our own glory in God and in all creatures" (WA 40:2, 325, 28–29; cf. LW 25, 313). All too often the best moral efforts of human beings are accompanied by a smug, self-satisfied, self-righteous attitude. And these efforts thereby became worthless in God's eyes: "No one is certain that he is not continually committing mortal sin, because of the most secret vice of pride. . . . [T]hrough it all works are made unclean and cannot stand in the light of God's just judgment" (LW 32, 91; cf. 31, 11). Luther calls pride a "most secret vice" because humans learn to disguise and hide it so well, often precisely beneath its opposite, humility (LW 21, 316). Indeed, pride is so pervasive that Luther can call it the root of all sin: "if pride would cease there would be no sin anywhere" (LW 31, 47).

A sixth way in which Luther speaks of the ultimate sin is as self-love (LW 31, 46–50). This, he can say, is "the beginning of all sin" (WA 7, 212, 7). God's demand on humans is that they act out of love for him and for their fellow human beings. Humans cannot do God's will in this regard precisely because they act out of self-love. It is this that blocks them, and it is this, therefore, that is sin in its most basic sense. "In everything that one does or leaves undone, one seeks one's own good, will, and honor rather than God's or one's neighbor's: that is why all one's works, all one's words, all one's thoughts, all one's life are evil and not godly" (WA 6, 244, 10–13). Ultimately, human egocentricity attempts to dethrone God: "Man is by nature unable to want God to be God. Indeed, he himself wants to be God" (LW 31, 10). What sin could be more fundamental?

Luther from time to time identifies each of these six—lack of faith, idolatry, self-justification, ingratitude, pride, or self-love—as the root of human sinfulness, as *the* ultimate sin. Is he wildly self-contradictory here? No, for in his mind they finally amount to the same thing. They are simply different ways of saying that humans "turn in on themselves" (*homo incurvatus in se*; LW 25, 345) and thereby turn away from God. These are different ways of looking at the ultimate sin from which all other "sins" proceed (LW 1, 150, 147–148, 162). Thus the true sickness of the human condition is not many, but one. All other particular "sins" are mere symptoms of this disease.

The particular sins, those forbidden in the Decalogue for instance, are manifestations of this one "sin." Luther's various expositions of the Ten Commandments emphasize this. In his Large Catechism, for instance, he makes the point that the first commandment is "the most important" (BC 392). In forbidding us to have other gods, it demands faith, that is, that you "entrust yourself to him [God] completely" (BC 388). This aligns us, as it were, with God's will and thus

fulfills all the other commandments: "if the heart is right with God and we keep this commandment, all the rest will follow on their own" (BC 392). And the contrary is also true: entrusting ourselves and our destiny to anything other than God results in the distortion of all our actions (BC 310).

How do we as humans come to understand the depth of our sinfulness? Already in his early Romans lectures (1515/16) Luther insisted that this cannot be logically deduced from observation of human nature. Rather it is revealed to us (LW 25, 215; cf. 32, 240). Right through to the late Smalcald Articles (1537), he insisted on the same point: "This inherited sin has caused such a deep, evil corruption of nature that reason does not comprehend it; rather, it must be believed on the basis of the revelation in the Scriptures" (BC 311). At the same time, it is important to realize that "revelation," for Luther, is not the mere imparting of abstract information. For it to be revelation, it must be experienced. This is what some modern interpreters have called Luther's "existential" understanding of revelation: revelation is not revelation apart from its impact on us. In the case before us, the issue of human sinfulness, he puts it this way: "This knowledge of sin, moreover, is not some sort of speculation or an idea which the mind thinks up for itself. It is a true feeling, a true experience, and a very serious struggle of the heart. . . . [I]t means to feel and experience the intolerable burden of the wrath of God. The knowledge of sin is itself the feeling of sin, and the sinful person is one who is oppressed by conscience and tossed to and fro, not knowing where to turn" (LW 12, 310). Far from being merely one further piece of information, this "knowing" of one's sinfulness is the kind that throws the knower into acute anguish.

It has this effect because it destroys our self-deception regarding some fragment of residual goodness at the core of our being. The doctrine of human sinfulness means, finally, that we sin in everything we do, even in our best and noblest moral acts. As Luther put it in 1518, "Free will, after the fall, exists in name only, and as long as it does what it is able to do [i.e., its very best], it commits a mortal sin" (LW 31, 40). A year earlier Luther had argued that "man, being a bad tree, can only will and do evil" (LW 31, 9). Even a "righteous man sins in all his good works" (LW 32, 83). Even our highest moral achievements, Luther was saying, are at best ambiguous mixtures of good and evil. Though they may be noble in the eyes of the world, they count for nothing before God. "Knowing" our sinfulness means knowing that our goodness is an illusion.

Indeed, Luther thought, this kind of knowing leads inevitably to despair. When a person understands the depth of his or her sinfulness, "despair follows, casting him into hell. In the face of the righteous God, what shall a man do who knows that his whole nature has been crushed by sin and that there is nothing left on which he can rely, but that his righteousness has been reduced to exactly nothing?" (LW 12, 310f). And this state of despair is essential. Despairing of one's own righteousness is the indispensable preparation for receiving the righteousness of another, from another. "It is certain," Luther said in 1518, "that a man must utterly despair of his own ability before he is prepared to receive the grace of Christ" (LW 31, 51).

More than a few modern thinkers, pop psychologists, and so on, have disparaged Luther's understanding of human sinfulness as an excessively negative, gloomy, and emotionally unhealthy estimate of human nature. Luther was convinced that if one is to err in this matter, it is better to err on the side of anthropological pessimism. After all, was this not the direction Paul himself took? The whole purpose of his letter to the Romans, Luther thought, was "to blow [sin] up [*magnificare peccatum*] . . . and thus to show that . . . Christ and

his righteousness are needed" (LW 25, 3). Magnifying sin magnifies the savior. Over and over again he accused the medieval scholastics of doing the opposite, minimizing sin (LW 1, 141). "[U]nless the severity of the disease is correctly recognized, the cure is also not known or desired. The more you minimize sin, the more will grace decline in value" (LW 1, 142). The tendency to downplay human sinfulness is itself an indicator of the boundless egocentrism and capacity for self-deception in the human person, that is, it is itself sin. And it is a sign of human ingratitude to God, an insult to the "suffering and merit of Christ" (BC 38). Why? Minimizing the sickness relativizes the importance of healing. And relativizing the importance of healing relativizes the importance of the healer. With Augustine and Paul (Gal. 2:21), Luther warns: if human nature is not in bondage to sin, "Christ has died in vain" (BC 311).

Theology Luther wore many hats during his lifetime—first that of monk, then husband and father, university professor, pastor, church organizer, political adviser, translator, publicist, counselor, and so on. But he was first and foremost a professional theologian. In 1512, despite .his great reluctance and protestations of unworthiness, he received the doctor of theology degree from the University of Wittenberg. To the end of his life he took this degree as confirmation that God had called him to this task, and he gave himself to it unreservedly.

How did Luther understand the nature of his discipline? This question is fundamental to understanding Luther, and yet the matter is highly resistant to facile slogans and easy formulas. Luther reflected on this, of course; indeed, he did so continually. But he never wrote a book, or even an essay, outlining his understanding of theology's presuppositions, assumptions, definitions, methods, and so forth. In reading Luther, we almost always observe the theologian doing what the theologian does. Only rarely does Luther give us a modest reflection on the nature of the discipline. Before looking at some of these reflections, we do well to begin with a more concrete question: what kind of theologian was Luther?

No one would argue if we describe Luther the theologian as prolific. He was driven by an unrelenting intellectual curiosity, and he studied incessantly, even in times of illness. His output was prodigious: commentaries, disputations, treatises, tracts, meditations, sermons, letters, translations, and so forth. These writings today fill 120 volumes in the modern critical edition (the *Weimarer Ausgabe*). Their quality is uneven, as Luther himself acknowledged. Some works were meticulously researched, carefully thought through, and beautifully written. Others were hastily dashed off and are relatively worthless.

It is often said, and not without warrant, that Luther was a "biblical" theologian. His academic appointment at Wittenberg was as professor of biblical interpretation. In this capacity, he lectured on the Bible continually. Another lifelong task for him was learning the biblical languages and translating the Old and New Testaments into German. From his detailed exegesis he drew theological conclusions. His favorite books—the Psalms, the Gospel of John, the Letters of Paul—occupied him endlessly, and he saw their riches as inexhaustible. In these ways he was a "biblical" theologian. (*See also* **Bible**.)

He was also a "controversial theologian," in the sense that his theology at many points was developed and worked out in the heat of controversy. Already in 1518 his views were viciously attacked by multiple opponents, and before long he had learned to hit back hard. In the 1520s his Catholic opponents were joined by others of various opinions and persuasions. Though he was now attacked from all sides, Luther remained largely undaunted, replying with a vehemence, vulgarity, wit, and polemical dexterity rarely matched in the history of Christian theology. In many cases, the urgency of the situation demanded that calm reflection and careful formulation of positions be set aside. This Luther was more than willing to do. Wisely or not, he frequently allowed his opponents to determine his theological agenda.

What about the term "systematic" theologian? Can this be applied to Luther? Here opinions differ, depending on what one means. If a systematic theologian is one who writes a single, unified, integrated, all-embracing theological work (like Thomas Aquinas or John Calvin or Karl Barth), then the answer is clearly that he was not. But on the other hand, if by systematic theology we mean a coherent and internally consistent set of theological ideas that are all related to, and governed by, a single, central theme, then Luther the theologian was undoubtedly "systematic." This uniting and controlling concept is often summed up in the slogan "justification by faith alone." Luther never tired of explaining it, for he believed it to be the heart of Christianity, the "gospel" as he called it. And Luther saw with an astonishing clarity its implications for every other Christian belief. In this sense, his theological thinking was systematic.

What then can one glean from Luther's scattered comments about the discipline itself? Luther is quite clear, first, on the subject matter of theology: "The proper subject of theology is man guilty of sin and condemned, and God the justifier and savior of man the sinner. Whatever is asked or discussed in theology outside this subject is error and poison" (LW 12, 311; cf. 12, 4). Theology, rightly understood, does not focus on God in himself, but on God in relation to the human. And it does not focus on the human in itself, but on the human in relation to God. To put this another way, theology studies humans—their guilt and their redemption; and theology studies God as the one who accuses and the one who acquits. Theology is thus the study of the distinction between law and gospel. It is the study of justification (LW 34, 147). Or, in Luther's shorthand, "Christ is the subject matter of theology" (WATR 2, nr. 1868, 242, 4).

How does one know anything about this subject? Luther's answer is that God has revealed himself, first and foremost in Jesus Christ (*see* **Christology**), and secondarily in the Scriptures (*see* **Bible**). Theology is therefore "biblical": "Scripture alone is the true lord and master of all writings and doctrine on earth" (LW 32, 11–12). Less authoritative resources for theology are the three classical creeds (*see* **Creeds**). For Luther, the articles of faith they express are a reliable distillation and summary of what is found in the Bible. The theologian then, in her quest to understand something about the human and the divine in relationship, turns to the Bible and the creeds.

What method is to be used in approaching these sources? Luther gives us no neatly laid out, step-by-step plan. We do get some hints in a rather cryptic, and undated, Table Talk: "What makes a theologian? (1) the grace of the Spirit; (2) *Anfechtung*; (3) experience; (4) opportunity; (5) concentrated study; (6) knowledge of the liberal arts" (WATR 3, nr. 3425, 312, 11–13). Whether one can read a "theological method" into this statement is debatable. A better place to start is with Luther's more extensive and carefully considered reflections in the preface he wrote for the 1539 edition of his collected German writings. Here he isolated and explained "three rules" for "the correct way of studying theology"—prayer, meditation, and *Anfechtung* (*oratio, meditatio, tentatio*) (LW 34, 285).

First, Luther argues, prayer—a turning inward—is necessary for this discipline because of its subject matter. Speaking of Scripture, he says, "not one [book] teaches about eternal life except this one alone. Therefore, you should straightway despair of your reason and

understanding. . . . But kneel down in your little room and pray to God with real humility and earnestness" (LW 34, 285). Prayer here means disposing oneself in humble, open receptivity to enlightenment by the Holy Spirit.

If the first "rule" turns the theologian inward, the second—meditation—turns one outward. By *meditatio* Luther does not mean introspection, or the attempt to empty the mind, or passive waiting for a new revelation from the Holy Spirit. His description: "Second, you should meditate . . . by actually repeating and comparing oral speech and literal words of the book, reading and rereading with diligent attention and reflection, so that you may see what the Holy Spirit means by them" (LW 34, 286). In other words, what Luther means by meditation here is assiduous study. This is obviously indispensable for understanding. Theologians, in other words, are scholars.

Luther did not understand this discipline as a "science," as scholastic theologians did. It was not, for him, a body of knowledge derived from "first principles" (in the Aristotelian sense). Rather Luther thought of it as an "experiential wisdom" (WA 9, 98, 21). This is reflected in his third rule for this kind of study: "Thirdly, there is *tentatio, Anfechtung*. This is the touchstone which teaches you not only to know and understand, but also to experience how right, how true, how sweet, how lovely, how mighty, how comforting God's word is, wisdom beyond all wisdom" (LW 34, 386–387). *Anfechtung*—the anguish of inner personal struggle with doubt and despair—this experience prepares a person for theological understanding. (*See also* **Anfechtung**.) One does not really become a theologian, Luther says (with some exaggeration), by reading and speculating, but rather by living, dying, and being damned (WA 5, 163, 28–29). "Experience alone makes the theologian" (LW 54, nr. 46, 7; cf. 32, 258).

More or less explicit within these "rules" for approaching Scripture and the articles of faith is what looks very much like an assault on reason. Some entries in Luther's Table Talk reinforce this perception. For example: "One ought not to criticize, explain, or judge the Scriptures by one's reason, but diligently, with prayer, meditate thereon, and seek their meaning. The devil and temptations also afford us occasion to learn and understand the Scriptures, by experience and practice" (WATR 2, nr. 1353, 67, 32–35). On the other hand, one also finds highly positive statements about reason in the Table Talk: "Dr. [Luther] was asked whether . . . reason has any value at all for Christians. He replied, 'Prior to faith reason is darkness, but in believers it's an excellent instrument. . . . Faith is now furthered by reason'" (LW 54, nr. 2938b, 183). In the face of such an apparent contradiction, what can be said about Luther's view of the role of reason in theology?

A full answer to this question, taking into account the whole of Luther's authorship, would be lengthy and complex. Here I want to take only an initial short step toward such an answer by suggesting that often what looks like an assault on reason in Luther is actually better understood as a polemic against literalism. One place this is evident is in Luther's 1531 sermons on the sixth chapter of the Gospel of John, an important but often overlooked text.

John 6:51 quotes Jesus as saying, "I am the living bread . . . and the bread . . . is my flesh." To make sense of this, Luther argues, one "must not follow his eyes or judge by appearances, confer with reason, or employ his other senses in this matter" (LW 23, 109). In other words, one must not take it in what Luther calls "a fleshly sense" (LW 23, 186) or "in a fleshly manner" (LW 23, 187)—what we would call the "literal sense." Many people do precisely this (and here Luther names "sacramentarians," "schismatics," "fanatics," "heathen," "Turks," "Jews"; cf. LW 23, 119; 23, 168–169). When they hear the word "flesh," they immediately think of the butcher shop and sausages (LW 23,

119). But in this way the literalists make nonsense out of everything: "This is the true meaning of eating and drinking. To eat is synonymous here with to believe. He who believes also eats and drinks Christ" (LW 23, 135). So too in early Christianity the Romans heard Christians speak of eating Christ's body and charged them with cannibalism (LW 23, 169). And the seventy-two disciples who abandoned Jesus (John 6:66–67) did so because they took his words about eating his flesh literally: "They left him [Jesus], even though he had so plainly told them several times that his words were not to be taken in a fleshly sense" (LW 23, 186). In the end, all these people make judgments on the basis of sense perception and reason. Or as Luther puts it, they are stuck "in the realm of reason" (LW 23, 169). In other words, Luther identifies "the fleshly sense" (i.e., literalism) with "reason." To truly understand, therefore, means the abandonment of "reason": "whoever would hear the word of Christ must leave this ass at home and not act and reckon according to reason" (ibid.). Clearly, what looks like an attack on reason is in fact a polemic against literalism. (*See also* **Reason.**)

What this suggests is that for Luther, religious language, whether from Scripture or the creeds, is not ordinary, common, everyday, human language. The meaning of a religious statement, therefore, is not obvious or self-evident or transparent. Translation is necessary. And precisely this is theology's primary function.

All Christians (or almost all), Luther thought, have taken the first steps in the discipline of theology: "We are all called theologians, just as we are all called Christians" (WA 41, 11, 9–13). Whenever Christians ask about what something means, they are venturing into theology. In Luther's Small Catechism, for instance, the first article of the creed is quoted—"I believe in God, the Father almighty, Creator of heaven and earth"—and then the question is asked,

"What is this?" or "What does this mean?" This question is asked because it is not self-evident or obvious. The answer that follows is "theological": it translates the religious language of the creed into ordinary, straightforward language (*BC* 354).

Already in some of his earliest writings, Luther noted the new and different language Scripture gives us for speaking about God (LW 14, 286). Later in his career he came back repeatedly to this language's new vocabulary. He did not mean that new technical terms are invented. Rather, as he put it, "all words in Christ take on a new meaning in what they signify" (WA 39:2, 94, 16–17). Speaking of ordinary words, he said: "in theology they become completely new words and acquire a new meaning" (LW 26, 267). Alternatively, Luther could also speak of "a new and different theological grammar" (WA 40:1, 418, 5–6; cf. LW 26, 267–268; WA 5, 27, 8–9; WA 6, 29, 7–8). The language of faith is a special language with its own vocabulary and grammar: translation is needed (WA 39:1, 229, 16–24). And this is theology's highest task.

Examples of this kind of "translation" can be found on almost every page of Luther's exegetical and doctrinal writings. Take for instance the "bosom of Abraham" mentioned in Jesus' parable recorded in Luke 16:19–31 ("the schoss Abraham" in Luther's translation). Reading this literally would clearly reduce it to nonsense; accordingly, Luther's exegesis translates: "So all the fathers who lived before the birth of Christ have gone to Abraham's bosom, that is, they died firmly believing this word of God and they have all fallen asleep, are preserved and protected in this word, and sleep in it until the last day as though the word were a bosom" (WA 10:3, 191, 24–28). All "interpretation" of Scripture by Luther inevitably involves such a translation process. The same goes for the articles of faith as found in the creeds. For instance, it is not obvious what the "descent into hell" or the "ascension" mean. Taking these doctrines literally, Luther thinks, spells disaster: translation is necessary. (*See also* **Descent into Hell; Ascension**.)

Luther was convinced that this discipline was the "queen" of all disciplines (LW 34, 128), that being a professional theologian was the most noble and exalted of all vocations (LW 12, 5), and that God had called him to it. He pursued it with enormous energy and focus; indeed, we could say that it became his lifelong obsession. The story was told (and there is no reason to doubt it) that Luther went fishing, and took his wife Katie along (or did she take him?). Even this became the occasion for a theology lesson (LW 54, nr. 3390b, 199–200)! He could not, it seems, give it a break.

Yet one also finds in Luther a kind of critical distance, a penetrating self-awareness, a genuinely self-effacing humility. Theology as a discipline, he thought, could never be mastered (WA 10:3, 63, 17–18), and he certainly laid no claim to such mastery. Many if not most of his own writings, he insisted repeatedly, were relatively worthless (e.g., LW 34, 283). His advice for those who have begun to think of themselves as accomplished theologians is famous: "take yourself by the ears, and if you do this in the right way you will find a beautiful pair of big, long, shaggy donkey ears. Then do not spare any expense! Decorate them with golden bells" (LW 34, 288). The vice of the theologian is pride, and this transforms one into an asinine fool.

Trinity   Luther had relatively little to say about the doctrine of the Trinity. This was not because it was unimportant to him, but rather because he accepted the traditional teaching entirely. Thus the Augsburg Confession of 1530, which he endorsed, said that the doctrine is "true and is to be believed without any doubt" (*BC* 37). Likewise, in the Smalcald Articles of 1537, Luther wrote, "These articles are not matters of dispute or conflict, for both sides [Roman Catholic and Lutheran] confess them" (*BC* 300). Accepting the decision of Nicaea and all three creeds, Luther affirms "three distinct persons in one divine nature": the unbegotten Father, the Son begotten by the Father, and the Holy Spirit who proceeds from both (ibid.). From Luther's point of view, this ancient teaching of the church needed no defense. Nor was he inclined to follow "the scholastic teachers [who] have attempted to make this understandable with very great subtleties" (WA 10:1:1, 181, 10–13).

Yet as Luther began to take more of an interest in Judaism and Islam in the 1530s, and as he also became increasingly aware of Michael Servetus's anti-Trinitarian speculations, he began to focus more frequently on the subject. Thus it comes up in his promotion disputations for doctoral candidates at the University of Wittenberg in the 1540s (as dean of the Theological Faculty, Luther drew up the theses for these disputations). Moreover, it is explicitly thematized in his various sermons for Trinity Sunday, in some of his later creedal expositions, and elsewhere.

Luther was convinced that the truth to which this doctrine points is found in inchoate form in the Old Testament, in the plural *Elohim* of Genesis 1:1, in the Prophets, and so forth (WA 42, 10, 11–14; 50, 278, 28–35). The Trinity is attested to even more clearly in the New Testament (WA 39:2, 382, 6–7). Finally, "at the time of Arius" the doctrine was explicitly formulated (WA 4, 365, 5–14). In the creeds, which gather up the disparate allusions of Scripture, the doctrine was given its definitive, technical terminology.

Yet this terminology—"Trinity," "substance," "hypostasis," "person"— is not absolute. In using it "we stammer and lisp as best we can" (WA 41, 270, 6–7). "Threefoldness" or "threeness" does not capture it adequately, nor in fact do the other terms. In a sermon of 1538, Luther said, "Call it some kind of

threesome. I have no adequate term for it" (WA 46, 436, 12). All are weak human attempts to capture a larger reality. Even the term "Trinity" is in principle replaceable, though extreme caution is needed so as not to distort the truth it points to (WA 39:2, 305, 16–20).

It could be said that in the history of Trinitarian doctrine, every theological contribution ends up emphasizing either the unity of the divine essence or the distinction of persons. Luther was so evenhanded on this that today Luther scholars disagree on where he came down. In my view, he stressed the unity more, especially in his sermons. In these he took pains to explain that while we attribute creation to the Father, redemption to the Son, and sanctification to the Holy Spirit, in reality all of God's works *ad extra* (i.e., toward creation) are undivided. What this means is that the three persons in fact create, redeem, and sanctify as a unity (e.g., WA 26, 500, 27–29; 37, 41, 25). Be this as it may, none of this qualifies Luther's firm adherence to the traditional dogma.

Also in keeping with the tradition, Luther was convinced that the Trinity is the highest, most sublime mystery— one that far transcends the capacities of human comprehension. Non-Christians find it foolish and offensive (WA 46, 550, 27–30). What should Christians say then, when asked by Muslims and others, "How is this possible? Respond with humility": Luther says, "I do not know" (WA 40:2, 253, 13). In the end, on this question reason must bow to the higher authority of faith.

Universal Priesthood Already at an early stage in his life, Luther experienced the Roman church as a uniquely powerful institution, exercising enormous influence over the hearts and minds of ordinary Christians. Those who functioned on the institution's behalf, the clergy, used their power in ways that he thought were profoundly oppressive. They were determined to dominate rather than serve the Christian community. Consequently this issue—the power of the clergy—loomed large on his horizon throughout his career.

One of Luther's major weapons for attacking this power structure was his concept of the universal priesthood of all baptized Christians. This was already operative, at least implicitly, in his Ninety-five Theses of 1517. By 1519 it had become explicit. Speaking of the power to grant absolution, Luther said, "where there is no priest, each individual Christian, even a woman or child does as much" (LW 35, 12). In other words, what priests do is something that all Christians can do. A move was afoot here to demystify and democratize, to "disempower" the clergy by empowering the laity.

In the following year, 1520, we find Luther giving a full-blown explanation of what he had in mind. In *A Treatise on the New Testament, that is, the Holy Mass* of that year, he grounds universal priesthood on the principle of an equality based on faith: "Each and all are, therefore, equally spiritual priests before God. . . . [A]ll Christian men are priests, all women priestesses, be they young or old, master or servant, mistress or maid, learned or unlearned. Here there is no difference, unless faith be unequal" (LW 35, 100–101). Also in that year, in *To the Christian Nobility*, he suggested that the inordinate power of the clergy is based on the church hierarchy's distinction between the "spiritual estate" and the "temporal estate." Obviously church leaders make this distinction to enhance their own power. But, Luther argues, "no one need be intimidated by it, and for this reason: all Christians are truly of the spiritual estate, and there is no difference among them except that of office" (LW 44, 127). Priests have no special power unique to them, not even a special relationship to God, but only a different job than the rest of us.

To illustrate, Luther used the revealing example of a group of laypeople marooned in the desert. There is no episcopally ordained priest among them. Who then will "baptize, say mass, pronounce absolution, and preach the gospel?" Anyone chosen by the group, Luther says (LW 44, 128). "For whoever comes out of the water of baptism can boast that he is already a consecrated priest, bishop, and pope" (LW 44, 129). Christians, by virtue of their baptism and their faith, all have the same power. They are radically equal in the eyes of God.

Later in his career Luther spoke less frequently and in a more guarded way about the universal priesthood. Certain "spiritualists" and "enthusiasts" seemed to him to be promoting the concept with chaotic consequences. Yet he never abandoned it (see, e.g., LW 13, 65 from 1530; LW 41, 154 from 1539). It was a permanent part of the arsenal Luther deployed to dismantle the clerical power structure he detested. In the end it meant that Christians are all spiritually equal, that vocations all have equal value in God's eyes, that the access of ordinary Christians to God is not controlled by an institutional hierarchy, and that grace is not mediated to the laity by a clerical elite.

See also **Ministerial/Pastoral Office; Ordination**

Vocation For about a thousand years before Luther, most Christians believed that God singles out some individuals, both male and female, and calls them to serve him in a special way. They receive a "vocation" to the religious life, whether as monks, friars, nuns, or priests. It is not difficult to see how this belief contributed to the emergence of the clergy-laity distinction within the Christian community, how it undergirded a two-class system in the church, and how, over the centuries, it fostered an ever-increasing power differential between leaders and followers. The traditional understanding of vocation, in short, eventually helped produce an oppressive "clericalism," which Luther grew to despise.

By 1520 he was prepared to undercut the entire edifice—what he saw as the exaggerated power of the clergy—by proposing a new understanding of vocation. In his *Appeal to the German Nobility* of that year, he did his best to destroy the conventional distinction between the "spiritual estate" and the "temporal estate": "It is pure invention that the pope, bishops, priests, and monks are called the spiritual estate while princes, lords, artisans, and farmers are called the temporal estate. . . . [A]ll Christians are truly of the spiritual estate, and there is no difference among them except that of office" (LW 44, 127). It is by virtue of their baptism that Christians all belong to the "spiritual estate" (cf. WA 34:2, 300, 23–24). But, Luther goes on to explain, they have different work, or offices: "those who are now called 'spiritual,' that is, priests, bishops, or popes, are neither different from other Christians nor superior to them, except that they are charged with the administration of the word of God and the sacraments, which is their work and office" (LW 44, 130). Just as clergy are "called" to their work, so too are members of the so-called temporal estate: "A cobbler, a smith, a peasant—each has the work and office of his trade" (ibid.). All Christians thus receive a "vocation" from God. And therefore, in God's eyes, all their work is of equal value, as Luther explained in *The Babylonian Captivity* (also from 1520): "the works of monks and priests, however holy and arduous they may be, do not differ one whit in the sight of God from the works of the rustic laborer in the field or the woman going about her household tasks" (LW 36, 78). All Christians are called to their work, and the work of each is equally important.

Here, in a nutshell, was Luther's new understanding of vocation, complete in its essentials in 1520. Its implications, worked out over the next two decades, were enormous.

First, since we are all called by God to our vocation, we are all doing God's work (WA 52, 395, 12–20). The work of the teacher, the full-time mother, the priest, the dentist—all of these are only different ways of "serving God." A person's job, in this sense, connects her or him to God. What, after all, does it really mean to "serve God"? In every case, Luther says, we "serve God" by serving our fellow human beings: "everyone must benefit and serve every other by means of his own work or office" (LW 44, 130; 21, 237). Thus the purpose of the work of every human being is the same: serving God by serving our fellow human beings in the way God has called us to do this.

At first glance, it appears to us that doing our work is the way we "earn" what we need to live. But if we look more deeply, Luther says, we will see that our work is a "mask" behind which God hides and freely gives people what they need to live (LW 14, 115). In fact, our very vocation is a gift from God. Our work, therefore, should make us happy: "Should not the heart leap and overflow with joy when it can go to work and do what is commanded of it, saying, 'See, this is better than the holiness of all the Carthusians'?" (*BC* 403). And all Christians should be content to serve God in the vocation to which they have been called. In a Christmas sermon of 1521, Luther emphasized this: "all works are the same to a Christian, no matter what they are. These shepherds [who came to see the Christ child] do not run away into the desert, they do not don monks' garb, they do not shave their heads, neither do they change their clothing, schedule, food, drink, nor any external work. They return to their place in the fields to serve God there" (LW 52, 37; cf. WA 12, 644, 29). Their work and ours, Luther says elsewhere, "is earthly, though also divine" (WA 34:2, 301, 21–22). All work, even work that seems to us "secular," has religious value.

If Luther's new understanding of vocation undercut the monastic impulse to flee from a wicked world, it also was an impetus toward a new ethic of work.

If Christians understand their work as service to God by way of service to their fellow human beings, then the criterion for moral judgment changes. As Luther argued in a sermon of 1523, "We owe nobody anything but to love and serve our neighbor through love. Where love is present, there it is accomplished that no eating, drinking, clothing, or living in a particular way endangers the conscience or is a sin before God, except when it is detrimental to one's neighbor. In such things one cannot sin against God but only against one's neighbor" (LW 28, 46). What counts, from a moral standpoint, is how well I do my work, that is, how well I serve my fellow human beings. Yet, important as our work is, it in no way "saves" us. The commandment to keep the Sabbath—to rest and let God work—is a weekly reminder that the significance of our work is penultimate (LW 53, 279).

The concrete historical effect of Luther's redefinition of vocation is hotly disputed among experts and will not be settled here. What seems clear is his intention. He wanted to undermine what he saw as the excessive power of the clerical establishment. He wanted to empower the laity to take charge of their own religious lives. And he wanted to give a religious valuation to work in the world. His new doctrine of vocation pointed in these directions.

War   An important aspect of Luther's social and political ethics (see **Ethics, Social/Political**) was his teaching on war. The remoter context in which this must be understood was a thousand-year-old tradition of just-war theory. The more proximate context was five centuries of crusades—Christian "holy wars" and apologias for them. The immediate context was the actual, incessant, and brutal warfare of one kind or another that engulfed early-sixteenth-century Europe. Seen against this background, Luther's views appear in part traditional and in part innovative.

Luther's most basic assumption about war is that it is evil: it is the work of the devil (BC 451); warmongers will have no place in the kingdom of heaven (LW 46, 118); peace is always preferable (LW 21, 39). The Christian starting point must always be opposition to war.

Yet, Luther held, some wars can be "just," and when they are, Christians can fight in them with a good conscience. In this, of course, he was taking his place in the tradition of just-war thinking that had dominated in the West for a millennium. From the time of Augustine, theologians had listed various criteria that had to be met for a war to be just. Among these criteria, Luther emphasized, first, "just cause": one must have this, Luther believed, but in itself this is not enough (LW 46, 121; 21, 39). For a war to be "just," it also must be initiated by legitimate authorities. As Luther explained in his 1529 treatise *On War Against the Turk*, it is the political leader's "duty, as a regular ruler appointed by God, to defend his own" (LW 46, 184). Thus the war against the Turks "should be fought at the emperor's command, under his banner, and in his name. Then everyone can be sure in his conscience that he is obeying the ordinance of God" (LW 46, 185).

Besides these criteria, Luther places an even stronger emphasis on a third: defense. When attacked by a foreign power, Luther explained in 1523, one should first extend an offer of peace. If this is rejected, then "defend yourself against force by force": "If you cannot prevent some from becoming widows and orphans as a consequence, you must at least see that not everything goes to ruin until there is nothing left except widows and orphans" (LW 45, 125). Starting a war, he bluntly stated in 1526, is always wrong (LW 46, 118; cf. 21, 39). Wars of "lawful self-defense" are the only just wars (LW 46, 121, 185), and thus war "should be waged only when it is forced upon us" (LW 46, 125).

Rulers are required by God to defend their subjects in this way (LW 46, 187,

121, 98), and subjects are mandated by God to take part. In this connection Luther frequently cites biblical passages such as Luke 20:25, Romans 13:1–4, and 1 Peter 2:13–14, passages he sees as requiring obedience and submission to political authorities. This last requirement makes it possible for Christians to participate—even enthusiastically—in a just war: "In a war of this sort it is both Christian and an act of love to kill the enemy without hesitation, to plunder and burn and injure him by every method of warfare until he is conquered" (LW 45, 125).

The Scripture passages demanding a citizen's obedience and submission to political authority were also used by Luther to prohibit all types of insurrection and revolt. Most notoriously, in his 1525 work *Against the Robbing and Murdering Hordes of Peasants*, Luther deployed these verses in condemning the peasants (e.g., LW 46, 51), regardless of the legitimacy of their complaints. As he said again in 1526 and frequently thereafter, "war and uprisings against our superiors cannot be right" (LW 46, 118). Tyrants ought not to be deposed (LW 46, 104–18).

Nevertheless, with regard to wars against a foreign power, Luther allows citizens the right to dissent. It may be difficult to assess a threat, and if people are unsure on this score, they may accept their leader's judgment and follow him into war (LW 45, 126). But if they are sure their leader is wrong, that is, that they are not being threatened by a foreign aggressor, they should not take up arms (LW 45, 125). This was Luther's position in his 1523 treatise on *Temporal Authority*, and he repeated it in his 1526 work, *Whether Soldiers, Too, Can Be Saved*: if you are convinced your prince is wrong in going to war, "you should neither fight nor serve" (LW 46, 130). In principle, Christians can be conscientious objectors.

From the outset, Luther was aware that this just-war tradition in Christianity is problematic, given the apparently pacifist orientation of Jesus, above all in the Sermon on the Mount (Matt. 5: "Blessed are the peacemakers"; "Turn the other cheek"; "Love your enemies"; etc.). By 1526 this pacifist challenge had been brought to the forefront of his consciousness by the early Anabaptists. In his work of that year, *Whether Soldiers, Too, Can Be Saved*, he himself formulated the issue. The question is "whether the Christian faith . . . is compatible with being a soldier, going to war, stabbing and killing, robbing and burning, as military law requires us to do to our enemies in wartime. . . . [On the surface the soldier's work] seems an un-Christian work completely contrary to Christian love" (LW 46, 95–96). Three years later, as he came increasingly to believe in the urgency of a defensive war against the Turks, his handling of the Anabaptist perspective was more dismissive: "there are some stupid preachers . . . who are . . . even so foolish as to say that it is not proper for Christians to bear the temporal sword" (LW 46, 161). Yet the theological/ethical problem would not go away: he continued to regularly bring up the issue until at least 1541.

The traditional solution had been to say that Jesus' pacifist-sounding strictures in the Sermon on the Mount were not requirements for all but rather advisory directives for those seeking Christian perfection. Luther abandoned this interpretation early on, and already in 1522 he was proposing another solution, namely his two-kingdoms doctrine (*see Ethics, Social/Political*). What this means, in summary, is that the Christian exists in two realms: first, the secular "kingdom of the world," promoting external righteousness and ruled by the sword; and second, the spiritual "kingdom of Christ," promoting true righteousness and ruled by the Word of God (LW 46, 99–100; 21, 105). Thus Christians combine "two persons" in themselves, two citizenships as it were, and it is of supreme importance to distinguish between the two (LW 21, 109). In the Sermon on the Mount, Christ is instructing his followers on how to live as members of the kingdom of Christ. But those strictures (e.g., love of enemies) certainly do not apply to one's life as a citizen of the secular kingdom (LW 21, 106–107). In other words, as Luther put it, "the Gospel does not trouble itself with these matters [the social and political order]. It teaches about the right relation of the heart to God" (LW 21, 108). For example, to turn the other cheek is admirable in the kingdom of Christ, but in secular society it is a foolish mistake (LW 21, 109).

Thus this distinction also makes it possible for the Christian to go to war with a good conscience. "A Christian may carry on all sorts of secular business with impunity—not as a Christian but as a secular person—while his heart remains pure in his Christianity as Christ demands. . . . Thus when a Christian goes to war . . . he is not doing this as a Christian, but as a soldier. . . . At the same time he keeps a Christian heart" (LW 21, 113; cf. 46, 99). He fights and kills not as a Christian but as an obedient subject of the secular ruler (LW 21, 110). Specifically as a Christian, he "should not make war or resist evil" (LW 46, 168). And as for the prince, king, or emperor, though he may be a Christian, it is not in that persona that he will declare war or lead his subjects into battle. Rather he will do it in his role as political authority (LW 46, 122; 46, 186). "[W]hat I want to do," Luther insisted, "is to keep a distinction between the callings and offices" (LW 46, 166).

The two-kingdoms doctrine also undergirded Luther's rejection of the "holy war" concept. In response to incessant calls for a new crusade against the Turk, Luther had said, already in 1518, "To fight against the Turk is the same as resisting God, who visits our sin upon us with this rod" (LW 46, 162). This article, condemned by Pope Leo X, had led some to believe that Luther was counseling pacifism. As he now explained in 1529, Christians were preparing to fight

"in the name of Christ," that is, as Christians, and this is what he was opposed to (LW 46, 165, 169). If Christians want to fight as Christians, their only weapons can be repentance, prayer, and reforming their lives (LW 46, 170, 184). But if they want to fight as obedient citizens of the empire, they can engage the enemy with all the weapons of war and do so with a good conscience. As for leadership in such a war, there too roles must be distinguished: "it is not right for the pope . . . to lead a church army, or army of Christians, for the church ought not to strive with the sword" (LW 46, 168). And on the other side, "The emperor is not the head of Christendom or defender of the gospel or of faith. . . . The emperor's sword has nothing to do with the faith" (LW 46, 185–186). Thus crusades of any type are out of the question for Luther: sharply differentiating the two kingdoms means that Christians can fight, but not as Christians, that is, not under the sign of the cross.

While Luther's two-kingdoms doctrine enabled him to criticize Christianity's four-century tradition of holy war ideology, he was unable in the long run to break with it decisively. Beginning in 1525 and increasingly as time went on, concepts integral to the holy war ideology crept back into his thinking on war.

The first such concept is that of martyrdom: when one who dies in a war is understood as a "martyr," we are adjacent to, if not in the midst of, holy war thinking. Already in 1525 in *Against the Robbing and Murdering Hordes of Peasants*, Luther describes those on the rulers' side who are killed as "martyrs" (LW 46, 53). The same language is used in Luther's 1529 *Army Sermon Against the Turks* (WA 30:2, 173, 25–26; 175, 19–20). And again in his 1541 *Appeal for Prayer Against the Turks*, death in this war is martyrdom (LW 43, 238). The argument, made elsewhere, that war is a purely secular affair (e.g., LW 46, 166–167) rings hollow if victims in that war are proclaimed martyrs.

Second, in holy war ideology the evil enemy assumes superhuman dimensions: in short, the enemy is not only our enemy, but an "enemy of God and a blasphemer and persecutor of Christ" (WA 30:2, 172, 19–20). To fight against the Turk is, Luther says, to fight against the devil (WA 30:2, 173, 3–5), or "Satan's army" (LW 43, 237).

A third aspect of holy war ideology that creeps back into Luther's thinking is that divine punishments and rewards are promised to the combatants in such a war. For those on "our" side, Luther says, it is a sin to submit to the enemy (LW 46, 193), and those who desert to the enemy's side "are surely condemned to hell" (LW 46, 196). On the other hand, already in the case of the Peasants' War, Luther says that those who die for the cause are rewarded with eternal life: "These are strange times, when a prince can win heaven with bloodshed better than other men with prayer!" (LW 46, 254–255). Of course, Luther occasionally suggests that they receive this reward because of their obedience to the emperor in accordance with Romans 13 (e.g., LW 46, 185). But more often, and especially after 1529, Luther simply promises heaven to those who are killed, without any such caveats (e.g., WA 30:2, 175, 9–10, and 19–20; 177, 9–10; LW 46, 185).

Fourth, and closely related to the foregoing, the cause for which one fights in a "holy war" is not merely secular: the enemy is not only threatening our land, our homes, our families, our lives, and so forth—the enemy is attacking God. From 1529 on, Luther becomes increasingly explicit on this score. The Turk threatens us, but he "also lays waste to the Christian faith and our dear Lord Jesus Christ" (LW 46, 174–175). Luther calls the Turk "the enemy of Christ our Lord" (LW 46, 175), the "enemy of God" (WA 30:2, 172, 19). Clearly the cause, in Luther's view, is a holy one. In one of his final statements on the subject, his 1541 *Appeal for Prayer Against the Turks*, he met the issue head on:

We are not fighting to win land and people, wealth and glory. . . . Rather are we fighting to establish God's word and his church. Especially do we fight for our children, for the coming generations. We are fighting that the Turk may not put his devilish filth and blasphemous Muhammad in the place of our dear Lord, Jesus Christ. That is the real reason and serious purpose for which we now fight, die, or live. This is certainly true. (LW 43, 238)

Here Luther's initial rejection of medieval Christendom's holy war concept is abandoned completely. If the cause for which one fights is holy, if divine rewards and punishments are at stake, if the enemy is identified with the demonic, and if casualties on "our" side are understood as martyrs—the war is a "holy" one.

In summary, Luther's view of war combined traditionalism and innovation. In no fundamental way did he move beyond the medieval just-war theory he inherited. In response to the pacifist challenge, posed by the Sermon on the Mount and pressed on his consciousness by the Anabaptists, he abandoned the traditional explanation, offering a new one on the basis of his two-kingdoms doctrine. Finally, with regard to the medieval holy war ideology, he tried to transcend it with the help of his two-kingdoms doctrine but ultimately failed to do so.

Women By today's standards, sixteenth-century Europe was unabashedly sexist and wholeheartedly patriarchal. The prevailing assumptions of the age were (a) that women were in every way inferior to men; (b) that they ought to be in every way subordinate to men; and (c) that their most basic purpose was to bear and raise children. Luther inherited these assumptions and never, in any fundamental way, challenged or transcended them. To him, and to almost everyone else in his age, they seemed self-evident.

For instance, the picture of the female sex that he painted in mid-career, in his Ecclesiastes lectures of 1526, remained constant from youth to old age:

> As a creature of God a woman is to be looked on with reverence. . . . But if a woman forsakes her office and assumes authority over her husband [she must be corrected]. For God did not create this sex for ruling, and therefore they never rule successfully [!]. . . . For she was created to be around man, to care for children and to bring them up in an honest and godly way, and to be subject to the man. Men, on the other hand, are commanded to govern and have the rule over women. (LW 15, 130)

The view sketched here was a commonplace in Luther's world, requiring from him neither defense nor elaboration.

The roots of this view, however, reached deeply into the Pauline and Augustinian subsoil of the tradition. These were explored by Luther perhaps most extensively in his late course of *Lectures on Genesis* (1535–45). Accepting the historicity of the Genesis account, Luther affirms that woman was created in the image of God (LW 1, 68). But on the question of whether God created her to be equal with the male Luther is unclear: sometimes he says they were absolutely equal before the fall (e.g., LW 1, 115; 1, 137), and elsewhere he speaks of her inferiority (LW 1, 68; 1, 151). In fact, he says, the serpent tempted Eve first precisely because of her weakness: had he approached Adam first, Luther thinks, he would have been told to "Shut up" (LW 1, 151). In any case, the fall is blamed on women, though, Luther adds, we should not despise them for this (LW 2, 29).

The fall brought about a change in women's status and role. Before the fall, childbirth would have been painless (LW 1, 133). Before the fall, the woman was needed for reproduction, whereas after the fall she was needed also for companionship, household management, and as an "antidote against sin" (LW 1, 116). And the fall brought with it a new kind of subordination. Whereas she was initially meant to "share in all the cares, endeavors, duties, and functions of her husband . . . the wife was [now] made subject to the man by the law which was given after sin. This punishment is similar to the others which dulled those glorious conditions of paradise. . . . There the management would have been equally divided. . . . Now the sweat of the face is imposed upon man, and woman is given the command that she should be under her husband" (LW 1, 137). Thus women's second-class status seems to have had its origin in creation (cf. LW 1, 68), and was dramatically worsened by sin.

Though Luther concedes that there are examples of women in the Hebrew Scriptures who "teach" and "rule" (LW 40, 389), he is much more interested in the example of Sarah, "deservedly held up by Peter (1 Peter 3:6) as a pattern for the entire female sex" (LW 3, 44). For "the chaste Sarah not only follows her husband but also respects him as a lord" (LW 3, 209). In contrast to the usual female weaknesses like "inborn levity," "disgraceful curiosity," and "garrulousness," Sarah embodied "the highest virtues of a saintly and praiseworthy housewife" (LW 3, 200). Perhaps the ultimate in submissiveness, she even "concedes the glory of fertility to her maid" (LW 3, 44).

Alongside this rather demeaning view of women, we also find in Luther frequent warnings not to denigrate the female sex. He was critical of the considerable literature of his day that vilified women (LW 45, 42). "Ungodly celibacy," he thought, had made matters worse in this regard (LW 1, 118). And he was critical of the Jewish prayer thanking God for creating them "as males and not as females": this is a "fool's boast," he said (LW 47, 140). That other traditional role model for women, Mary, stood for Luther as a warning against males exalting themselves by casting aspersions on women.

For it was Mary's "deep insight and wisdom, that God is the kind of Lord who does nothing but exalt those of low degree and put down the mighty from their thrones" (LW 21, 299).

Luther was wholly traditional in his view that the primary purpose of the female of the species was the work of motherhood. However, his new understanding of vocation raised the status of motherhood to that of a divine calling. It is not the case, Luther taught, that God calls some women to serve him in a special way (i.e., in the convent) and leaves the rest to their own devices. Rather, God calls almost all women to the estate of motherhood; and since he does, in his eyes it is of equal dignity with any other vocation. Indeed, because of this, the most menial household tasks "are all adorned with divine approval as with the costliest of gold and jewels" (LW 45, 38). Since God calls women to motherhood, "all the works, conduct, and suffering of that estate become holy, godly, and precious" (LW 45, 40). The work of a mother is more holy in fact than that of the cloistered nun, whose calling is in any case dubious (LW 45, 41), and more holy too than the work of a pope (LW 3, 202). Luther's theology thus overturned conventional ways of thinking about holiness, and gave a new value and dignity to "women's work."

Yet the long-term consequences of the Reformation for the status of women in the West remain a matter of debate. For alongside Luther's revaluation of women's work came another, more ambiguous development. Luther's campaign in the early 1520s against celibacy and against the monastic life eventually had the effect of closing the convents in large parts of Europe. This development narrowed the lifestyle choices that women could make: whereas previously they could choose marriage or the convent, now for many marriage became the only option. This too must be taken into account in assessing the Reformation's impact on women's place in society.

As for the role and function of women in the church, while it was inconceivable to Luther that women would become leaders, he laid the theoretical groundwork for this (much later) development. For he explicitly included women in his concept of the "common priesthood of believers" (LW 39, 234). This concept entailed, among other things, the view that all Christians by virtue of their baptism are capable of doing what priests do: the ministry of the Word and sacrament. Thus, Luther held, women are capable of preaching (LW 30, 54, and 135), but should not unless they are called (LW 30, 55). Paul's strictures against women preachers notwithstanding (1 Cor. 14:34), Luther could conceive of occasions when women would be called to this, in nunneries, for instance (LW 30, 53), or if no suitable male was available (LW 36, 152). The same principle is applied to the administration of the sacraments: women are not generally called to it, in Luther's opinion, but they are capable. And he could conceive of emergency cases in which they would perform this function (LW 41, 154; 40, 23). In principle, at least, women can do all that men do in the church.

Gender bias and patriarchal attitudes in Luther? Obviously and without a doubt. Misogyny too? No. The late Middle Ages and the Reformation produced a fair number of writings deeply imbued with male hatred and fear of women. But Luther's works are not among them. Indeed, everywhere in these writings there is evidence to the contrary: in the loving, respectful, gently teasing tone of his letters to his wife Katie (e.g., LW 50, 208–212); in his bitter grief over the death of his daughter (LW 54, nr. 5494, 430; nr. 5496, 432); in his affirmation of the goodness of human sexuality; in his extravagant praise of marriage; in his contention that women have a right to sexual fulfillment (LW 6, 103; 45, 19); in the many respectful and serious letters to women who asked for advice; in his extended marveling over the miracle of conception and childbirth (e.g., LW 1, 126); in his (perhaps clumsy) attempts to comfort women in the pain of childbirth (LW 45, 39–40); in his 1542 booklet of consolation, *Comfort for Women Who Have Had a Miscarriage* (LW 43, 243–250); in his opinion that "the saddest aspect of warfare" is the wholesale rape of women on the losing side (LW 2, 377); and so forth. All this, combined with the total absence of hateful statements about women, suggest no trace of misogyny is to be found in Luther. Indeed, how could there be, in a theologian who identifies women with motherhood, and does not hesitate to draw an analogy between motherhood and God (LW 45, 43)?

Worship   Already during Luther's lifetime his followers adopted a new form of worship. This differentiated them in a visible way from the church "under the papacy," as Luther called it (e.g., BC 301). Thus a substantially revised cultus became one of the hallmarks of the Reformation. What precisely Luther had to do with this development is complex. To summarize, we can say that he showed little concern for the particulars of Christian worship except when, in his estimate, forms of worship contradicted his basic theological position.

Traditional Roman Catholic worship, of course, centered around the sacramental system. As early as 1520, in his *Babylonian Captivity of the Church*, Luther drastically downsized this (LW 36, 11–126; for details *see* **Sacraments, General**). Baptism and eucharist (and penance for a short while) retained their status as "sacraments." In 1523 and then again in 1526 Luther wrote new and revised orders for baptism (LW 53, 96–103; 106–109; *see* **Baptism**). In 1523 he wrote *An Order of Mass and Communion for the Church at Wittenberg* (LW 53, 19–40), and in 1526 he published his *German Mass and Order of Service* (LW 53, 61–90; *see* **Lord's Supper**). Some rites were no longer regarded as sacraments

and yet retained their importance: thus in 1529 he wrote new orders for marriage (LW 53, 110–115; *see* **Marriage**), confession (LW 53, 116–118; *see* **Penance**), and ordination (LW 53, 122–126; *see* **Ordination**). As for confirmation, he conceded that this rite may have some value (LW 36, 91–92; *see* **Confirmation**). Extreme unction, however, should be discontinued (LW 36, 119–120; *see* **Extreme Unction**). Thus Luther's new "sacramental system," in terms of its prominence in the worship of the church, was a shadow of its former self.

At the heart of the traditional cultus was the mass—the worship centerpiece par excellence. What began in the first century CE as a simple celebratory meal had developed, by Luther's time, into this religion's central rite, accompanied by elaborate theological explanation and lavish liturgical embellishment. For the average layperson, "worship" was unimaginable without it. It is estimated that in the Castle Church in Wittenberg (with its nineteen side altars), a total of some nine thousand masses were celebrated in the year 1519 alone. Luther effectively put an end to this. In 1523 he reported that he had been trying "to wean the hearts of people from their godless regard for ceremonial" (LW 53, 19). Daily masses, he announced, had been discontinued at Wittenberg (LW 53, 30), and they should be discontinued elsewhere (LW 53, 37–38). Why? Because "the Word is important and not the mass" (LW 53, 13; cf. 53, 30). In fact, the only indispensable elements of Christian worship are preaching and prayer (LW 53, 11). Preaching is "the highest office in Christendom" (LW 39, 314), and the most important part of worship (LW 53, 68). Thus, for Luther, preaching replaced the eucharist as the core of corporate devotion.

This is not to say that the Lord's Supper was now insignificant. Rather, what Luther called for was a reformed eucharist, with nonbiblical accretions excised (LW 35, 81), with Christ's words of institution spoken aloud (LW 35, 90), with the laity receiving the cup (LW 36, 27–28), with private masses eliminated (LW 53, 32), in the vernacular for those who did not know Latin (LW 53, 63), and so forth. By far the most important "reform," however, was Luther's adamant rejection of all references to the mass as "sacrifice."

With this last issue, we have arrived at the heart of Luther's understanding of worship. In Luther's languages, the terms for worship were *cultus Dei* and *Gottesdienst*, both meaning "service of God" or "divine service." What is crucial to understand, Luther said repeatedly, is that in worship humans do not serve God, but God serves them. Humans do not give anything to God, but rather God gives everything to them (LW 35, 85–87; 53, 11; 53, 25–26; BC 301–5; etc.). The only possible way in which humans can be said to "serve" God is through service to their fellow human beings (LW 44, 130; 21, 237). And the only thing they can possibly "give" to God in worship is gratitude for what he gives to them (LW 53, 81). The mass, as it was celebrated "under the papacy," was understood as our sacrifice to God, and this was "the greatest and most terrible abomination" (BC 301). It entailed an implicit denial of justification by grace alone (*see* **Justification**).

True worship is thus the primary context in which God's gift—the gospel and grace of Jesus Christ—comes to us. If this is the case, it makes little sense for worshipers to show up out of obligation. Rather, they ought to come "because they are troubled by the consciousness of their sin, the fear of death, or some other evil, such as temptation of the flesh, the world, or the devil, and now hunger and thirst to receive the word and sign of grace and salvation . . . so that they may be consoled and comforted; this was Christ's purpose, when he in priceless love gave and instituted this supper" (LW 53, 32; cf. 53, 34). Human need—existential, emotional, spiritual—is what should drive Christians to worship.

The fulfillment of our need should evoke profound gratitude. That too is to be expressed in worship. And when hearts overflow in spontaneous thanksgiving to God—this should not be excessively reined in by rules. Liturgy, Luther says repeatedly, should not be made into law. In 1523 he composed his own *Order of Mass* only after repeated urging (LW 53, 17), and he stressed throughout that all are free to adopt whatever order they want (LW 53, 20, 25, 28, 30–31, 37, 39). In his *Christian Exhortation to the Livonians Concerning Public Worship and Concord* of 1525, he counseled in this regard not to make "dictatorial laws opposed to the freedom of faith" (LW 53, 46). And in his *German Mass and Order of Service* of 1526, he advised pastors to disregard this order if they prefer a different one (LW 53, 62). The only guideline Luther insisted on was this: "the orders must serve for the promotion of faith and love. . . . As soon as they fail to do this, they are invalid, dead, and gone" (LW 53, 90).

Suggestions for Further Reading

Althaus, Paul. *The Theology of Martin Luther*. Trans. R. Schultz. Philadelphia: Fortress, 1966.

———. *The Ethics of Martin Luther*. Trans. R. Schultz. Philadelphia: Fortress, 1972.

Bayer, Oswald. *Theology the Lutheran Way*. Trans. J. Silcock and M. Mattes. Grand Rapids: Eerdmans, 2007.

———. *Martin Luther's Theology: A Contemporary Interpretation*. Trans. T. Trapp. Grand Rapids: Eerdmans, 2008.

Bornkamm, Heinrich. *Luther in Mid-Career, 1521–1530*. Trans. T. Bachmann. Philadelphia: Fortress, 1983.

Brecht, Martin. *Martin Luther: His Road to Reformation, 1483–1521*. Trans. J. Schaaf. Minneapolis: Fortress, 1985.

———. *Martin Luther: Shaping and Defining the Reformation, 1521–1532*. Trans. J. Schaaf. Minneapolis: Fortress, 1990.

———. *Martin Luther: The Preservation of the Church, 1532–1546*. Trans. J. Schaaf. Minneapolis: Fortress, 1993.

Dieter, Theo. *Der junge Luther und Aristoteles: Ein historisch-systematische Untersuchung zum Verhältnis von Theologie und Philosophie*. Berlin: de Gruyter, 2001.

Ebeling, Gerhard. *Evangelische Evangelienauslegung: Eine Untersuchung zu Luthers Hermeneutik*. Darmstadt: Wissenschaftliche Buchgesellschaft, 1969.

———. *Luther: An Introduction to His Thought*. Trans. R. Wilson. Philadelphia: Fortress, 1970.

———. *Lutherstudien II: Disputatio de Homine*. Tübingen: Mohr, 1977.

———. *Luthers Seelsorge: Theologie in der Vielfalt der Lebens-situationen, an seinen Briefen dargestellt*. Tübingen: Mohr, 1997.

Edwards, Mark U., Jr. *Luther's Last Battles: Politics and Polemics, 1531–46*. Ithaca, NY: Cornell University Press, 1983.

Gerrish, Brian. *Grace and Reason: A Study in the Theology of Martin Luther*. Oxford: Clarendon, 1962.

Ghiselli, Anja, Kari Kopperi, and Rainer Vinke, eds. *Luther und Ontologie: Das Sein Christi im Glauben als strukturierendes Prinzip der Theologie Luthers*. Helsinki: Luther-Agricola-Gesellschaft, 1993.

Grane, Leif. *Modus Loquendi Theologicus: Luthers Kampf um die Erneuerung der Theologie*. Leiden: Brill, 1995.

Gritsch, Eric. *Martin—God's Court Jester: Luther in Retrospect*. Philadelphia: Fortress, 1983.

Hagan, Kenneth. *Luther's Approach to Scripture, as Seen in His 'Commentaries' on Galatians, 1519–1538*. Tübingen: Mohr, 1993.

Headley, John. *Luther's View of Church History*. New Haven: Yale University Press, 1963.

Hendrix, Scott. *Luther and the Papacy: Stages in a Reformation Conflict.* Philadelphia: Fortress, 1981.

Hirsch, Emanuel. *Lutherstudien.* 2 vols. Gütersloh: Bertelsmann, 1954.

Holl, Karl. *Gesammelte Aufsätze zur Kirchengeschichte*, Vol. 1: *Luther.* Tübingen: Mohr, 1927.

————. *What Did Luther Understand by Religion?* Ed. J. Adams and W. Bense. Trans. F. Meuser and W. Wietzke. Philadelphia: Fortress, 1979.

Junghans, Helmar. *Der junge Luther und die Humanisten.* Göttingen: Vandenhoeck & Ruprecht, 1985.

Karant-Nunn, Susan C., and Merry E. Wiesner-Hanks, eds. *Luther on Women: A Sourcebook.* New York: Cambridge University Press, 2003.

Kolb, Robert. *Martin Luther as Prophet, Teacher, and Hero: Images of the Reformer, 1520–1620.* Grand Rapids: Baker, 1999.

Lindberg, Carter. *Beyond Charity: Reformation Initiatives for the Poor.* Minneapolis: Fortress, 1993.

Loewenich, Walther von. *Luther's Theology of the Cross.* Trans. H. Bouman. Minneapolis: Augsburg, 1976.

Lohse, Bernhard. *Martin Luther: An Introduction to His Life and Work.* Trans. R. Schultz. Minneapolis: Fortress, 1986.

————. *Martin Luther's Theology: Its Historical and Systematic Development.* Trans. R. Harrisville. Minneapolis: Fortress, 1999.

Mannermaa, Tuomo, and Kirsi Stjerna. *Christ Present in Faith: Luther's View of Justification.* Minneapolis: Fortress, 2005.

Martikainen, Eeva. *Doctrina: Studien zu Luthers Begriff der Lehre.* Helsinki: Luther-Agricola-Gesellschaft, 1992.

McGrath, Alister. *Luther's Theology of the Cross: Martin Luther's Theological Breakthrough.* Oxford: Blackwell, 1985.

McKim, Donald K. , ed. *The Cambridge Companion to Martin Luther.* New York: Cambridge University Press, 2003.

McSorley, Harry. *Luther: Right or Wrong? An Ecumenical Theological Study of Luther's Major Work 'The Bondage of the Will'.* New York: Newman, 1969.

Oberman, Heiko A. *Werden und Wertung der Reformation: Vom Wegestreit zum Glaubenskampf.* Tübingen: Mohr, 1966.

————. *Luther: Man Between God and the Devil.* Trans. E. Walliser-Schwarzbart. New Haven: Yale University Press, 1989.

Ozment, Stephen E. *Homo Spiritualis: A Comparative Study of the Anthropology of Johannes Tauler, Jean Gerson and Martin Luther (1500–1516) in the Context of Their Theological Thought.* Leiden: Brill, 1969.

Pelikan, Jaroslav. *The Christian Tradition: A History of the Development of Doctrine.* Vol. 4: *Reformation of Church and Dogma.* Chicago: University of Chicago Press, 1984.

Pesch, Otto H. *Die Theologie der Rechtfertigung bei Martin Luther und Thomas von Aquin: Versuch eines systematisch-theologischen Dialogs.* Mainz: Matthias-Grünewald Verlag, 1967.

————. *Hinführung zu Luther.* Mainz: Matthias-Grünewald Verlag, 1982.

Peura, Simo. *Mehr als ein Mensch? Die Vergöttlichung als Thema der Theologie Martin Luthers von 1513 bis 1519.* Mainz: Philipp von Zabern, 1994.

Raunio, Antti. *Summe des Christliche Lebens: Die 'Goldene Regel' als Gesetz der Liebe in der Theologie Martin Luthers von 1510 bis 1527.* Helsinki: Universität Helsinki, 1993.

Rupp, Gordon. *The Righteousness of God: A Reconsideration of the Character and Work of Martin Luther.* London: Hodder & Stoughton, 1953.

Russell, William R. *Luther's Theological Testament: The Schmalkald Articles.* Minneapolis: Fortress, 1995.

Schwarz, Reinhard. *Fides, Spes, und Caritas beim jungen Luther unter besonderer Berücksichtigung der mittelalterlichen Tradition.* Berlin: de Gruyter, 1962.

Steinmetz, David. *Luther and Staupitz: An Essay in the Intellectual Origins of the Protestant Reformation*. Durham, NC: Duke University Press, 1980.

———. *Luther in Context*. Bloomington: Indiana University Press, 1986.

Wicks, Jared. *Man Yearning for Grace: Luther's Early Spiritual Teaching*. Philadelphia: Coronet, 1969.

———. *Luther and His Spiritual Legacy*. Wilmington, DE: Glazier, 1983.

Wingren, Gustav. *Luther on Vocation*. Trans. C. Rasmussen. Philadelphia: Muhlenberg, 1957.

Zur Mühlen, Karl-Heinz. *Nos Extra Nos: Luthers Theologie zwischen Mystik und Scholastik*. Tübingen: Mohr, 1972.